The

George 'Shrimp' Simpson joined the Royal Navy in 1914 but saw out the years of the First World War in a battleship gunroom where his most dangerous adversaries were the midshipmen. He soon recognised the value of submarine warfare and had a distinguished career in that service. He moved to New Zealand after the War where he died in 1972.

PERISCOPE VIEW

*A Memoir of the 10th Submarine Flotilla
at Malta 1941–1943*

GEORGE SIMPSON

New Introduction by Jeff Tall

Seaforth
PUBLISHING

Copyright © George Simpson 1972
Introduction copyright © Jeff Tall 2010
This edition first published in Great Britain in 2010 by
Seaforth Publishing,
Pen & Sword Books Ltd,
47 Church Street,
Barnsley S70 2AS

British Library Cataloguing in Publication Data
A catalogue record for this book is available from the British Library

ISBN 978 1 84832 054 3

First published by Macmillan London Ltd, 1972

Despite extensive inquiries it has not been possible to trace the copyright
holder of *Periscope View*. The publishers would be happy
to hear from anyone with further information.

Printed and bound by the MPG Books Group, UK

FRONTISPIECE
The author as a Commander before the War

NEW INTRODUCTION

Periscope View is the story of Rear Admiral George 'Shrimp' Simpson who, between 1941 and 1943, commanded the Tenth Submarine Squadron in Malta at a time when the island was under the severest attack by the German Fliegerkorps X, operating only sixty miles away in Sicily, and when his men were suffering a fifty per cent casualty rate. It was vital to the allied war effort in the crucial arena of the Mediterranean that both Malta and the Fighting Tenth keep going. They did, and the Allies were eventually able to attack the 'soft underbelly' of the Axis powers.

The early chapters of the book present an autobiographical picture of the development of a future wartime leader of men. Simpson describes his hatred of bullying, his dislike of tradition for tradition's sake that stultified creative thought, and his conviction that boredom was anathema to the naval soul. The middle chapters deal with events that were to shape Simpson's own destiny and that of hundreds of young men under his command, half of whom were to lose their lives in battle. He pulls no punches in his views about the conduct of the early days of the War. The final chapters portray the panoply of events, often harrowing, that surrounded the seige of Malta and the submarine operations that played a crucial role in the defeat of Rommel's army in North Africa.

Unlike the battle of the Atlantic, which was a battle for strategic naval domination of the Atlantic Ocean, the battle of the Med was predominantly a campaign to secure the Mediterranean Sea for advantages in the land wars which were fought around it, particularly North Africa. The Northern African campaign was strategically important for both the Allies and the Axis powers. The Allies used the campaign as a step towards a second front against the Axis powers in Europe, and it helped to ease Axis pressure on the Eastern Front. The Axis powers had planned to dominate the Mediterranean through control of the Suez Canal, and to follow a successful campaign in North Africa with a strike north to the rich oil fields of the Middle East, and a strike east towards India and their Japanese allies. So rather than being a sideshow or strategic dead-end, the Mediterranean was the pivotal theatre of the Second World War in Europe.

Malta, situated in the central Mediterranean but only sixty miles from Sicily, was crucial as a static aircraft carrier and as a naval base, particularly for submarines, because of its proximity to Axis re-supply lines. It is said that by failing to capture it, Hitler lost the War strategically. It can equally be said that but for the brilliant leadership of men like Shrimp Simpson, and the astonishing courage of the Maltese and their boarders, the Allies could easily have lost the battle of the Mediterranean.

Simpson, having volunteered for submarines in 1921, never looked back, and his natural skill and enthusiasm saw him rise rapidly in submarine circles. He was promoted Commander in December 1936, and was in command of HMS *Porpoise* when the Second World War started. He had close contact with Captain Philip Ruck Keene, his Captain(S), and a man who showed Simpson a flotilla of the highest morale. Simpson wrote: 'I watched his methods.... He had a flair for knowing what mattered, how much it mattered, and putting things in their correct priority, and for cutting through time-wasting formality.... His boyish enthusiasm led him naturally to foster and encourage the young in his command'. Simpson caught the eye of (then) Vice Admiral Sir Max Horton, Flag Officer Submarines, during an inspection visit to Harwich, home to the Third Submarine Flotilla based on HMS *Cyclops*, and soon afterwards he was appointed to command a small group of submarines that were to operate from Malta from January 1941.

Simpson established his flotilla headquarters (The Tenth) at Lazaretto on Manoel Island in Malta. He and his small staff team, made up of like-minded 'can-do' individuals, quickly, and often nefariously, put in place offices, messdecks, and workshops. Under relentless bombing by the Luftwaffe they dug into the hillside and created a cinema and bars for recreation and a sickbay, and above ground they created a farm populated by pigs, rabbits and turkeys. All this activity was driven by Simpson's determination to provide the very best facilities for his crews who he knew would be operating under the severest stress whilst at sea, and would be longing for proper rest and recuperation when in harbour. He never forgot Max Horton's exhortation to treat his COs as 'Derby winners'.

At the same time as creating base facilities, Simpson had his submarines to deploy, and it should be borne in mind that he was only a Commander at this time. His brief from his Commander-in-Chief, Admiral Cunningham, was succint and to the point and ended with the exhortation: 'If you don't get results and don't dispose your forces to suit me I will soon let you know. Until then you have a free hand to act as you think best to achieve your objectives'. A free hand brought with it massive responsibility to harry the enemy all the way from Italy to North Africa; to mine all Rommel's embarkation and discharge ports; to launch commando raids and other special operations to keep the enemy hopping.

Simpson's style of leadership was to underpin the Flotilla's success, for after a year or so of operations it gained the sobriquet of 'The Fighting Tenth'. In his own words: 'I must observe that in this command I attribute much of our success to the fact that I lived and messed amongst my officers and throughout the whole of March 1942, when the officers' quarters were demolished, I messed on the general mess-deck with the men'. This arrangement was unusual to say the least, and it could have had the opposite effect to relaxing his officers and men, but as one of his staff officers observed, 'full justice can never be done to this galvanic and dynamic little freckle-faced man. His strong sense of justice and humour, coupled with an innate knowledge of human nature led to a flotilla which would have followed him cheerfully to kingdom come and back had he ordained it. He made allowances for youth and inexperience, and for the excitement of the moment. He never reprimanded – he simply pointed out errors and omissions'.

One of his COs, Lieutenant Commander Alistair Mars DSO DSC RN of HMS *Unbroken*, confirms the success of the arrangement. 'The wardroom mess of the submarine base in Lazaretto, under the friendly but shrewd eye of Commander Simpson, was soon to become the melting pot of submarine thought as fresh but battled-hardened blood and talent poured in from the west, to mingle with their astute and phlegmatic colleagues from the east. It became an exchange mart of tactical thought, adventure and experience, both policy and determination fused to a granite which the enemy could chip but never smash'.

Not only was the support for his officers a fundamental element for success, but also the Flotilla's deliberately relaxed attitude to discipline was another major contributing factor. Simpson just wanted his men back after the necessary run-ashore, whatever their physical and mental state. As Lieutenant Commander Ben Bryant DSO**DSC RN observed: 'Dreariness led to staleness; staleness to being a second or two slower, the second or so that made the difference between success and failure, survival or destruction. All COs needed something to help them unwind. Alcohol could serve that purpose; so could other things but they were neither available, nor easily transportable and accommodated'.

Indeed Simpson went to great lengths to ensure that there was sufficient 'lubrication for relaxation' available. On one occasion *Turbulent* was joining Malta from Beirut and Simpson sent her a signal giving her the route to take. Having given a series of positions and times he added 'and bring plenty of booze so that we can have a good time'. This signal happened to be monitored and Shrimp was taxed by Flag Officer Malta with the frivolous use of the ether. Far from being abashed he stood his ground and said (more or less)

Sir

I would have you know that in all the time I have commanded the Tenth Submarine Flotilla never have I known anything like the disastrous series of misses that have occurred during this last month. This has coincided with the Lazaretto's supply of refreshment being completely exhausted. The two matters are not disconnected. I consider that anything to relieve the staleness of my overstrained COs is a matter of the most vital importance.

As well as cleverly working out a safe passage for his submarines to take in and out of Malta, Simpson also knew that if the enemy's surface forces could be dispersed, their efficiency would suffer. Accordingly he disposed his submarines as widely as possible, though always with the primary aim of catching the enemy's convoys as they sailed south from the Italian mainland. His COs knew that he had them constantly in his thoughts while they were on patrol. As his Assistant Paul Thirsk explained: 'Shrimp would pore over the night's signals... he would then proceed to dictate signals to make whatever adjustments to his submarines' dispositions he thought necessary.... It was typical of him, and well appreciated by his Commanding Officers, that his first consideration was to engage the enemy more closely and do as much damage as possible. But it was equally realized that he had a masterly grasp of operating conditions and would never unnecessarily hazard a submarine or put her into danger.... It occurred to me that this total rapport between Shrimp and his COs was the basis of a mutual trust and respect which was reflected in the Flotilla's achievements.... Amid all the death and destruction in the central Mediterranean in those days his light hearted touch was irresistible'.

The individual stories of triumph and loss related in the book play havoc with the reader's emotions – what such incidents must have done to Simpson's emotions can only be imagined. Mars comments: 'It says much for the steadfastness of Shrimp's men that not one man ever shirked a patrol deliberately. There were isolated incidents of stress-related mental disturbance; it would be astounding if there were not. In *Upholder*, during the depth charging that followed her attack on *Conte Rosso*, one man had to be forcibly restrained from trying to escape through the lower conning tower hatch. While *Urge* was being hunted, a hardened leading stoker, with years of submarine experience, temporarily went off his head and strode up and down the Control Room reciting the Lord's Prayer out loud. But the vast majority took their cue from their Captain(S) and turned their inner doubts and fears into a positive drive to defeat the enemy'.

Gradually events took their toll on Simpson's stamina and Ben Bryant observed: 'As I said goodbye to Shrimp, I noticed how grey his hair had gone since he had been our Commander(S) in the old *Cyclops* at Harwich three years ago. On him had fallen most of the strain.' Another CO observed: 'With these terrible decisions on one pair of shoulders he should have been twice as tall and twice as broad. How could one man take all that he did and survive for so long?'

Just before he returned to the UK the strain on Simpson showed in his words. 'I loathed the way in which it had developed during the past two months on the Palermo-Tunis route. Instead of some respite afforded by the relief of Malta and the success of our armies there was that growing gnawing anxiety every hour of day and night over how my men were standing up to the strain of operating within a narrow channel with barely sea room to manoeuvre, ceaseless enemy air patrols overhead and convoys to attack which now contained invariably twice the escorts than there were targets'. It was time to hand over the reins, which he did to Captain George Phillips DSO GM RN on 30 January 1943. On his way home he was sunk onboard HMS *Welshman*, but that is another story.

Periscope View is the story of how a handful of submarines changed the course of the War. For sixteen momentous months Malta Force submarines struck out into the unknown from that isolated island – to stop enemy supplies from reaching North Africa. Half of all Axis shipping was sunk: half of our submarines failed to return.

Jeff Tall, OBE
Commander Royal Navy (Retired)
Former Director of the Royal Navy Submarine Museum

FOREWORD

by Vice-Admiral SIR JOHN ROXBURGH
K.C.B., C.B.E., D.S.O., D.S.C.
Flag Officer Submarines

As I sit here at the desk from which 'Shrimp' Simpson retired from the Royal Navy as Flag Officer Submarines eighteen years ago, I count myself privileged to have been asked by the publisher to write a foreword to this absorbing book.

Periscope View is Shrimp's professional autobiography and covers his opinions on submarine development between the two world wars. It goes on to offer some salty comment on higher policy towards our own submarine service in the inter-war years which resulted in its neglect. Finally it details the record of the 10th Submarine Flotilla fighting under his command from Malta in 1941–1942. It is our loss that it does not also tell of his subsequent service in the Western Approaches, in New Zealand, in Germany and finally as Flag Officer Submarines.

Few officers (and Shrimp was only a Commander at the time) can have been given such an unfettered directive to operate an important command as he was in January 1941 by Admiral Cunningham from his headquarters in Alexandria, 'If you don't get results and don't dispose your forces to suit me I will soon let you know. Until then you have a free hand to act as you think best to achieve your objective.' The results Shrimp achieved with his submarines from Malta undoubtedly prove what a sound leader he was.

This is a serious historical work which needed to be written; we are fortunate that the man who was at the centre of submarine operations from Malta was persuaded to undertake it. It also includes some nice touches of humour and demonstrates Shrimp's eminently practical approach to the human problems with which he had to contend. It shows too, his quiet understanding of the officers and men who served under him. What it does not really show is the immense strain that he underwent during his two years in command of the submarines throughout the siege of Malta, for Shrimp was always the most modest of men.

Shrimp was ever an engaging and friendly personality, full of fun, with a twinkle in his eye, and yet, with his craggy face and thickset sturdy figure, gave one a feeling of solid dependability and confidence. I first met him when I arrived in Malta as a young 'spare' Commanding Officer in October 1942 aged twenty-three. He soon gave me command of a submarine and despatched me on patrol in the Sicilian narrows which turned out to be a somewhat trying experience. Shortly before I was due to go on my second patrol, again in the same area, we were having a convivial evening in a submarine alongside Lazaretto; impulsively I pulled out a photo of my wife of six months and pressed it on Shrimp (who was unmarried at the time), 'bequeathing' her to him should I fail to return. He gravely accepted the photo, subsequently returning it to me with due ceremony when I next got back to Malta after a successful and rather happier patrol. The two were due to meet for the first time later this year when Shrimp was hoping to be back in this country for the publication of his book. Alas, fate has decreed otherwise.

The view through a periscope can often be cloudy and indistinct; in *Periscope View* it is sharp and clear. This book will be read with delight by all those who knew and took part in the events covered; it deserves to and will also I am sure be enjoyed by a far greater circle.

John Roxburgh

Fort Blockhouse, Gosport, Hants
15 May 1972

AUTHOR'S PREFACE

In his absorbing and authoritative book *The Swordbearers*, Corelli Barnett, in studying naval leadership in the First World War, has this to say (amongst other things) in his concluding paragraphs. 'The British general decadence had the same roots as the defeat at Jutland – the propagation of social and emotional values unrelated to the hard facts of power and survival. The superiority of the gentleman over the industrialist was accepted, as was the arts over science; of status, right and tradition over function.'

Again on the following page:

There was nothing accidental, nothing of bad luck, nothing of blame on individual officers in what happened at Jutland; nor in what happened in the forty odd years after Jutland. It was part of the vast process of dissolution that began about 1870, when the British first forgot that life is a continued response, with daily new beginnings; that nothing is permanent but what is dead. British decay began when the British forgot the sources of their power and even denigrated them. It is an astonishing indictment of British parliamentary government in its supposed golden age that, in the critical years from 1870 to 1914, the dominating political topic was not the modernisation and mobilisation of British resources for a desperate struggle for survival – but the future of Ireland, than which no matter could be of lesser relevance and importance.

I joined the Royal Navy in 1915 and was retired in 1954, so my service experience covers the period that has earned Corelli Barnett's censure. I found his remarks and scholarly argument fascinating.

I interpret his message to imply that since he finds that the British nation had become decadent, it follows that the Royal Navy was decadent in 1916 and for some forty years afterwards as a natural consequence. My opinions formed throughout my service by practical experience and an inquisitive mind lead me to rather different conclusions. I consider that the 'decadence' reflected in the disappointingly poor performance of the Navy in the First World War was certainly caused in part by the factors he has enumerated, but his analysis is a great over-simplification; the Navy's troubles lay chiefly within its own bounds.

The Service troubles born at the turn of the century continued to harass the Navy with declining influence until the experience of the Second World War laid the ghost.

I am sure that the Navy's performance during the Second World War showed a revival in spirit, initiative and fighting qualities that equalled if not exceeded that of any other period in its long history. Those involved at all levels did not fight for glory, did not worship tradition or any other false god. They were educated men who fought dispassionately and successfully for the survival of their country, and cooperated unselfishly with their sister Services.

Of course there were initially a few in senior positions who had learned nothing, but they faded out during the course of the war.

My service has covered the slow change which transformed the Navy from a wealthy, aged and puzzled Goliath to an impoverished youthful and confident David. I had the good fortune in the last war to command the submarines based at Malta throughout the siege. Subsequently, until the war ended, I commanded the largest escort vessel base in Western Approaches, so I had an exceptional opportunity to study the young commanding officers and their ships' companies who retrieved the Royal Navy's lost laurels with superb elan.

I write this book as a duty and as a tribute to my men of the 10th Submarine Flotilla at Malta, of whom more than half were killed in action, and amongst whom, in over two years of intense activity at sea and enemy bombardment in harbour, I never had one single man who shirked a patrol despite our crippling casualties.

This book concerns people not machines, and sailors not ships. I have quoted names where it has suited me without in my opinion being either fulsome or foul. I believe that if the people of Britain knew more about the Royal Navy and its recent achievements they would be more inclined to regard this great Service as a lasting national asset, rather than a traditional ghost slain by progress and redundant due to brotherly love!

PROLOGUE

HAVING written my preface and then the book which has taken me a long time in preparation and execution, I have received unstinted assistance from many sources and in particular from the Naval Historical Section of the Ministry of Defence who have answered innumerable questions of detail to cross check my memory of this personal narrative.

The views expressed are entirely my own.

The bibliography and acknowledgements will show the sources I have referred to, and I have found several books to be quite inaccurate regarding events in the Mediterranean during the siege of Malta.

I have been largely guided by the monumental and brilliant work of Captain Roskill's *The War at Sea*, Vols. 1 and 2, which I have been unable to fault even in the smallest detail of personal experience. So it is with trepidation that I have dared to disagree with him on one issue: the initial stages of the Invasion of Norway. The cause of my disagreement is solely due to what I feel has been left unsaid.

I have been critical of decisions at the top on two other counts and with the benefit of hindsight this can be churlish. I hope I have not been irresponsible. The book was originally to have been only about submarine operations from Malta during the siege 1941–1942, but I continually came up against two basic questions. Why had I been operating a very few submarines (average number at sea less than four) which were operationally inferior to the German U-boat and, why were we continually bombed?

It just makes nonsense to write about Malta in 1941 and 1942 without comment on these two points, and this leads to criticism, for I have no intention of whitewashing a situation which I regard as having been unnecessary and very wrong. To avoid appearing to have a chip on my shoulder I have written my experience in the Royal Navy which had a bearing on how the first happened, and

I have endeavoured to leaven the loaf with reminiscence both grave and gay.

The result is largely autobiographical, but through it runs a dominant theme showing how enemy naval development in the First World War rendered the Grand Fleet impotent. Circumscribed by tradition and lacking vision we nearly lost. Then followed the doldrums of peace and finally the Navy's resurrection in the crucible of the Second World War.

My two questions when put in a general form, rather than a petty personal point of view, read rather differently as follows: Why did the Board of Admiralty from 1918 to 1939 virtually ignore a future German U-boat threat, in particular after Hitler's seizure of power in January 1934? Why was it Government policy between 22 June 1941 (invasion of Russia) and 7 November 1942 (decision at Alamein) that the R.A.F. based on Malta were to give priority to the offensive against Axis shipping and ports instead of securing and protecting this unique base for fast, radar-fitted gunships of the Royal Navy to operate from, with large numbers of submarines and torpedo carrying planes to operate beyond the perimeter of the surface force's radius of action?

These two questions are no doubt too 'hot' for an official historian to tackle just yet. So far they have hardly been referred to. Some people will be inclined to counter regarding the second that we had neither the fighters nor the ships at that time. This I will show to be quite untrue.

Regarding the second question I must make it clear from the start that I am not indulging in an inter-Service bicker, or implying that the R.A.F. (or the Air Council) were to blame for the policy adopted over Malta. This was a Government policy which at the time seemed to me sheer lunacy and still does.

To show the extent to which this remarkable 'cart before the horse' policy was also held outside R.A.F. circles I quote from *A Sailor's Odyssey* (page 350), by Admiral of the Fleet Lord Cunningham.

I could never agree that the primary duty of the Royal Air Force in Malta was to defend the island. In my considered opinion it had the equally important function of making use of the ideally situated base for offensive air action against the enemy besides working in close cooperation with our surface ships attacking the convoys to Libya. The Navy, by itself could only interrupt the Axis communications with Tripoli. It could not stop them.

That makes it clear that, so far as the naval C.-in-C. was concerned, the R.A.F. should pursue an *ad hoc* opportunist policy at Malta during the war, and on this one point I cannot agree with my great commander-in-chief. Such an equivocal policy must fail, and it did and nearly lost us the war.

ACKNOWLEDGEMENTS

Sources studied to check my memory have either been identified in the narrative or appear in the bibliography.

Corroboration or opinion sought by correspondence has been acknowledged in the narrative.

Here in New Zealand I am deeply indebted to Mrs Joan Johnson who typed the original manuscript with accurate and punctual enthusiasm. I also thank my daughter Tania whose youthful opinion, criticism and help have assisted me.

In Britain two officers from my staff of those war days are responsible for the book appearing in print. Lieutenant-Commander Lord Hardinge of Penshurst, now of Macmillan and Co., suggested that I undertake the task and his patience, encouragement and criticism have been invaluable. Commander W. J. N. Rutherford undertook the very considerable task of editing my diffuse manuscript. I thank them both.

The Naval Historical Branch of the Ministry of Defence under the direction of Rear-Admiral Peter Buckley have answered my innumerable questions both fully and promptly. I am most grateful.

70 Kiripaka Road   G. W. G. Simpson
Whangarei
New Zealand

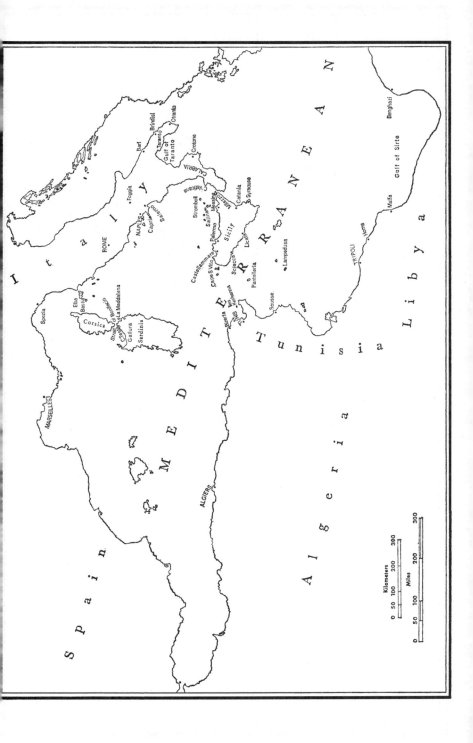

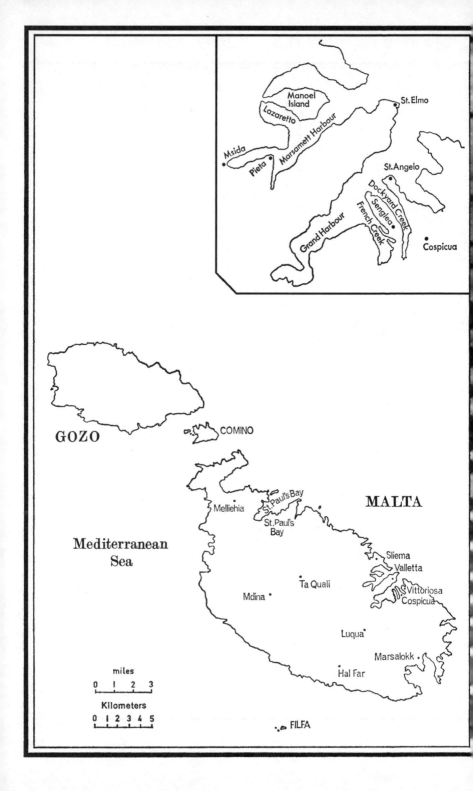

1

My career in the Royal Navy started in the bitter aftermath of the reforms introduced by Fisher and during the stalemate at sea that opened the First World War. It is important to understand the several strands that composed the Navy of those days.

When it was finally agreed in 1914 that I should sit the examination for entry to the naval college, my father had to find a person of sufficient influence to sponsor me. Our family had no naval or political connections so he asked a friend and cricketing companion if he would do it. This was my first introduction to Captain Douglas Nicholson, then Captain of the Royal Yacht, who very kindly became my patron.

Although Nicholson came from a military family – his father was a general, four of his brothers were in the Army and another was in the Navy – he was not a forceful 'fire-eating' character but an officer of the greatest integrity and completely devoted to the Service. He commanded HMS *Agincourt* at Jutland, was later promoted to Rear-Admiral and commanded the second division of the 4th Battle Squadron until the end of the war, flying his flag in *Colossus*. He retired in 1922 as an admiral and at intervals throughout my career I would hear of or from him.

Early in 1939 I had a few days' leave and, feeling that war was imminent, decided to visit him in Devon for what was, in fact, the last time. He was delighted to see me and, as usual, we had a long conversation about the Navy and the rights and wrongs of various decisions. Just as I was thinking of leaving I asked him 'What is your opinion, sir, of the Fisher–Beresford controversy which seems to have bedevilled the Navy before World War I?'

His gentle expression clouded as he walked towards the window facing the sea and, with his back half towards me, he spoke slowly and deliberately for about ten minutes, never mentioning Beresford at all but with a tang of contempt in his voice and hatred on his face. 'Fisher achieved two things. Firstly he split the Navy into two camps from top to bottom with such effect that for over a decade no officer dared express an opinion on a naval matter in a mess, or in a ship, or in a club, or even in a drawing room. Secondly, by one impetuous act he put the whole Navy out of date in a year. You have only to read Admiral Tirpitz' memoirs to understand that the German Navy was many years behind ours until 1906, but then by this act they were only one year behind; even our world-wide docking facilities were made useless by the building of *Dreadnought* and her successors.'

He became more and more unreasonable, stating that Admiral May had been the architect of a balanced fleet with world-wide supply and docking facilities. I suggested that surely Fisher's introduction of oil, the turbine and the new education system, his interest in aircraft and submarines, and his correct anticipation that our naval interest in the war would not be world wide but in the North Sea, had been of essential value. Sir Douglas would have none of it. 'I don't remember him for those things,' he retorted. 'He was an evil man and he split the Navy from top to bottom.'

Thirty years had not been enough to erase the hatred for Fisher caused by his actions before the First World War, and it was still strong enough to make a quiet, experienced, and very senior, officer utter wild statements. Fisher, however, was not the sole instrument of change since the last fifty years of the nineteenth century witnessed the introduction of two scientific and industrial developments which also affected the nature of the Royal Navy – steam and wireless telegraphy. Most of the effects of the latter were on strategy but it did put an end to the world wide wanderings of independent commands 'showing the flag' while really enjoying a leisurely, but disciplined, yachting trip with all the privileges accorded the White Ensign.

The change from sail to steam meant that although the same number of seamen were required to fight the ship in action, very few were required to work the ship at sea. It also meant that nobody needed to go aloft in foul weather and therefore men and midshipmen could not work together in mutual danger, nor could they show off their prowess by 'skylarking' in the rigging in harbour. Progress in this material matter was therefore in danger of breeding the most dangerous virus that can assail shipborne life – boredom.

A congress of bored ships lying at anchor (as opposed to lying alongside) in a port, has always been disastrous. The causes of mutiny in a navy may be eradicated or corrected by improvement in service conditions, but the wind that fans the spark to flame is boredom. Whilst I know from experience that this has been so in the Royal Navy I suspect that it played its part in 1917 and 1918 in both the Russian and German fleets.

There was no need to take any steps to prevent the officers becoming bored because they could easily be disciplined – put ashore, put on half-pay, or sent to rot in an almost forgotten outpost. But for the seamen there were in those days two principal ways of preventing boredom without spending money: providing more work (either necessary or invented and if possible on an intership competitive basis), and giving the sailors lots and lots to talk and laugh about.

Work had been provided by the introduction of a large variety of general drills which replaced sail drill (some of them being good and some particularly futile), and intership sailing regattas, and pulling regattas, on which executive officers, with increasing fanaticism, wagered their promotions; a habit that persisted unabated until the mid thirties.

The main entertainment of the sailors in the years following the turn of the century was, however, provided by two major performers who first served together as Commander-in-Chief and Rear-Admiral Mediterranean – Fisher and Beresford. The variety and absurdity of their performances left an atmosphere of expectant mirth and chatter on the lower deck, of wonderment and apprehension amongst the junior officers, and of either active intrigue or sullen disgust amongst the senior officers.

The Fisher–Beresford feud is well documented, but its effect and its extent are not widely appreciated. Nowadays it is not easy to understand how two public figures at the top of their profession could behave as they did, but one can well imagine the partisan comment and laughter on the lower deck, and the spirited brawls ashore on a Saturday night, relieving any sense of boredom.

The fact remains that Fisher towered above his contemporaries and either dominated or removed his subordinates. Despite his ruthless and often evil methods, one is forced to the broad conclusion that without him the reforms would have been niggardly and inadequate if left to the conservative opinions of contemporaries who lacked Fisher's vision and unequalled prestige.

The matter that concerns us here, however, is not the material excellence or the disabilities of the Grand Fleet as created by Fisher but the state of mind of the officers and men of the Navy as a direct result of his impact, his methods and his feuds. The restrictions and limitations imposed on the spirit of the Navy by Fisher outlived his ships. Flag officers and captains were unused to uninhibited cooperation and the use of initative. The junior officer had been denied the education of argument and dissent and had become inarticulate. Finally the dismissal of Beresford and the retirement of Fisher in 1909 had taken from the lower deck its Punch and Judy Show. This was the Navy, with material faults known to him, that Jellicoe was ordered to command on the outbreak of war, the plum job which he accepted with such reluctance. And this was the Navy that I joined in 1915.

2

THE naval colleges at Osborne and Dartmouth, where I spent two and a half years, were administered on naval lines by officers who for one reason or another were not required at sea. The scholastic teaching was by civilian masters and excellent. The naval training seemed to be left to the term Chief Petty Officer, who was always accessible, full of common sense and helpful.

Considering it was wartime it seemed remarkable that at neither college did the captain or any naval officer address the cadets on any subject until in September 1916 Commander Arthur Marsden (later M.P. for Battersea) arrived at Dartmouth. He walked with a limp from a leg wound and was the sole survivor of the destroyer *Ardent*, sunk at Jutland. We were marched onto the College 'quarterdeck' to hear what this war hero had to tell us, and it can be well imagined how eagerly we four hundred cadets listened. He said, 'When you get to sea you will soon learn that the British sailor is a very discerning and critical fellow, so it is up to you whilst at College to make the very best of your schooling so that you may be able to lead these fine men with confidence based on sound knowledge!' This was the sole theme for a ten-minute talk; no mention was made of Jutland or of any sea-going experience; we were bitterly disappointed. I asked my friend Cadet Wheeler, who had a more mature experience than I, how we could be so let down, had we not joined the Royal Navy and had not a great victory just been won? 'Well, I think the trouble is,' replied Wheeler, 'that for the captain to be the sole survivor is not in the best traditions of the Service.'

This was the only occasion I was to hear a naval officer address an audience, or a ship's company, throughout the whole war, until Armistice Day 1918 when our captain spoke to the ship's company and read us the armistice terms. There were several reasons for this. There was nothing whatever to say. As a result of the Fisher-Beresford quarrels officers were scared of expressing any views that could be out of line with current doctrine, whilst the excuse reigned supreme that the Navy was the Silent Service, so to put forward any ideas, or in fact to talk, was bad form and against tradition.

During 1917 the Admiralty decided to augment the fleet by sending 240 cadets to sea in September, instead of the 110 who were due to be promoted midshipmen. About 1 September orders arrived that I was promoted to midshipman and appointed to HMS *Superb*. It was natural and true that I was thrilled – it slightly offset the shock of my brother's death at Ypres in August, and gave me a personal pride that I was to serve in his stead.

On 24 September 1917, having been very sea sick crossing the Pentland Firth in the mail ship *King Orry* in heavy weather, I climbed aboard *Superb* over the stern boom just before midnight. I was sixteen and three months, five feet two tall, with a treble voice and full of hope and expectation.

At the naval colleges I had been introduced to the catchword 'tradition' and on going to sea I was to feel the full impact of this word, with its limitless interpretations and abuses. The true description of naval tradition corresponds exactly to the theological one, viz, 'Doctrine, supposed to have divine authority but not committed to writing' – 'supposed' being the key word. After forty years' experience of it I can see the advantages enjoyed by the German Imperial Navy in 1914, or the R.A.F. in 1939, by their freedom from this harlot of the vocabulary.

What happened to me and my contemporaries as midshipmen was immensely important in those impressionable years, it was also the main reason why I and many others sought the refuge of submarines as a career and blessed our choice. Since the abolition of sail, gunroom life had largely lost its meaning and, without the elements to contend with, boredom resulted in bullying to a greater or lesser degree throughout the Service.

All cadets at Dartmouth had been appointed to ships for the fleet mobilisation of July 1914, and when the fleet dispersed to war stations the cadets (some aged fourteen) were promoted to midshipmen and remained on board. When I went to sea this 'vintage' of young officers were the sub-lieutenants of the gunrooms of the fleet.

The battle cruisers based on Rosyth were in sight of civilisation and its amenities. They had also seen more action. The battleships at Scapa Flow lay at anchor in the gale swept Flow, with one permissable landing place on one low, treeless, uninhabited island, Flotta. There was a daily wireless bulletin, there was no shipboard cinema and in my experience no shipboard games. Officers and lower deck did not play games together in those days. Speech broadcasting was not invented until the mid twenties and talkies were fifteen years away. A canteen ship visited once in two months and the ship with a theatre for amateur theatricals never came alongside any ship I served in.

There was one football field for about 40,000 men on Flotta, and since the soil was peat and rainfall heavy it was seldom fit for play. In fact very few sailors ever went ashore. Most midshipmen landed once in two or three weeks for a walk. There were two things which broke the ghastly unimaginative tedium – going to sea and coaling ship. The chief recreation in the wardroom was auction bridge, in the gunroom auction bridge and the gramophone, and on the lower deck sleeping.

Naturally every midshipman, on promotion to sub-lieutenant took all steps possible to leave the fleet for other service and, if he could, to join a wardroom. Vacancies in destroyers, submarines, R.N. Air Service, minesweepers, coastal motor boats or Mediterranean service would take most; cruisers, the least popular alternative, would take the balance after leaving the bare requirements for battleship and gunroom purposes. In every walk of life there are the five per cent of duds, and so it was that the five per cent of failures who were under report (quarterly to the Admiralty) had to be in battleships or battlecruisers where an officer of post captain's rank could report upon these frustrated failures, who were both bored and angry. I spent my first four and a half years at sea in three battleships, one destroyer and one cruiser and during that time I was shipmates with eleven executive sub-lieutenants only one of whom was promoted to lieutenant, the other ten being retired as sub-lieutenants.

Tradition ordained that children go to sea, but since they were no longer the protégés, or junior relatives, of senior officers and could no longer acquire the agile techniques of sail, nor in the lower rates sit as powder monkeys on powder casks in battle to keep the sparks out, duties had to be invented for these children. They ran messages, made watchkeepers cocoa and attended school with shipborne schoolmasters. Their activities were designed to allow officers already bored with too little to do to do less and less.

The duties of the wardroom officers in capital ships at sea were sinecures compared with those of their contemporaries in destroyers, submarines, small craft and flying. Whilst in harbour these duties were child's play, which is why they were often carried out by midshipmen. One example will suffice. During the last four months of the war I watched my contemporary, junior midshipman A. R. Higgins of HMS *Benbow*, who was 'tankey' (navigator's assistant), wind and compare the chronometers daily and keep the chronometer log, correct all charts and sailing directions, and write up the fair log which he also initialled with his own impeccable version of each officer's signature. As he explained to me, 'It saves them having to sign the thing, they only have to check what I have written.'

The hugely fat, prematurely aged, Navigating Commander, long past hope of promotion, had thus reduced his work to a weekly visit to the chronometer-room to coincide with captain's rounds on Saturday, and a daily visit to the chart-room just to check that the work was being done. As we were a private ship he had virtually no staff duties. At sea he had considerable responsibility, but under the eye of an experienced captain; the time spent at sea by a capital ship in 1918 was perhaps ten per cent of the year.

Under these circumstances I joined *Superb* in September 1917 with high hopes. I will confine my remarks to what happened to me, remembering thankfully that, since my small size deterred bullying and my agility helped in not being last in most activities, I lived a favoured existence.

Officers' quarters were under the fo'csle deck, the gunroom being immediately forward of the wardroom. Midshipmen took their meals and lived in the gunroom during waking hours and slept in hammocks in an area below the gunroom. The space allotted and food provided were quite adequate. On our first morning Midshipman Sitwell took charge of us and explained our duties. Our schooling until Christmas was to be engineering and we would do some harbour watchkeeping to learn ship routine. My cruising station when the fleet was at sea was submarine lookout in the foretop with Midshipman Thomas, R. N. R. My battle station was in Y turret on the quarterdeck. Sitwell then handed us an exercise book and told us to study it.

The 'Gunroom Standing Orders' were concise and sufficiently personal to be easily remembered. After fifty years I can recall them with fair accuracy.

(1) On guest nights every officer in the gunroom will drink His Majesty's health in wine.

(2) Any midshipman exceeding his monthly wine bill of 10s. will receive twelve cuts.

(3) The stakes at auction bridge shall be sixpence per hundred and are to be entered in the mess card book and credited or debited to the monthly mess bills.

(4) Any midshipman who fails to pay his mess bill at the end of the month in full will receive twelve cuts.

(5) 'Brightwork Stations' will be exercised under the direction of the senior wart from 0830 to 0850 daily. All bare metal surfaces are to be maintained in a state of high polish.

(6) During non-working hours from 1530 daily or from noon on make and mends (half holidays) a duty wart is to be in the gunroom to carry out the orders of the seniors. His duty ends when the last officer has quit the mess for his hammock.

(7) 'Gunroom Evolutions'. All warts are to be conversant with the following evolutions:

At any time	Breadcrumbs
	Dogs of war
During dinner	Fork in the Beam – last wart out six cuts
	Provide Bumph – last wart home six cuts
After dinner	Scuttle drill
	Angostura Trail encouragement
	Running Torpedoes as necessary

Signed: Mess President

Sitwell continued his explanation. There were two sub-lieutenants and the senior, who was mess president, had been appointed away; this was a pity because he was a pleasant officer and only exercised evolutions on the weekly guest night. When he left life would change, since the junior sub. was bad tempered and would be a bully. It was particularly necessary to understand the 'evolutions' procedure since this was a potent method of inflicting punishment.

If the sub-lieutenant shouted 'breadcrumbs' it meant that a conversation was about to take place which warts must not hear, so all warts stopped their ears with their fingers. If the sub-lieutenant then said 'O.K. cancel breadcrumbs' and you took your fingers out of your ears you got a dozen with a dirk scabbard across the backside for listening. Fingers must be kept in the ears until a senior snottie came and removed them.

If the sub-lieutenant of the mess wished to remove anybody from the mess he would shout 'Dogs of War' whereupon all warts would growl. He would then order 'Out Mr X' and all warts in the gunroom at the time would eject Mr X, and if he resisted hotly the sub-lieutenant might add 'debag Mr X' and he would be ejected without his trousers.

'Fork in the beam' meant that whilst the sub-lieutenant was eating his evening meal he might at any moment thrust the fork in his left hand into the wooden beading supporting the horsehair settee upholstery behind him. Every wart then scrambled for the door and the last to get through it got six cuts after dinner. However if he stuck the fork into the horsehair settee and not into its wood, any wart who left his seat got six cuts; alternatively if the sub changed the knife to his left hand and stuck that into the woodwork any wart who moved would get six cuts. (This was by far the most popular evolution since it gave a quick return in thrashings due to its permutations and it made the evening meal a burden for all warts.)

At the order 'Provide Bumph' every wart jumped from the dinner table and dashed to the gunroom W.C. (which was some sixty yards away through three bulkhead doors), seized a handful of toilet paper, and dashed back, placing the prize on the dinner table beside the mess president. The last home was thrashed after dinner.

After dinner, 'Scuttle drill', forced us all, one wart at a time, to stand on a chair by the ship's side. On the word 'go' we would go through the scuttle, reach to the next scuttle and pull ourselves out of one and back into the mess through the other. This was seldom exercised since only tall warts could span the distance; the opportunities for hitting a disappearing backside were obvious.

For 'Angostura Trail', the selected wart was blindfolded, and a zigzag line was spilt on to the lino deck covering from an angostura bitters bottle. The wart was placed at one end of the trail and a crust of bread at the other. On hands and knees, with nose to the deck, he would follow the trail by smell and when he deviated from it or hesitated too long his upturned backside would be thrashed. The evolution was over when the wart had sawllowed the crust.

Someone said, 'What's all this in aid of?' and Sitwell replied, 'Oh, they are traditional, you know.' I have heard that in the days of sail and wooden walls if the sub-lieutenant was entertaining senior officers, or needed to be alone, he would stick a fork into a beam in a well known prominent position and other officers junior to him would not enter until he had removed it. This was the only 'evolution' with any early naval usage.

Sitwell explained that there was only one punishment for warts, and that was to be beaten, the question being whether six or twelve with the scabbard were administered. If a wart failed in some duty, or was considered by a wardroom officer deserving of punishment, then the mess president was told to beat the offender. This did not often happen but he felt that the quiet time we were having would shortly change. He emphasised that only the president of the mess could beat anyone.

The first days were interesting, everything was new to me, but I was apprehensive and decided never to ask questions in the gunroom since I had found a source of information that would never think me a fool or hurt my pride or beat me for my ignorance. In Y Turret Chief Petty Officer Goble, a 'Gunner's Mate', was 'Captain of the Turret' and explained my duties to me simply. He was a fine looking man with a trim red beard and fierce eyes, who spoke quickly and urgently. 'Lieutenant Carter commands this turret and sits up there and controls the gun fire if in action we go into independent firing. You sit up there beside him and work that rate clock, it's easy, sir, and you are second in command of the turret, but if Lieutenant Carter is killed you're sure to be killed too, but don't you worry, sir, I'm Captain of the Turret and I will go on firing and make my own corrections. We'll be all right.' He was so frank and direct that I felt I could safely ask him to help me to understand all those things I wanted to know which I dared not ask any officer. This he agreed to do, remarking 'I would not have come up through the gunroom for all the beer in Pompey.' I found out later that a year before he had lost his son in *Hampshire*, sunk with Lord Kitchener on board, to the west of the Orkneys.

Within a week a rumour was circulating the gunroom, brought by the senior snottie running a picketboat. He had heard that there had been a spot of bother in the flagship of our battle squadron, HMS *Hercules*. He gathered that midshipman Gordon Cumming, who had come to sea ten days before us, had fallen foul of the junior sub of the *Hercules* who had beaten him, and had indicated that he intended to beat him daily as a matter of routine. We never learned details except that on being told that he would be beaten immediately, junior wart Gordon Cumming had drawn a bayonet from his coat and stabbed his assailant repeatedly on the face and chest. This news was discussed by senior snotties as well as warts, since there was a fine legal point which was sure to come out in the court martial; if wart Gordon Cumming had assailed the mess president then, of course, he deserved to be keelhauled, but the beating by a junior sub was against tradition. If that gained ground no wart would be able to sit down.

We were to be disappointed. Apparently a junior wart was so unimportant that he had no right to be heard. No court martial took place but Gordon Cumming's elder brother was asked whether his younger brother was insane; we understood that Lieutenant Gordon Cumming thought not, and his younger brother was sent home to his parents. This incident was very important to us as young officers. We understood quite clearly that the mess president alone enforced discipline in any manner he chose without any question; this traditional arrangement had been abused and the issue fobbed off. Where did we stand now? We wondered.

Soon after this episode our easy going mess president left the ship and his embittered deputy took over. A few days later our subdivision of four battleships was ordered to escort a Scandinavian convoy and *Superb* put to sea in rough weather. My night cruising station was in the searchlight control mounted on the after funnel and the sulphurous fumes made me very sick.

Next day continued rough. I had the afternoon watch and was sitting in the gunroom, unable to eat lunch, when the sub-lieutenant said, 'Midshipman Thomas, which wart has the after-noon watch with you as submarine lookout?' 'Simpson,' said Thomas. 'Well, here's a cigar for the little bastard. See he smokes it and bring me back the butt at the end of your watch.' 'Right,' said Thomas, catching a large cigar, and we set off.

It was far too rough to go by the normal route, climbing the rungs outside the port or starboard strut, so we went down to the main deck, entered the foot of the hollow mast and climbed the hundred odd rungs to the fore top to take over the two seats from the midshipmen of the forenoon watch. 'You look out from right ahead to sixty degrees to port and I will cover the same sector to starboard,' said Thomas. 'All right,' I said in my squeaky voice, 'but can you tell me what a periscope looks like?' Thomas replied petulantly, 'How the hell should I know? Nobody's ever seen one. Stop asking bloody stupid questions and get busy smoking this cigar.'

Smoking was forbidden until you were eighteen years old, so I was inexperienced. I found the foretop sweeper's bucket, placed it between my knees and lit up, and then alternately drew on the cigar and vomited until an hour later I gave the butt to Thomas. I felt very weak and empty and could hardly see out of my eyes but by four o'clock, when our reliefs arrived, I was sufficiently recovered to be feeling sick again. I said tentatively to Thomas, 'Please let me go first down the mast; you see, I might be sick.' 'Certainly not.' said Thomas. 'Haven't you learnt yet that the senior officer goes first,' and he disappeared below, followed unsteadily by me. I had got down about twelve rungs of this vertical swaying tube when I gasped, 'I'm going to' and was very sick. We entered the gunroom and Thomas went up to the sub-lieutenant and gave him the cigar butt. 'What the hell's happened to your cap and face and shoulders, you're filthy?' So Thomas explained. 'Oh,' said the sub-lieutenant to me, 'you must learn not to insult a senior officer. Bend over,' I got half a dozen.

Two days later the weather still continued rough but I had got over sea-sickness and was feeling fit. I had just eaten tea before going to the top for the first dog watch, and got on to the settee from my place to walk round the head of the table, which was the only way out. At that moment the ship gave a lurch to starboard, I lost my balance and the point of my shoulder cracked the glass over the signed photo of the King. 'Come here you bloody little wart,' shouted the sub-lieutenant. 'First you vomit over a senior officer and now you insult the monarchy! Bend over.' I got a dozen.

About a month later in harbour I really earned a thrashing. For engineering instruction one morning I had been given a torch and told to go to a boiler room with the fires drawn and trace certain steam pipes. It was dark and snug up there on top of the boiler so I lay down on the main steam pipe and went to sleep. I woke with a torch shining in my eyes and the voice of the Senior Engineer inquiring after my health. Temporary Engineer Lieutenant Commander Earnshaw was in private life a professor of marine engineering at Victoria University, Wellington, New Zealand, and seemed ignorant of what my traditional punishment was. Instead of reporting me to the sub-lieutenant he said, 'You will have to make up for lost time, snottie. Report to the engineer's office at 4 pm daily for a week and fire the furnaces and trim the bunkers under the duty chief stoker until 7 pm, in whichever boiler room has steam.' I replied, 'I am sorry about this, sir, but please may I stoke from four to eight?'

'Why?'

'Well, sir, then I would miss gunroom dinner and evolutions and could have watchkeeper's supper in peace at eight fifteen.'

'All right, then report to the office at five and stoke until eight.'

That was the happiest week I had in the *Superb*. I learned a lot and made some friends amongst the stokers.

The organised sadism of gunroom evolutions is self evident from their advertisement in 'Gunroom Standing Orders', but the last one, 'Running Torpedoes', deserves special comment.

It was held that 'Running Torpedoes' in *Superb's* gunroom was impossible because the 'torpedo' must inevitably be killed. The sub-lieutenant argued that this was surmise and that a practical test was necessary. So one evening after dinner he ordered that the mess be prepared for this evolution and the mahogany dining table be put diagonally across the mess and two leaves be taken out. Then pointing to a rather fat youngster he said, 'And that wart will be the torpedo.'

The wart to be the torpedo took off his jacket and lay on his stomach with chin braced up and head back and hands clenched behind his back. He was at the far end of the table against the bulkhead, with about twelve midshipmen each side of the table. The act was for the torpedo to be propelled at such a speed down the table that, provided he kept his chin up, then the fall on to the deck would be taken on his chest. If however he lost his nerve and used his hands to break his fall, he got beaten.

The senior midshipman of the mess then said to the sub-lieutenant that he must point out that since the table had been shortened it was not possible to get up enough speed to prevent the torpedo merely smashing his face on the deck, whereas if the two leaves were put back into the table then the speed would be adequate but the gap at the end inadequate and the torpedo must inevitably break his neck on the far bulkhead. 'That has yet to be proven,' said the sub-lieutenant, 'so we will have a dry run. By that I mean that the torpedo will be propelled at full speed, with the table short as it is now, and the two biggest snotties at the receiving end are to catch the torpedo in mid-air. I shall then be able to judge speed, trajectory, angle of impact and all the data we require for this important experiment.' So the torpedo hurtled down the table, was safely caught and his hands were still clasped in mid-air. 'I must point out,' said the senior midshipman, 'that our mahogany dining table is now ruined – the torpedo's shirt buttons have scoured a furrow right down the middle.' 'How damnable,' said the mess president. 'Take his shirt and vest off.' So the torpedo, nude to the waist, was replaced in the firing position. 'Stand by for second dry run. Fire!' The torpedo re-mained where he was. 'What the hell's happening down there? I said Fire!'

The torpedo, sweating with fear, was firmly stuck to the table and could not be moved horizontally. The sub-lieutenant, to my surprise and relief, looked quizzically at the problem then said, 'Replace all gear. I want a bridge four!'

The inevitable showdown with this tyranny occurred in mid-February 1918. The sub-lieutenant, drunk with power and liquor after the evening meal, accused the whole mess of laughing at him. 'Fall in and I'll flog the lot of you', he yelled. Fortunately Bowen, the one stripe paymaster and far the oldest member of the mess, was present and said, 'We've had enough! Lock him in his cabin, and two keep watch on it until he's asleep.'

It was a stormy night, and midwinter, but our prisoner threat-ened revenge and opened the porthole in his cabin. Stating that he would swim to the gangway and report mutiny he dived through only to stick at the knees. Surgeon Lieutenant Law R.N.V.R. had joined the ship a few weeks before from Guy's Hospital and

Bowen asked him to attend to this urgent case. Law, a big man, went into the cabin, seized the ankles and pulled the patient back into the cabin. The doctor then knocked the patient unconscious with a right to the chin, screwed up the porthole, placed the body on the bunk, locked the cabin, dismissed the sentries and returned to the wardroom.

Superb paid off at Newcastle the first week in April and until then an uncanny peace reigned. The sub-lieutenant never again spoke in the mess and spent most of his time in his cabin.

At the end of April I joined HMS *Dreadnought* sent north from duty as flagship of the Thames force to take the place of *Superb* in the Grand Fleet. She had been refitting in May 1916 so missed the battle of Jutland but before that she had established a record which has never since been equalled. She was, and is, the only battleship world wide that sank an enemy submarine in war.

In mid-March 1915 the Grand Fleet had been carrying out exercises in the North Sea and when about fifty miles south of Scapa, at noon, the Fourth Battle Squadron was detached to Cromarty. During this manoeuvre torpedo tracks were seen and then a periscope fine on *Dreadnought*'s port bow. It appears that the U-boat lost trim after firing. *Dreadnought*'s ram lifted her out of the sea and the 'U-29' on her conning tower was clearly read. The significance of this sinking was not immediately realised but the commanding officer had recently transferred from *U9*. In fact he was Lieutenant Otto Weddigen, who had sunk the cruisers *Aboukir*, *Hogue* and *Cressy* on 22 September 1914 and the cruiser *Hawke* on 15 October, following with successes in the first U-boat campaign against British trade routes. Lieutenant Weddigen was the first German U-boat ace, and a formidable one, whose name was recalled by Doenitz in 1935.

The midshipmen's lot on board *Dreadnought* was in complete contrast to *Superb*. The senior sub-lieutenant, under report as usual, awaited the war's end with cynical indifference. I was told that this intelligent but lazy youth had wrecked his career by a disastrous marriage at the age of eighteen. Our life was free and easy in the gunroom, but the lieutenant responsible for midshipmen's training disapproved of our happy freedom and itched to beat us, which was against regulations. He contrived to satisfy his urge by composing an eighty-page book entitled 'Regulations for Midshipmen's Instruction' and at regular intervals sent for an individual and pointed out some infringement, awarding as punishment one week's morning watches standing from 0400 to 0800 on the roof of the foretop. This was a vicious punishment, particularly in high winds or driving rain at Scapa with only the stump mast to cling to. He would then add, as a gracious after-thought, 'Or, alternatively, if you take this cane to the wardroom bathroom I will give you six now and we will say no more about it.'

We midshipmen studied his technique with organised collusion. Six weeks after I had joined midshipman Watkinson burst into the gunroom and shouted, 'I've got him. He has just given me six without the option of a week's morning watches so after being beaten I said I would at once report him to the Commander. He's in a panic and said he thought the alternative was understood. What do we do, chaps?' The officer was informed that provided he never again punished any of us himself we would not report the matter. This he accepted. For the few weeks remaining the midshipmen served with enthusiasm and a sense of voluntary good behaviour.

I served three months in *Dreadnought* before she paid off, having proved too slow for fleet duties. I had now been at sea in the Grand Fleet ten months and within the 'warts' world', to which I had been consigned for training and 'the invaluable experience of active service', I had seen authority twice grossly abused and twice peremptorily deposed; the first time by violence, the second time by blackmail. On both occasions I had enthusiastically partici-pated at 'wart level'.

I transferred to the battleship *Benbow* in mid-August 1918, wondering what was in store. The contrast was complete. There were officers in the wardroom who would laugh with us rather than at us, who visited the gunroom and even dined with us on guest nights. The sub-lieutenant was under report as usual but was an amenable nonentity. I was told that *Benbow's* gunroom had come through the usual troubles but that in early 1916 the Captain becoming aware of bullying, ordered the gunroom doors to be removed for a year; the sub-lieutenant had retaliated by ordering that the duty wart should stand at the door holding a newspaper with arms outstretched, whenever he was in the mess during this year, to restore his privacy. When I joined this was but a distant memory of the 'bad old days'.

In three months the war was over. The Fleet was at Rosyth when, at 11 am on 11 November the ship's company assembled on the quarterdeck and Captain Waistell read us the armistice terms and emphasised their sweeping character. On 21 November the Grand Fleet steaming east in two columns six miles apart sighted the light cruiser *Cardiff* at 8.30 am, heading west between our lines. Out of the mist, forty miles east of May Island the High Seas Fleet followed, led by *Seydlitz* – fourteen capital ships, seven light cruisers and forty-nine destroyers in line ahead. Their station keeping was good, their appearance filthy. It looked just what it was, a convoy of scrap iron on its way to the knacker's yard. Our fleet reversed course, turning inwards, and steamed on either side to the anchorage in Largo Bay. There were thirty-seven British capital ships, six American and one French, a force over three times the size of our opponent.

After the excitement of seeing these almost mythical ships for the first time, a sense of fiasco crept like fog over us all. For the Commander-in-Chief, and those who with him had borne great responsibility, this must have been a bitter and certainly not a glorious climax. This surrender followed by internment at Scapa Flow was a far greater achievement than it appeared. For over four years our naval enemy had the initiative to break out and seek action at a moment and under conditions of his choosing; he had failed to do so.

As we came to anchor just before noon the Commander-in-Chief signalled, 'The German flag will be hauled down at sunset today and will not be hoisted again without permission.' As soon as boats were out a party of marines left our ship to inspect *Grosser Kurfürst* to check that gun breech blocks were inoperative and magazines empty. On return the Marine subaltern visited the gunroom and told us, 'When we got on to the quarterdeck four seamen delegates with red arm bands met us – the poor bums have mutinied.' At sunset I watched the German flags come down with admirable precision. It seemed then an act of dramatic finality.

It was just fourteen months since I had gone to sea. I had seen no gun fired in anger nor any weapon used offensively. I had seen no sign of any enemy above, upon or below the sea, until that morning. I had never seen my Commander-in-Chief and no Admiral had ever visited a ship I had served in. For this squalid experience I got two medals.

3

DURING my remaining three years as a midshipman I was eight months in the destroyer *Whitley* and then returned to battleship life in *Benbow* in the Mediterranean. The varied and interesting service in the post-war chaos steadily erased the disillusion which Grand Fleet inactivity had caused.

Whitley's active service, with Admiral Cowan's Baltic Force successfully establishing the independence of the Baltic states, followed by *Benbow*'s unsuccessful efforts to bolster General Wrangel's Crimean front and equally unsuccessfully to try to thwart the rejuvenisation and modernisation of Turkey by Kemal Ataturk further confirmed my conviction of the importance of light forces and the ineffectiveness of the unhandy pompous progress of the battleship.

In late 1920 *Benbow* was back in Malta. Five of us sat our examination for sub-lieutenant and passed. We spent a month on board awaiting orders to return to Britain and were given odd jobs within our capability. One was watchkeeping in harbour between 10 pm and 6 am and one evening I was walking the quarterdeck with the quartermaster, Petty Officer Miller, whom I knew and liked. Miller, looking ashore to the waterfront on the Valetto side said, 'Look, sir. See that bright light just gone on there? That's my girl-friend just come in; now that everything is quiet here, sir, would you mind if I just slipped ashore to see her? I'll be back by three, I promise you, sir.'

I replied primly, 'But Miller, I always thought you were a married man. I'm sure you have told me so.'

'Well, I suppose I am, sort of.'

'How do you mean sort of? You are either married or you aren't.'

'Well, sir, since you don't approve of my going ashore I'll tell you what I mean by "sort of". I'm a countryman from Devon and I fell in love with a lass from my village and we were married as soon as I was an able seaman. That was in 1909. After ten days together I bids her farewell, and serves my three years, and am taking passage home when due to some sickness on the Australian station my draft is sent to Sydney, and I am still on the South Pacific Station when war breaks out in 1914. So then, of course, any entitlement to leave is washed out and I starts another commission, but I gets back to the old country in early 1917 and gets ten days leave and goes on with my honeymoon where I'd left off eight years before.

'Of course, barracks drafting office don't want the likes of me around, I might be expecting some soft job like the drafting office for myself which might disturb someone, so I am posted to the Mediterranean immediately; so after minesweeping and such like I find myself in this battleship and I shall take my discharge in a few months, when my thirtieth birthday comes round. Well, sir, that's what I mean by "sort of" and as the saying goes "A slice out of a cut cake is never missed!" '

The impressionable years were behind me, I had formed the opinion that battleships and battle cruisers were considered dominant in the Royal Navy because they provided the most jobs for the most senior officers. They were of little use for fighting because they were too valuable to lose. So in peace time nobody took any notice of them.

I also knew that in war it was much more important to make a hole below an enemy's waterline than above it, but for some reason admirals did not think so; that the best young officers came from public schools and the worst from the naval colleges; and that the lower deck of the Royal Navy was unbeatable in loyalty, courage and good humour.

I cannot have entirely wasted my time at sea since I thought much the same on retirement.

I joined submarines in October 1921.

In November Britain proposed, at the Washington conference, that submarines be abolished – which was naturally disregarded by all other powers.

In the first post-war naval exercises submarines operated realistically with surface ships in fleet manoeuvres. It was particularly unfortunate that *K5* was lost during fleet exercises in January

1921 and *L24* in similar circumstances in January 1924, whilst *H42* was sunk in collision with a destroyer off Gibraltar in April 1922. From these sinkings there were no survivors. There is no doubt that these losses during fleet exercises weighed heavily against future participation of submarines in full scale fleet co-operation which meant that submarines were to lack realistic practice, while the fleet would consequently be encouraged to discount the submarine.

I was happy in submarines from the start. Everything that everyone did was necessary and part of the whole common sense technical routine to keep the submarine and its weapons one hundred per cent efficient. If a man was casual, lazy or ignorant, his mess mates quickly summed up his failings, and if he did not correct them he was endangering all on board and he would find his way back to the spare crew (who in those days did not get submarine pay). The danger inherent in the service was used to enhance morale and comradeship. Nobody was bored and defaulters or punishment were rare.

My first years were in the L class, a medium-sized all-purpose submarine, well tested during the last year of war. I served on the China station from 1923 to 1926 where the Fourth Flotilla was based from the time the Japanese alliance ceased after the 1921 Washington Conference. The Fourth was our premier flotilla and all commanding officers and most first lieutenants had war experience. Our flotilla was a band of enthusiastic submariners, but in 1923 our peacetime limitations were made clear. On 31 August Tokyo and Yokohama were struck by a severe earthquake. The flagship HMS *Hawkins* and all other available cruisers and sloops went at full speed to assist the Japanese people, but Admiral Leveson left us at Wei Hai Wei because of our slow speed and small manpower. The disaster was on too large a scale for us to be of any use.

After two interesting and happy years as the junior officer of *L15* I was appointed first lieutenant of *L7*, then completing a long refit in Hong Kong dockyard. It was late April 1925 before I met my new Captain who had just arrived on the station. *L7* was to undock the day before the depot ship *Titania*, with Captain *S4* on board and eight submarines in company, sailed north 1,300 miles to our summer exercise base at Wei Hai Wei.

It had been arranged for *L7* to provision ship, adjust compasses, embark torpedoes and ammunition and the many other chores, ending with a test dive to check water tightness and diving mechanism during a two-day programme, sail independently the day after *Titania* and join the flotilla off the Shantung peninsula. This meant that we would miss the exercises on passage north, which ended with firing a practice torpedo at the depot ship. The *Titania* only conducted exercises at sea twice a year, so to lose this early opportunity of proving his skill was a severe disappointment to my Captain, since our frequent exercises with cruisers and sloops were not witnessed by Captain *S4*. My Captain boldly asked permission to postpone the test dive until we were on passage, in an endeavour to sail with the flotilla, and this was allowed, on his own responsibility.

After clearing harbour *L7* went ahead of the flotilla, carried out a successful trial dive in slow time and rejoined off Taiwan. Approaching the latitude of Shanghai the submarines were sent ahead to their attack positions for the following day and that evening my Captain sent for me and said, 'Now that our test dive is over there is to be no more hanging about on the surface. In future when the klaxon goes you are to dive the submarine at an angle of ten degrees, that is my standing order.'

I replied, 'Since the diving angle gauge only registers up to nine degrees, because the propellors come out of water then, would it not be better to dive at eight degrees, sir?' I knew that the correct practice was five degrees for efficient diving. He retorted: 'As the gauge only registers to nine degrees, amend my order to: The submarine is never to be dived at an angle of less than ten degrees. I will tell you soon enough if we are steeper than I wish to be.'

All this puzzled me; up to this moment everything since he had joined had gone without a hitch, but now that we were to do a simple exercise he seemed all tensed up and finding fault. I knew *Titania* was due to pass about 8 am so imagined we would dive about two hours before that. I returned to the mess and turned in. I was wakened before midnight and told that the Captain wanted me on the conning tower. On arrival he beckoned me aft, so that nobody could hear us and said, 'When do you finish charging batteries?'

'I shall continue a charge on both engines until 0400, sir, then I think they will be well up.'

'Very good, that suits well,' said the Captain, and continued, 'from now on there's to be no more so called peacetime routine; my submarine is to be trained and kept in a state of readiness for war, so at some time between 0330 and 0400 when the ship's company is at watch cruising stations and two-thirds of them asleep, I will press the klaxon and I want this submarine of mine to be taken down as smartly at night as she might need to be in emergency at war – do you understand?'

'In that case may I break the charge at 0300, sir, to cut out one complication?'

'Certainly not, what the hell for? I suppose the next thing you are going to say is that you have not trained the crew! Is that your trouble, Number One?'

'No, sir, but we have new officers and more than half the ratings are new to *L7*, which was in dry dock this time last week, so I think that your intention to dive during the middle watch from watch cruising stations with a charge running on both engines is premature. I don't think it is fair to the crew.'

'Well, the crew can learn tonight how I intend to go on. Remember not a word to anyone, and not less than ten degrees bow down. That's all.'

I put down for a call at 0300 and went to sleep.

I have to explain a technicality here. The submarine had been charging its batteries as it travelled north through the night and was near the end of the charge at 0300: for this reason the battery voltage would be about 240 volts instead of the 220 volts for which all minor electrical machinery and the lighting was designed. This difficulty was overcome in L class submarines by driving a double-ended armature, feeding in battery voltage one end and taking out a steady 220 volts the other end to supply the fuse panel and switchboard for all minor electrical circuits. This double-ended armature was, sensibly, called the reducer, and it weighed about half a ton. It was situated behind the hydroplane standards and mounted with its axis in the fore-and-aft line of the submarine. Because we were on charge all auxiliaries were running off the reducer.

At about 0345 I was standing in the control room when the klaxon blared. I told the duty watch in the control room to take her down right away and opened the main vents. Everything happened in copybook fashion, and the two awakened watches took up their diving stations quickly. I kept the fore planes at dive until the bubble was passed nine degrees and told the second coxswain to keep that angle on until we reached forty feet. *L7* was diving normally except for bow down angle, and I doubted whether she would be controllable since in my opinion both propellors and the after planes must be out of water.

Just as the Captain arrived in the control room the reducer burst into flames; he leaned towards the switchboard and broke the reducer switch, plunging the submarine into darkness and preventing the second coxswain from taking the dive rudder off the fore planes. It was too late to try to put machinery into hand operation, everyone was holding on with one hand to something overhead since the angle was too steep to stand on deck. As I tried to reach the twenty-volt secondary lighting switch I was hit behind the knees by one of several objects flying through the darkness from the stoker's mess and I ended up at the bottom of the periscope well. The Captain made the reducer switch again, the lights went on and flames shot two feet out of the front end of the reducer. He broke the switch and put the lights out once more.

This time the electrical fire had caught the paintwork and the smoke was making us cough. Someone with a torch had found me and pulled me back on deck. The Captain ordered a pyrene to be played on the flickering reducer, stopping the flame and giving off a gas that seemed pungent and deadly. At this stage I got the secondary lighting on. *L7* was evidently stopped about thirty-five degrees bows down with 130 feet showing on the control room gauge.

The coxswain, Chief Petty Officer Gadd, hanging from a pipe gripped by his left hand, had his right hand on the after hydroplane control wheel. He suddenly said, 'My wife has always told me I'm a bloody fool, she'd have a good laugh now if she could see me, stuck in the mud ten thousand miles from home!' Nobody laughed or said anything.

From now on the Captain did all the right things, and there was need for quick action since the smoke and fumes were stifling and getting worse. Main ballast tanks were blown from forward to aft in succession but we remained stuck. Astern power was used at about three-quarters power, on port then starboard propellers alternately, for fully ten minutes. We were then about to start the slow laborious job of pumping out fresh water and fuel when the angle suddenly came off and $L7$ was on the surface after a predicament lasting twenty-five minutes.

The Captain opened the conning tower hatch, started main engines and the atmosphere cleared. Shortly afterwards we dived again but at a five-degree angle and, on a flat calm morning, carried out a skilful attack, our torpedo passing under the *Titania's* bridge. $L7$ surfaced and took station astern and continued north with the flotilla.

When the reducer was cool enough it was examined and the defect was easily found. All heavy electrical motors were mounted in submarines with their axis in the fore-and-aft line of the vessel and, to prevent the armature slipping if the submarine took up an excessive angle, annular distance pieces were fitted to keep the armature central; these were missing.

As a result, the armature at full revolutions had been torn and short circuited by the brushholders. I naturally suspected the mistake had occurred in the Hong Kong dockyard electrical shop, but it could have occurred earlier in a British yard or even at the manufacturers.

Twenty-five minutes on the sea-bed in such circumstances is something to be avoided and I knew that the reason was due to the Captain being too demanding; nevertheless we had had the good fortune to have found out this defect in shallow water; if it had happened in a depth of over four hundred feet the submarine would have collapsed. Alternatively had the submarine been handled normally the fault would probably never have shown up. The important outcome to my mind was to make a full report to Captain $S4$ on arrival in port.

Before noon, I took my report on to the conning tower and gave it to the Captain, who read it and, looking angrily at me, said, 'I see you have written from $L7$ to Captain $S4$. Do you really imagine that I shall report this type of incident to the Captain S? Just because as first lieutenant you have failed to inspect the machinery with efficiency and now wish to fob off your mistakes on to a wretched Chinese electrician. No, the type of report that I shall send to Captain S is to make an unseen attack on a flat calm day and put a torpedo plumb under his bridge when he is standing on it! That is the type of report to make!' and he flung my report over the side.

The signalman, the look out, and the officer of the watch were no more impressed than I was; he was apparently so obsessed with his own advancement that he would not allow experience to assist, or possibly save, the lives of his flotilla mates. On arrival in port I went to his cabin and gave him a letter explaining that I had a duplicate. In it I told him that I intended forthwith to inform all first lieutenants of the flotilla of the defect in $L7$'s reducer and the circumstances of the discovery so that they might inspect their own. If he objected I wished to see Captain $S4$ to state my case. He made no comment and I made my report to my contemporaries.

I have recorded this incident to show how an officer of professional ability could fail due to the tensions of 'promotionitis' causing him to behave irrationally. It was this type of unpleasantness that the Monsell reforms removed in 1933, by changing the regulations for the selection of officers for promotion to the rank of Commander and to the rank of Captain.

Throughout the nineteenth century the old custom of promotion due to influence from family connection died very slowly. Admiral of the Fleet Sir Henry Keppel, who died in 1904, wrote at the end of his career, 'I never got a step that was not a "job".' This custom was succeeded before 1900 by the consideration of an officer's career from the confidential reports of his Commanding Officers, with a covering opinion by his Commander-in-Chief at the time that his name came before the Board of Admiralty for consideration; and this was only once for each step.

Although a death blow to nepotism, the reform was too rigid. A sub-lieutenant of brain and diligence could advance the date of his promotion by six months by gaining first class certificates in all professional courses. But the date he was promoted Lieutenant became his 'basic date' from which all subsequent promotion was calculated. He then served eight years as a lieutenant and a further six years as a lieutenant commander; and after fourteen years and perhaps a few months his name came before the Board of Admiralty for inclusion, or not, in the promotion list which was sent out by Whitehall radio station on 30 June and 31 December annually, and still is. If his name was not on that list he could continue to serve in his original rank up to the time of full pension, usually in shore or depot ship appointments suited to his rank and experience.

The same routine applied for promotion to Captain after precisely eight years in Commander's rank.

The most obvious shortcoming was that it allowed no opportunity for the really outstanding officer to gain young promotion. All Commanders on promotion were within a year of thirty-five and all Captains within a year of forty-three; but this was one of the lesser evils.

The Navy needed the best officers to be promoted but this did not necessarily happen, as can be seen in the following example.

Imagine that of ten lieutenants six had basic dates in the period from January to June 1918 and four in July to December 1918. The six would hear their fate on 30 June 1932 and the four on 31 December 1932.

Suppose the first six were all good officers deserving of promotion, but on promotion date there was only a requirement for two. After searching deliberation the Board of Admiralty made their decision, which had all the unsatisfactory features of compromise, and four good officers were relegated. Of the four in the second half of the year suppose one died in 1925, one retired to a directorship in his father's firm, and another's eyesight had failed, rendering him unfit. The fourth might be the least satisfactory of all ten, a mediocrity but with nothing whatsoever against him. For two vacancies there would be one candidate, and he would be promoted.

This was not all; obviously it was supremely important to be in 'a promotion job' under the notice of an admiral of real influence at the Admiralty when your turn came. So obviously it was good to be First Lieutenant of the Fleet flagship on the Home or Mediterranean stations and bad to be the captain of a sloop on the South Africa or East India station. This led to jockeying for certain appointments and the bad feeling and jealousies that go with wangling.

The Monsell reform was simple and effective. Every officer entered the zone for promotion four years before his final chance, so that he had eight opportunities for promotion to Commander and again to Captain. Not only did this ease tensions and remove jockeying for plum appointments, but it also meant that exceptionally able officers could gain several years seniority, in fact it was just possible to become a post captain at thirty-five, which was young enough but not too young.

This change at once eased tensions and prevented all contemporaries being in cut-throat competition. It greatly improved social life and allowed wives to be their charming selves instead of part of the rat race. It transformed the atmosphere within the Service and did immeasurable good.

4

AFTER three years abroad I returned to a scene of appreciable naval building activity. The battleships *Nelson* and *Rodney* were nearing completion. The ten County Class cruisers with eight inch guns were coming forward annually, as were the first post-war destroyer flotillas and the necessary tugs and auxiliaries for base duties. When I arrived at Chatham in 1926 to join *L18* as first lieutenant I found the first post-war, general purpose, submarine *Oberon* nearing completion. *Oberon* was followed by five other O class and six P class submarines, and the splendid depot ship *Medway*. (This new depot ship and submarines were destined to replace the ageing L class flotilla in the Far East in 1929.)

In 1926 the 'No war for ten years' policy governed all financial approval for defence spending, which made this naval programme a remarkable achievement on the part of the Board of Admiralty under the leadership and prestige of Lord Beatty. I and my contemporaries took the Navy's privileged position as a matter of course; the plight of the Army and the R.A.F. passed us by.

In the middle of 1927 I arrived at Fort Blockhouse to spend three months with three other contemporaries doing the submarine Commanding Officer's Course, sometimes called the Periscope Course. This was a particularly happy experience, almost devoid of bookwork, and was a concentrated effort to develop in the students a sense of location and a clear mental picture of one's own position relative to a target which is to be attacked by torpedo throughout that time when the submarine is being manoeuvred blind, since the periscope can usually only be used for less than five per cent of an attack. This sense of relative position in the Captain's mind's eye is what the success and the safety of the submarine chiefly depend upon. It should be quickly developed in the simple case of a merchant ship steering a straight course at slow speed, first sighted many miles distant, but the sense must be developed so that the Captain will act both correctly and immediately when confronted with, for example, an aircraft carrier escorted by eight destroyers zigzagging at twenty-five knots in a visibility of only two miles.

This flair for holding a correct mental picture comes easily to some people, but most can with practice become safe rather than brilliant submarine captains; the one essential was constant and frequent practice. Today, with an attack team and computer to assist, things may be different but then a good eye, self confidence and an ability for mental arithmetic were sufficient to give proficiency.

At Blockhouse we gained this attack sense and self confidence chiefly through a large instrument called the attack teacher, which simply meant that the student entered an underground full scale working model of a submarine's control room, and when he looked through the periscope he gazed at a complete surround of canvas realistically painted to represent sky, horizon and sea. From one section, moving on a clockwork trolley, came his target doing any speed and zigzag, either alone or escorted, which the instructor may have set on the clock. That was all that there was to it in my day, but of course refinements to make the instruments more realistic were steadily added.

After the first month of the course we went to sea once a week to carry out attacks on a slow sloop, which gave the necessary practice in sea conditions and the avoidance of merchant shipping, but for one sea attack each week we would experience about eight attacks on models with infinite variety. The instrument therefore was of very considerable importance and since the officers of foreign navies building submarines in Britain were trained on it, its renown was not confined to Fort Blockhouse.

The four of us passed our tests and I joined my first command, *H49*, at Portland in December 1927. The H class submarines were of American design, built under licence in Britain in 1917, and like the L class were destined to fight in both wars. The flotilla's duties were cooperation with HMS *Osprey*, the shore-based anti-submarine school at Portland, and our close and friendly liaison taught us the limitations of asdic as a submarine locating instrument and its value to a submarine as a source of accurate information about enemy surface vessels which could be acquired without use of the periscope. Working in close accord with *Osprey's* officers and scientists was first class training for developing cunning in avoiding asdic location by the use of tide rips, other shipping, depth, and holding trim stopped, to quote some factors. It was apparent that local knowledge counted for a lot, rather like local knowledge on a golf course.

The impression I gained at first hand during 1928 was that the anti-submarine specialists and scientists could never make asdic into more than a close range and unreliable location device, whereas its introduction to the submarine would vastly improve the efficiency of that vessel in both attack and escape.

It was a matter of routine that submarine officers after one year in command reverted for two years service in capital ships, in order to keep in touch with the main stream of naval affairs. The prospect of 'big ship time' as it was termed, filled me with dismay. As my year neared its end I read in an Admiralty Fleet Order that one executive Lieutenant was required to learn Russian during 1929. Although quite useless at languages I applied successfully.

Three months' study in London University and a preliminary examination was followed by a journey to Tallinn, Estonia. To visit Helsinki across the Gulf to the north was only a twenty minutes journey by air, and I took a week-end holiday there, I had an introduction to the commissionaire of the Societenhusen Hotel, who was an ex-colonel of the Imperial Russian Army. The first evening my friend took me to the Russian Officers' Club to play bingo and meet the Russian speaking community. I met about five retired naval officers there and each one enquired enthusiastically, 'How is Max Horton? Tell me please about him.' I did not know the formidable Horton in those days, but was able to assure them that he was prospering in the Navy. Their high regard for him was most marked.

My week-end visit paid an interesting dividend six years later.

I passed my interpreter examination in November 1929, a qualification which I failed to keep up and which I barely have had occasion to use. Whilst I had postponed my battleship appointment I found that I had in no way shortened it, and before Christmas 1929 I joined *Nelson*, flagship of the Home Fleet, for a two year commission.

I was with a splendid company of officers and men in the most modern and powerful battleship afloat, but I had been wholly prejudiced against battleships. I thought them a useless waste of money. I felt it was most unfortunate that the admirals who commanded fleets invariably flew their flags in battleships. I could not see their wartime use, and on completion of my service in *Nelson* I thought the same.

My war action station could not have been bettered. I controlled the port six inch battery; added to which there was much gunnery practice and a liberal ammunition allowance. Nevertheless it seemed plain to me that *Nelson* had much to fear in war from a submarine, while a submarine had nothing whatever to fear from *Nelson*. What, I wondered, did we build and plan the composition of our fleet for – was it to beat the enemy or for social duties?

I found that although my messmates in the wardroom were good company, and the gunroom seemed a happy and civilised place, the same problems persisted. How could 1,300 men and over 100 officers be sensibly and objectively employed in peacetime? What would *Nelson* do if there was ever another war? How many cruisers or destroyers or coastal motor boats or submarines could be built for the cost of *Nelson*? How many officers and men on board had ever served in a submarine? About six, I supposed.

At that time, 1930, there were over seventy officers in the wardroom, seventeen of whom were executive lieutenant commanders. Of course several of these were on the staff, but all the same it seemed to me much like a full strength battalion with seventeen majors. The staff at this time were giving much thought to a mythical weapon called the 'B' bomb. It was understood that sticks of these bombs would be dropped ahead of the fleet and keep bobbing up and down, and some were sure to explode right underneath a ship where there was no armour and be lethal. On the other hand it appeared to be thought that if a submarine pumped a salvo of torpedoes into a battleship it would be inconvenient but no more, because she had side armour. Such was staff gossip.

In 1931, in order to employ part of our passage time to the West Indies usefully we held a paper tactical exercise. Officers in their cabins exercised varying commands of the Red and Blue fleets, which were at war. Each officer plotted the movements of both fleets on a chart in his cabin and manoeuvred his command by writing out a signal and sending it to the exercise control in the staff office. Rear Admiral Colvin, the Chief of Staff, was umpire. Each player knew as much or as little of enemy movements as it was thought he would know in war by signals brought by messengers to his cabin.

During the course of this exercise I was commanding the Red submarines and the Blue battlefleet steamed straight through my submarine disposition. I received a signal, 'One hit is awarded on one Blue battleship. Speed of Blue fleet is reduced by two knots.' I went round to the umpire and said, 'Sir, I quite see that one does not wish to prejudice the exercise at this early stage, but please tell me what you consider a realistic damage assessment would be?' Admiral Colvin, a very able officer, replied, 'On the contrary, Simpson, I think the award of one hit generous. Your flotilla has been out of sight of land for forty-eight hours so none of your submarines would know where they were.' I was quite speechless with rage, but this was an ordinary opinion for a senior officer. In their minds an anti-submarine school was improving a thing called an asdic so there was no more need to worry, the present headache was air attack and the 'B' bomb.

Ship's duties, after command of my own submarine, seemed paltry. Initiative was not encouraged; I remember our first port of call on this West Indies visit was Barbados and from there we were to go to Dominica, 150 miles to the north west. I asked permission to sail a cutter with a volunteer crew of young seamen, leaving Barbados twelve hours before *Nelson* and arriving about twelve hours after her. The month was March when tornadoes are unknown and there is a trade wind to ensure good sailing conditions. The Commander thought the proposal quite mad and took the matter before the Captain who said that he really could not take the risk. We must remember that the pulling regatta was in June, when the cutter was of real importance. The only officers in 1930 who sailed and were interested in yachting were the Royal Engineers; the Royal Navy Sailing Association was just starting.

In February 1932 I joined the submarine *Thames*, the first of the new Thames class, building at Vickers Armstrong, Barrow. Commander Claud Barry was captain and so I had the unusual experience of going back once more to the duties of first lieutenant, but was assured that my appointment was a good one. It proved both an invaluable and happy experience.

Barry, the winner of a D.S.O. in command of submarines in war, was very senior for this post, but had been appointed because of its special features. He had recently served in the Admiralty on the material side and was in part responsible for the Thames design and was its keen protagonist. I found him delightful to serve, being clear in what he wanted and trusting his subordinates to get on with the job. He was not a clever man and was as full of enthusiasm as he was lacking in imagination.

This submarine *Thames* (later followed by *Severn* and *Clyde*) was built for speed. Her main diesel engines could be boosted by smaller high speed diesel engines driving rotary fans which could give a supercharge air intake pressure of five pounds. To accommodate the engines and give a hull design to make the best of her 10,000 horse power required great length. The resultant graceful monster was 346 feet long and 2,000 tons displacement and about twice the cost of a standard 'S' class submarine; all this size and expense for an estimated 21 knots.

After a few days and a thorough study of the submarine I said to Commander Barry, 'What is this submarine designed for? She offers a huge target to the enemy, she cannot be quick and handy when turning submerged, she costs double an ordinary submarine and she cannot accompany the fleet, since battleship speed is now 25 knots?' Barry looked rather upset and changed the subject. Next day he said to me, 'To answer your question about *Thames*. Whilst I am in command she is the fastest, cleanest, most efficient and most beautiful submarine afloat! I will have no criticism of her, Number One.' I remark upon this incident because it is a good example of what could and occasionally did happen in submarine construction, the enthusiasms of individual submarine officers at that time carrying too much weight, opinions changing, leading to inconsistency and finally a showdown.

The building and fitting out of *Thames* was a fascinating task, particularly at Vickers Armstrong with their wealth of experience and immense pride in the finished vessel. There is one important difference in the acceptance trials of a surface ship and a submarine at any shipyard in Britain. For ships the builders provide the crew for trials. For submarines the Navy must provide a fully trained crew on board for diving the submarine, whilst the builders will have their own steaming party for checking the correct operation of all machinery. By July 1932 we were doing trials for a week up the Clyde and finally our diving trial. The *Thames* behaved beautifully.

During the acceptance engine trial Commander William Jameson, our splendid engineer officer, did not get his full horsepower, so it was agreed that we return to Barrow for a week to make engine adjustments, then go to sea for engine trials only, and if successful our Captain would sign the acceptance form; the Vickers steaming party would disembark into a tug and we would depart to Campbeltown to work up.

A week later the correct horsepower was achieved and *Thames* stopped and all our friends from Vickers stepped over to the tug at about noon on this calm summer's day with the Isle of Man in sight to the north, leaving only the crew of 76 on board, and we felt very empty and spacious since during trials 130 had been our complement.

The captain said, 'We will now shut off for diving and go slow ahead both engines and then dive when I press the klaxon. After we have caught a trim I will surface and we will go north to Campbeltown, happy in the knowledge that we have the finest submarine in the world.'

The klaxon blared, engines stopped, main vents opened, the motors went ahead, the hiss of air escaping from the tanks subsided as the captain arrived in the control room. 'Check her at five degrees,' I said to the coxswain. Claud Barry stood beside me watching events and happy that this dream ship was now all his.

'Take her down, Number One,' said my captain. 'Don't be afraid of the damned thing.'

'But she is going down,' I replied.

'Nonsense, the depth gauges show surface,' replied Barry.

'I can feel her going down, sir, please check through the periscope.'

'Oh, yes, up periscope, let's have a look.' Ten seconds elapsed before Barry could look through the periscope, then he yelled. 'Blow for Christ's sake! Blow all main ballast! It's pitch black down here! Bring her up, Number One! Surface! What the hell's happening?'

We surfaced promptly. What depth we had been to was never known, but less than 300 feet or the stern would have started those frightening noises like pistol shots when the shape changes under pressure.

There were eleven depth gauges in *Thames* throughout the length of the submarine. Each depth gauge was connected to the sea by a quarter-inch diameter copper pipe, which had a two-way tap at both the instrument end and on the pressure hull, so that by giving either tap a half turn the instrument could be shut off. The pressure hull tap would only be shut off if the pipe were fractured due to depth charging, so would not normally be used at all in peacetime. We found that all eleven depth gauges were shut off on the pressure hull, an operation which would have taken the saboteur about six hours in our opinion, and must have been done one night during the previous week.

Commander Jameson and I wanted this sabotage reported by wireless to Vickers and the Admiralty to give detectives full knowledge. However Commander Barry thought otherwise and only reported the matter by letter to the shipwright foreman, Mr Baxter. The management of Vickers and the Admiralty were never informed which I consider wrong. How can an evil be stamped out if authority does not know it exists?

My time in *Thames* with Barry was particularly happy. The ship's company were a splendid crew and the distances we covered between the Gulf of Bothnia for a cold weather cruise to Socotra south of Arabia for hot weather were considerable.

When we were at Malta Commander Barry said, 'I have invited Admiral Sir Roger and Lady Backhouse to lunch on board *Thames* on Sunday. Now this is really important. Sir Roger was Controller when *Thames* was designed and Lady Backhouse launched her; so just lay on the best lunch you can, tell Flack I expect everything to be just so, there will be just the four of us.' Able Seaman Flack was a torpedoman, but because he was a good hearted fellow he had volunteered to be officers' cook. His equipment was primitive, one griller, one hot plate and an electric kettle. I thought I had better plan for safety and arranged the menu – tomato soup, cold ham and tongue with salad, ice cream and coffee.

Our distinguished guests arrived, conversation seemed laboured. I had a premonition of doom and on orders from Barry, Flack arrived with two plates of soup for the Admiral and his lady. Barry looked at the immaculate, stalwart Flack with shocked surprise and in a loud aside said, 'Flack, your thumb's in the soup,' and Flack replied, 'Quite O.K., sir. It isn't really hot.' I sensed that even that would not break the ice and it didn't.

I left *Thames* at the end of 1933 and joined 'Greenwich' for the 1934 Staff Course.

The 1934 Staff Course of about forty naval officers, with the important addition of two soldiers and two airmen who had recently completed their service staff courses at Camberley and Andover, assembled at Greenwich College in January. I think the very real value of the course derived about equally from the people, places and opinions met and visited and the actual course of study. This gave me some insight into the problems faced by the other services. For example, during the summer leave the Aldershot Command held a short exercise at battalion, and then at brigade level, and naval staff students had the opportunity to attend.

At 5 pm on the final day the Commander-in-Chief, General Gathorne-Hardy, a tall, slim, Guards officer with sweeping mustachios, who had watched the exercises mounted on a splendid chestnut charger, attended a meeting at which all officers and N.C.O.s from the Brigade were assembled in a local hall. Smiling and debonair, the C-in-C entered and mounted the stage to give a commentary and some mild criticism on the exercise just completed. Suddenly his expression clouded.

'Captain Smith?' he inquired.

'Sir,' said a voice.

'Stand up, sir,' and an officer stood up.

'Tell me, sir, is it an overdeveloped sense of humour or just crass stupidity that persuades you to mount an anti-tank gun up an oak tree?'

Smith replied, 'On my sector of the front, sir, two tracks likely to be useful for a quick advance of enemy mechanised vehicles converged. There was no cover and no time to dig in. There was a large oak tree in full leaf commanding both tracks so I put my mauve flag and anti-tank guns crew up it. To what extent my action was practical I cannot say, since I have never seen an anti-tank gun nor have I ever been told what weight this weapon may be or the probable calibre of the ammunition.' He remained standing.

'Sit down, sir,' said the Commander-in-Chief and left the hall.

I said to the officer sitting next to me. 'I think the Commander-in-Chief was a bit tough on that officer, what is a military opinion?'

'Yes, I think so too. The fact is that neither our Commander-in-Chief nor anyone else in the Army has seen an anti-tank gun, the phrase is a mere cliché. Maybe Smith had a bright idea.'

So far as I could gather an infantry battalion had a rifle and bayonet for each man and two Lewis guns, one for stripping for instructional purposes and one for firing. I understand that the same applied in September 1939. How the Army maintained morale I do not know, but it did.

During this year at Greenwich one hour was devoted to submarines and not one minute to the 1917 U-boat crisis or to subsequent anti-submarine measures to prevent its recurrence. Three days' study of the Battle of Jutland took place, attended on the last day by a captain of a surviving battle cruiser who came up from his golf club to be with us. During the discussion on the last day Commander Gerald Hoare-Smith (a student) surprised us by stating that he had been a junior officer serving in a destroyer flotilla in the rear of the British fleet, and that it was not until reading the papers on return to Rosyth that his ship had any clue that there had been a battle at all. This gave a practical example of the state of fleet communications at the time.

The Naval Staff Course was, however, invaluable to all of us. Its strength lay in the wide ranging lectures given by experts on Trade, Economics, International Law, Army, Air Force and many other subjects outside our experience.

5

BEFORE my next submarine command I needed to requalify on the attack teacher, so in January 1935 I joined Fort Blockhouse for this, preparatory to the command of *L27* at the end of March. On entering my cabin one Friday afternoon during the first week of February 1935 I found a large envelope on my desk containing a quarto size school notebook with a covering letter attached and eight folded drawings on tracing paper. On the outside of the envelope was written, 'To be posted to me by the morning post on Monday without fail.' I had not been expecting this with any certainty, but had been hopeful since I knew of its existence and asked the privilege from a friend, who must obviously remain nameless. My trip to Helsinki in 1929 was bearing fruit.

Dear Georgi Robertovich, when I had the pleasure of meeting you again recently I was surprised to learn that the Royal Navy is unaware of the German U-boat activities under cover of the Finnish flag which have persisted over several years and have now reached the stage of training officer personnel.

At Turku (also called Abo), the naval base in south-west Finland, is the German controlled Crighton Vulcan shipyard where three U-boats of 500 tons have been built under German supervision to German design and specification. They were commissioned about 1931 and were followed some two years later by a small submarine of 250 tons and another very small one of 100 tons.

In return for the expertise afforded in building this substantial defence against any Soviet naval threat from Kronstadt (which is the only fear we Baltic states feel today) the Finns allow the German Navy to appropriate one of these U-boats for training officer cadets for the future U-boat arm with the proviso that one Finnish officer, the navigator, be an integral part of the

German crew. Although these U-boats are based at Turku they carry out sea exercises from Hango some fifty miles southward and the pilotage is intricate.

In the two years 1933 and 1934 a German accommodation ship *Grille* has arrived at Hango in May bringing 35 officer cadets and their submarine instructors. The routine has been that during the ice-free months ending late September every trainee serves about two weeks in each role; seaman, stoker, wireless, acoustics, torpedo, artificer, petty officer, etcetera. Then through the officer duties with the brightest achieving command experience.

The result is, my friend, that whilst you suppose that the Germans under the Treaty of Versailles have no U-boats and no U-boat potential, they have today 70 young officers trained in modern submarines of their own design whose acoustic capability gives directional evidence of slow propeller beats at ranges far exceeding periscope visibility.

This notebook and drawings are my copies from a friend's, which I made during a visit to Turku. They comprise the specification of a proposed U-boat of German design which is yours for the week-end. If your report is to be accepted you must disclose my identity, but I rely that my identity be restricted to a personal statement to your admiral and not allowed circulation with your report since subsequent disclosure might well prove fatal to me and to my family at some future date.

The notebook was the specification of a proposed U-boat of about 750 tons designated A1. It was written in Russian, but whenever the script was purely technical the script was in English due to the more sophisticated technical vocabulary of English at that time. This made its translation by me quite straightforward. I got to work immediately and co-opted the help of the constructor and his draughtsman on the admiral's staff and sought individual advice in the interpretation of some of the working drawings on unfamiliar techniques.

By Sunday evening the task was completed. The specification translated and all drawings copied and understood. The resultant bulky folio I took to the office of Flag Officer Submarines, Rear-Admiral Talbot, who sent it immediately to the Director of Naval Intelligence, Admiral Dickens.

About a week later Admiral Talbot sent for me and showed me an enthusiastic letter he had received from D.N.I. and I felt that my good fortune and the small team's week-end work had been both useful and appreciated.

During the ensuing years I have occasionally wondered the true identity of *A1* for foolishly I got a mental fixation that the U-boat whose secrets I had so busily deciphered that weekend was Finnish, but she never appeared in *Jane's Fighting Ships*. In 1970, through the diligence of the Naval Historical Department of the Ministry of Defence, who had been put on the right trail by their counterpart in Germany, the thesis by Dr Allison Savile (Appendix 1) gave the answer. *A1* was the 'type designation' allocated in 1933 by the Germans for a prototype 750 ton U-boat – in fact the U-boat that was to prove our chief naval antagonist throughout the Second World War. The accommodation ship *Grille* was in fact an acoustic laboratory to develop the technique of massed U-boat attack against merchant shipping.

It was in June 1935 that I made the only practice attack on a capital ship that ever came my way. It very nearly caused my removal from submarines.

There were rules for practice attacks on the fleet which stated that the ideal range was between 1,000 yards and 1,500 yards; this would be inside the destroyer A/S screen, normally stationed at between 2,000 and 3,000 yards. The exercise orders stated that if the range when torpedoes would be fired was over 1,000 yards, the submarine should surface on her attacking course and signal the target's estimated course and speed. If however the attacking submarine was closer than 1,000 yards the submarine should fire a smoke candle from her submerged position, go deep for safety and then surface and make her claim when it was established that the last surface ship had passed.

I thought these rules the chief cause of capital ship ignorance of submarine capability. My two years in *Nelson* had taught me that long range attack made little impact on big ship staff officers, whilst the appearance of a smoke candle nearby made even less, the usual comment being, 'I wonder which way the submarine is pointing!' In rough weather the smoke candle was sometimes not seen.

The truth was that the exercise regulations misled the fleet into false security and conversely were highly discouraging to submarine crews who were led to believe that it was difficult to attack a capital ship, or even dangerous.

Captain *S2* (Captain G. R. S. Watkins) sailed his five submarines from Tobermory in Mull to spread on an east-west line to intercept the Home Fleet on passage from Scapa Flow to Portland. The Commander-in-Chief, Admiral The Earl of Cork and Orrery, was better known to me as the impetuous Ginger Boyle who much preferred action to supposition, so I had decided to surface and make a claim whatever the range, always provided I was sure it was safe to do so.

It so happened that on the day visibility was good and the big ships came my way with *Hood* leading; then *Renown*, *Rodney* and *Nelson* (C.-in-C.) in the rear. The Fleet was doing that annoying zig-zag of four turns of twenty degrees each in one direction and then four turns back again. I surfaced *L27* on *Hood*'s beam 250 yards off track going full speed astern on both propellors. My signalman flashed our estimates to *Hood*, and yelled down the voice pipe in great excitement, 'We've sunk the *Hood*, she can't get away from this one.' But I was watching *Renown* and saw with dismay that she put her helm hard over to swing under my stern. I rang down full speed ahead and passed through the line with the certainty that I would be accused of 'hazarding my submarine.'

We arrived at Portland some hours after the fleet and I could imagine the indignant comments from the captains of *Hood* and *Renown*, and if it was established that I had behaved dangerously, I would be peremptorily removed from command and from submarines. I went at once to Captain Watkins who ordered his boat to call on the C.-in-C., although it was 9 pm. He came back just before midnight and said, 'All is well, but it is a good thing I went over to your support, *Hood* had accused you of surfacing within fifty yards of her. C.-in-C.'s assessment is,' and he read from a piece of paper, ' "I adjudge *Hood* sunk. *L27* carried out a good attack of a type unsuited to peacetime exercises." ' There was no comment or censure about my contravening orders, he had seen the attack himself and thought it safe.

I have quoted my experience at length as a typical example of how ineffective asdic screen was, which on that particular occasion was attributed to a heavy swell; how big ships reacted to a close attack, and the career risks run by commanding officers who tried to operate realistically.

In August 1935 the Home Fleet submarines sailed for Aden, following the Italian attack on Ethiopia. Our depot ship HMS *Lucia* with Captain *S2* on board led us out, and had been given orders that he was to take every step to avoid being identified as British by any vessel encountered. The steps taken were simple, we kept well to the west of the normal traffic route from Ushant to Gibraltar and passed through the straits of Gibraltar at night. However we passed close to tunny fishing boats on several occasions and on orders from Captain *S2* hoisted the French colours. This annoyed me very much; it seemed that units of the Royal Navy could no longer ride the seas proudly, but in case of objection from the League of Nations we had to creep about off trade routes and when sighted by fishermen masquerade as Frenchmen. Or was this secretive nonsense just the vagary of a spineless government? After arrival at Malta we became British again.

On board the Mediterranean Fleet Submarine depot ship Captain D'Oyley-Hughes sent for me and in the course of conversation told me that he had proposed to the Commander-in-Chief that submarine shelters should be cut into the rock under Valetta from Marsamxett Harbour.

On passage to Port Said *L27* and one other submarine were detached to approach within five miles of the channel buoy off Alexandria to simulate laying mines; a flotilla of destroyers and two flying boats were to try to locate us on our mission. Lieutenant Commander Sprague and I had no difficulty in gaining our positions undetected. On coming to the surface we were ordered to Alexandria for the night so that when we arrived at Port Said next day *Lucia* and the remaining submarines were already through the Suez Canal. A highly objectionable sight met us at the entrance to the canal. The battleship HMS *Barham* was moored on the north side and at right angles to the shipping passing in and out; just ahead of *L27* was a large Italian transport full of troops bound for Eritrea, she had a list to port as two or three thousand Italian troops lined the port gunwhale to jeer at the men on board *Barham*. How they howled! I did not believe then, and I do not believe now, that *Barham* was left at Port Said to be insulted on the orders of that wise and great Commander-in-Chief, Mediterranean, Admiral Sir W. W. Fisher. I feel sure that the government, having rejected naval intervention as a possible means of implementing League policy, and because the Air Council had said that the Fleet could use up its anti-aircraft ammunition in ten minutes, had still wished to advertise the 'British Sea Power' in which they had lost faith. So it was that a British battleship was moored at Port Said to be jeered by every Italian troopship.

An Irishman came on board as canal pilot for *L27*. 'Please take her through, Captain,' he said. 'I can never remember what to say to make a submarine go astern.' We rejoined *Lucia* at Suez and joined the East Indies Squadron under Admiral Rose at Aden. Our journey from Plymouth had indeed given food for thought.

On the evening of 31 December I was sitting in the wardroom after dinner when a sub-lieutenant burst in. 'You're promoted to Commander, sir!' he shouted, and a slight celebration started. That night I thought to myself, 'You had a lucky break over that report on the German U-boat falling into your lap, and that was a well spent week-end which followed.'

In late March 1936 I left *L27* at Aden and in August joined the Operations Division of the Admiralty. The Director and his Deputy were both Captains and in the operations office were six Commanders. The Operations Division dealt with current events, the practical application of Admiralty policy, and with liaison between the ships at sea and the Board of Admiralty.

Because of this liaison role, one of the six Commanders was always on duty day and night throughout the year. This individual, 'The Duty Commander, Admiralty', was the only person continually on duty in any government department except Scotland Yard, and since his duty was to give the Press what assistance or guidance he could, the position was no sinecure.

Each Commander had his normal working hour desk job, concerned with the type of ship with which he was best acquainted, and I had been appointed for submarines and submarine depot ships. For this reason I was the officer within the Admiralty to give a submarine opinion on a staff matter, whereas my colleague the submarine Commander in D.N.E. (equipment) would be sent for on a 'nuts and bolts' matter. In this advisory duty we both represented the Flag Officer, Submarines, at Fort Blockhouse, with whom we kept in touch.

I had been at the Admiralty about six weeks when Captain E. G. H. Bellars, the Director of Training and Staff Duties, sent for me. He said, 'Now that the German U-boat programme has been going for a year and a half I find myself handicapped in advising on training by knowing nothing about these U-boats; for instance it would make a vast difference to me if I knew whether the U-boats were fitted with asdic.'

I replied, 'Well, sir, as you will know, the German U-boat programme and training started four and a half years ago. The Admiralty has the specification of one and it has highly sensitive hydrophones fitted around the conning tower. I speak from memory, sir but I think there are sixteen, each covering an arc of $22\frac{1}{2}$ degrees. They are primarily for passive listening and under favourable conditions will record the direction of the beat of a ship's propeller far beyond visual range. Concurrently they can be used simultaneously or selectively to transmit messages either broadcast or directionally within their arc for many miles submerged, as we can with asdic. In fact the function is similar to asdic except that their submerged array is designed for locating and attacking shipping and our surface force array is designed for locating and attacking U-boats. Also of course it gives in this paper the frequencies used in this particular U-boat, which gives a good clue to what they are up to.'

'Indeed,' said the Director of Training and Staff Duties, 'but I wonder what paper you refer to, for it is certainly one that has never been seen in this department; what paper are you talking about?'

'Well, sir, I had the good luck to get the information and I wrote the paper about February the 10th, 1935.'

'In that case perhaps you could find it and have it directed to me forthwith,' said Captain Bellars eagerly.

'Yes, I will, sir,' and I went back to my desk and telephoned the registry of N.I.D. (that is to say the office which keeps track of all secret and confidential papers in circulation within the Naval Intelligence Division). I said, 'Please refer to the first half of February 1935 to new papers being received into N.I.D. and give me the Admiralty number of a paper received from Admiral Submarines about the second week in February.'

'Yes, we have an entry, its number is M.02187/35.'

'Thank you. Please tell me where it is now according to your registry.'

'Well, according to this it is in room X on floor Y.'

'Thank you. Please tell me the date it is minuted to room X on floor Y and is this room part of N.I.D.?'

I got a reluctant reply that the room was indeed within N.I.D. and that the paper had entered that room in early 1935. So I set off down the passage and entered the room presided over by a Commander I knew very well who denied all knowledge of the paper I sought and added, 'After all, I've been here over a year!'

One wall of this dingy den supported a large brown stained wooden cupboard reaching nearly to the twelve-foot distant, dirty ceiling.

'What's in this?' I enquired.

'Well, I'm not quite sure, but there's nothing in there that matters. I've never looked.'

'Well, let's look now.' I said, so we turned the key and there it was, lying on top of a shelf with lots of other papers on it, amongst other shelves and piles of other papers, unmistakably easy to recognise because of its roll of eight drawings, four feet long attached to it. 'I wonder what else is in this cupboard?'

'Well, my predecessor told me there was nothing in this cupboard that mattered!'

'Never mind about the rest, but Captain Bellars wants this paper within an hour,' (and he got it).

This was only the curtain raiser to the pantomime caused by 'Top Secret M.02187/35'.

The public knows all about 'Blinker Hall' and naval intelligence during the First World War. Also about 'Room 39' and naval intelligence under Admiral Godfrey during the Second (not forgetting Ian Fleming). So it seems reasonable to mention that vital time for intelligence, just prior to a war, when that Admiralty department was manned by 'no-hopers'. The Commander in 'Room X' may not have been energetic, but what of the clerk in the registry who allowed a Top Secret document, addressed by his Director to the following Departments: 'Equipment', 'Tactical Division', 'Torpedoes and Mines', 'Training and Staff Duties', 'Naval Construction', 'Signal Division' and 'Plans' and minuted, 'This interesting and comprehensive report on German submarine policy'—etc. etc., to lie for twenty months on the shelf of a wall cupboard without checking its whereabouts or its progress? Is it not strange that the Director himself who thought so highly of the report on reading it should not have spoken to one director of the seven departments to which he had minuted the paper to enquire what he thought of it?

The truth I suppose lies in the fact that the subject was submarines – a type of vessel which hardly merited remark, and which fortunately had been neutralised by asdic!

I returned to my desk and my routine duties and thought no more of M.02187/35 after the phone call I received from Captain Bellars, thanking me and expressing great interest. I was frankly puzzled on one count; obviously I had not been promoted to commander because of this report, and I could imagine no other reason.

It was early December 1936 when Commander Vivian, who was Admiralty Press Liaison Officer, called into Operations Division one Friday afternoon and said, 'Who's Duty Commander over the week-end?'

'I am,' I replied.

'Well, I have promised Lieutenant-Commander Kenneth Edwards, naval correspondent for the *Morning Post*, these papers. He will call on Sunday morning to take them away with him. Here they are.' He gave me a large buff envelope.

I knew Kenneth Edwards only slightly, for although he was a submarine officer he had retired in favour of journalism after successfully completing his first year in command, and we had never served together in the same flotilla. I was of course fully aware of the need for frankness, firmness and caution when dealing with the Press. I had now been four months in the job, and had found that the telephone could be unsatisfactory or dangerous as a method of communication since there could be misunderstanding; on the other hand if you talked to a press man face to face and individually there were no misunderstandings.

Edwards was conducted to my office by an Admiralty messenger and I gave him his papers and he remarked that the previous week he had visited Fort Blockhouse where he was a life member of the Wardroom Mess. He continued, 'I was talking to T who told me that you had written a most interesting and authoritative paper on the new construction of German U-boats. He told me that you had written it nearly two years ago but that since then he had heard no more about it. He said that this surprised him because there was a very remarkable hydrophone array which pointed to thorough suitability for a U-boat campaign against shipping. Please tell me about the report.'

I replied, 'T had no right whatever to mention this report to you, and no doubt he told you that he helped me to prepare it. I suppose nobody can prevent you from using your honorary membership for your own purposes?'

'I think you are being rather unfair to me and unreasonable in suggesting I am just a snooper feathering my own nest. After all the Press has a duty to inform the public of the truth. Is that such a disgraceful and underhand thing to do?'

'No, provided you don't go nosing around wishing to find out about Top Secret Admiralty papers. I don't think it right that an officer who retires to journalism should take advantage of life membership of his mess. If you had become a doctor, a parson or anything else O.K., but for a journalist it would be different.'

'All right, we can disagree over that, but will you answer just one simple question that I wish to ask? It has nothing to do with any report you have written, and please give me any reason you have for your answer.'

'All right, I'll try.'

'Right. In the event of war between Britain and Germany in the next decade do you think Germany would wage unrestricted U-boat warfare on British shipping?'

'I'll answer that. Yes I do, and my reason is best explained in the form of a parable. You are a young lad and your father has a dispute with his neighbour who is very rich and owns a hell of a lot of land. This dispute leads to a fight and the neighbour starts throttling your father. Your father's arms are shorter than your neighbour's so he can only threaten but not quite reach the neighbour's throat, so your father suddenly raises his knee and kicks the neighbour in the crutch. The neighbour shouts blue murder and calls in all the locals and says your father is a cad.

'Public opinion is against your father, who however continues to be strangled. Twice more your father raises his knee in this unethical manner and the last time nearly kills his opponent. Finally, your father is so out of breath he collapses on the floor. Your father never quite gets over this and dies. Your neighbour is badly knocked about, but he is still a strong fellow with very long arms and as you grow up you find you are broader and thicker and stronger than he is and you dislike your neighbour very much and decide you will fight him again and win this time – what then are you going to do, if you have learned anything at all from experience? You will kick him in the crutch so hard that you kill him, and of course you will have made that decision before you pick a quarrel to start the fight. I am very happy to tell you this since it is no profound secret but normal human action and reaction which can be observed in the slums of any city.'

'You've made no mention of culture or the League of Nations,' said Edwards and bade me farewell.

On Monday evening I returned home to Guildford for a day's leave after my week-end of duty, then caught the train on Wednesday morning and on the London tube saw the usual three feet by two feet Press headline posters. There it was large as life on the Tory blue poster of the *Morning Post*:

NEW GERMAN SUBMARINES
DESIGNED FOR COMMERCE DESTRUCTION
POWERFUL HYDROPHONES FOR
LOCATING SHIPPING

I felt a bit sick. I had been badly let down, and when I entered 'Ops' office all my colleagues were laughing and saying that this was a gaffe on someone's part that would rock the Admiralty, particularly since it was probably true. Captain Palmer, the Deputy Director came in and, in high spirits, said, 'The German Naval Attaché has just been to see D.N.I. and is absolutely livid, and D.N.I. has sent for Kenneth Edwards to ask for an explanation. I was told that Wassner looked apoplectic with anger. It'll be interesting.'

Later in the morning Palmer returned to the office and said 'Edwards, I am told, merely says that a year ago he wrote the same article, but nobody took any notice, and he adds quite reasonably that what was news a year ago can be appropriately resurrected, the only change is that today the editor picked on his article for the daily poster. However the very latest is that Wassner has come storming into the Admiralty again, and he is now in with D.N.I.' I carried on with my work, thinking to myself that what I had said to Edwards was fair enough, it was my opinion, and what Edwards had said about the public knowing the truth was fair enough too, so there was no problem and it would do Wassner good.

However Captain Palmer re-entered bubbling with news and thoroughly enjoying himself. He said, 'Captain Wassner completely blew up when he went to see D.N.I. just now, he said that Commander Hill on the Admiral Submarines Staff paid a visit to Kiel last week, accompanied by Admiral Tom Troubridge [Naval attaché Berlin]. Wassner says that Hill was visiting Kiel as a guest of the U-boat arm who wished to purchase an attack teacher from the British and to offer in exchange a "depth keeping trainer". Captain Wassner now says that Commander Hill not only turned down the exchange proposal but has shown the type of officer he is by abusing hospitality and on return to Britain he has told this pack of lies to the *Morning Post*.'

This last development put a completely different light on the whole episode. J. A. C. Hill was a personal friend of mine and he had done very rightly in refusing to part with the attack teacher 'know how' and design. So I got up and walked to the room of my Director, Captain Knox-Little, and told him the whole story. There was nothing petty about Knox-Little and he laughed and said, 'Well, to put people at the top in the know I shall now go and tell them. I doubt if they will think it funny, Simpson.'

I was then told to go and see D.C.N.S. The Deputy Chief of Naval Staff was Admiral Sir William James ('Bubbles' to his contemporaries). He could not have been nicer, and told me that newspapermen became an increasing menace the older one got. Unfortunately the truth or accuracy of a remark had nothing to do with discretion. Usually the only way to be discreet was to keep your mouth shut. 'I enjoy company and conversation, Simpson, but I am often worried whether I have been discreet, so my advice is to say nothing and know that you have been discreet.' I returned to my office.

By now the buzz was travelling around the corridors that Simpson in 'Ops' was the cause of this serious gaffe and diplomatic crisis. I no longer felt upset and I felt that what Edwards had written might do good. Just before lunch Commander Vivian, the Press Liaison Officer, came to my desk. 'I say, Simpson, I am terribly sorry about this ghastly business, but I am sure it will all pass over; for God's sake realise that in a few weeks people will have forgotten about it, and don't do what the engineer officer did over the K boat plans.'

'What did he do?' I inquired.

'Well, having lost them, he got into a bath and opened a vein.'

'I won't do that! Why the hell should I?'

The New Year opened on a happier note. On 1 January my Director sent for me and, laughing, handed me a sheet of paper.

'Here's the end of the story, Simpson, and I'm glad it has all turned out happily. What the hell's in this "comprehensive report" that's caused all this flapdoodle I haven't the vaguest idea, but I'm glad it's all dead and buried now.'

31 December 1936

M.02187/35

CONFIDENTIAL

Sir,

I am commanded by My Lords Commissioners of the Admiralty to acquaint you that they have read with much interest the report on Finnish, German and Latvian submarines which was rendered by Commander G. W. G. Simpson, R.N., in 1935, whilst serving under the Rear Admiral (Submarines).

Their Lordships consider that great credit is due to Commander Simpson for the time and trouble that must have been entailed in collecting the information and in preparing such a comprehensive report, and they are causing a suitable notation to be made in his record.

I am to request that Commander Simpson may be informed accordingly.

I am, Sir,
Your obedient Servant,
(sd) S. H. PHILLIPS
DIRECTOR OF OPERATIONS DIVISION

I remain convinced that no 'Lord Commissioner of the Admiralty' read my paper, but I treasure this memento to my only personal initiative into the intelligence world.

It seems reasonable to observe that Admiral Troup (Director of Naval Intelligence) would have been in a better position to confront the angry and dissembling Captain Wassner if he had read M.02187/35. Unfortunately his predecessor had put it in D.N.I.'s out-basket twenty-two months before.

6

In August 1938 I joined the submarine minelayer *Porpoise*, as her captain, at Devonport and was quickly ordered to go, in company with *Cachalot*, to Rosyth to embark mines. *Cachalot*, under the command of my old friend Commander Robin Conway, was a sister submarine – 1,500 tons, fifteen knots, and armed with a salvo of six torpedoes as well as fifty mines carried externally.

Conway and I were both playing hockey on 27 September. As we walked off the field a car drew up and inquired for us, and we were taken immediately to the C.-in-C. Scotland's office. The Admiral gave us each an impressive sealed envelope marked 'Not to be opened until signal received from Admiralty', 'Most Secret', and 'To be kept in safe until opened'. He added, 'I have been told to sail you forthwith for Blyth to rendezvous with Captain *S3* at 0800 tomorrow. *S3* is on his way now from Portland. It is a foul evening and full ebb tide, can you sail immediately? There appears to be an emergency.' We sailed half an hour later having gathered that the Fleet was mobilising for war.

As we approached Blyth on the Northumbrian coast from the north we sighted the *Titania* with Captain Jock Bethell in command arriving from the south. *Titania* had two L class and four H class submarines in company. She stopped engines and the pilot cutter went alongside. An aged pilot climbed the jumping ladder and on meeting the commander said, 'Hello, Commander, is Shanks Willis still Captain?' This ancient pilot had taken *Titania* out of Blyth in December 1918, accompanied then by two L class, four H class and three J class submarines. Seeing what was apparently identical hardware approaching Blyth to continue the conflict he enquired rather naturally whether the brains behind the machine remained the same. However the lugubrious 'Shanks' Willis had joined his forefathers some years before.

Alongside at Blyth, Conway and I boarded *Titania* and reported to Captain Bethell, an officer of great experience and full of practical common sense. His first question was, 'What do you think of your war orders?' So we both explained that they were in our safes and naturally we had not opened them since we were told not to.

Jock Bethell looked surprised. 'Look, these are war orders, and they are obviously written by some officer at the Admiralty who knows nothing about submarines. Do remember that in war you must know what your orders are before leaving harbour and not be told by some chair-borne official at the Admiralty to open envelope X and get on with it, because if you have that sort of trust you won't live a week in wartime. These orders are not written by Flag Officer Submarines; they are just an ad hoc bright idea. I have of course opened and read all the orders for all my submarines and I don't like yours, so go back now and read your operation orders and both write individual commentaries on them and come back here in two hours and discuss them.'

I found that I was to lay mines across the approaches to the Ems, whilst the intrepid Conway was to press on eastwards and lay north of Wilhelmshaven in the approaches to the Weser. These orders sounded sensible until a study of the chart showed that the positions selected for the lays were in fifty feet of water. The minimum depth required to cover the submarine when submerged and still allow depth to manoeuvre was seventy feet. So we returned to Jock who said, 'Good. Now my orders to you are that you should lay these mines to the north and west of the positions given, *provided* visibility allows you to fix where you have laid them, *provided* there is adequate depth of water during approach and lay, and *provided* both of you return here safely. I am not going to lose one-third of our total submarine minelaying force during the first week of war due to stupid orders stupidly labelled. The next lot of orders will be issued by Flag Officer Submarines, so we won't have any repetition of this suicidal stuff.'

Neville Chamberlain returned from Munich with 'Peace in our time' on 1 October. The crisis was over. Our submarine concentration at Blyth was ordered to disperse to our peacetime dispositions. On the way south I heard with concern that Duff Cooper had resigned as First Lord. He had replaced Sir Samuel Hoare halfway through my time at the Admiralty and even I, as the junior naval officer there, felt the difference. I cannot imagine how great was the relief felt by heads of departments. Sir Samuel Hoare's minutes were long, his writing almost illegible, and after they had been deciphered there was still no decision. Duff Cooper wrote in beautiful calligraphy 'Yes. D.C.', 'No. D.C.', 'This has my full support. D.C.', etc. In my opinion he did everything right and his resignation at this time struck me as particularly ominous.

Porpoise called with *Cachalot* at Portsmouth to disembark our mines, but I was ordered to take on fifty dummy mines to carry out a special investigation, whilst Commander Conway was briefed to prepare his submarine for a scientific survey unconnected with national defence.

A small anti-submarine sloop HMS *Puffin*, manned by the A/S school and fitted with their latest equipment was to do a very simple test. From the longitude of Lulworth Cove in Dorset two lines were drawn on the chart, two miles apart running eastward for twenty miles. The northern line passed four miles south of St Alban's head. These two lines represented an imaginary, swept, i.e. mine free channel. On a given day *Puffin* was to be on patrol within this channel. I was told to take *Porpoise* into the channel from either end and lay my fifty mines across the channel near its midpoint and then withdraw without being detected during daylight hours on the day selected.

I dived *Porpoise* at first light well clear of the eastern end of the channel and watched *Puffin* sweep the channel towards me and turn at the end to retrace her steps, sweeping at about ten knots. I followed at a good submerged speed and when she turned east again off Lulworth Cove some two hours later, I was near the position I was looking for.

In the autumn of 1932 the *Thames* left Portland for Portsmouth and the captain had naturally laid off a course straight for the Needles despite a strong southwesterly blowing against an ebb tide. After all *Thames* had a displacement of 2,000 tons and was 340 feet long; there was no reason to avoid the St Alban's race. When we reached it though, *Thames* rolled slowly, but heavily, to port and, instead of righting herself, hesitated before going over further to about thirty degrees. She hesitated again before continuing to port and, as everything movable in the submarine crashed from starboard to port, I stood off the wall of the wardroom. Lazily she righted herself, having gone over to seventy-two degrees when in full buoyancy.

The shelf of St Alban's had caused a huge wave to follow us, at our speed, from the starboard quarter. The officer of the watch saved himself by embracing the periscope, the signalman and lookout were washed overboard and drowned. Although the cause was a fluke synchronisation of vessel and wave speed, it was obviously something which should not have happened and was later rectified quite simply.

I had remembered this natural hazard and decided to use it as a hiding place by going to the bottom, bows into the tide and filling tanks until I had substantial negative buoyancy. The shingle swept past us rattling on our pressure hull and making a great hullaballoo; it was evident that we were in the right spot for maximum current and eddy, but we watched the compass with some anxiety, for had *Porpoise* slewed beam to current we would have rolled to an awkward angle and been difficult to control.

After an hour we estimated *Puffin* would have passed. We came to periscope depth and continued westward for a couple of miles to the position of our mine lay. Having laid our mines, we carried on west and cleared the channel south of Lulworth well ahead of *Puffin*, who was by now overtaking us on a westerly course, but we were outside asdic range. I continued to Portland and reported where the mines were; they were swept and recovered as evidence of our success in the exercise. The essence of the exercise was that *Porpoise* had to be in the channel during one sweep by *Puffin;* probably we would have been located had there been no St Alban's race, but we merely made use of the local hazards and won.

Conway brought *Cachalot* to join the Flotilla with some complicated gadgetry fixed in his control room. This bulky, valuable and delicate machinery was on loan from the Dutch Government so that the Royal Navy could play its part in carrying out the world wide gravity survey which had been quite widely progressed by Dutch submarines. We were told that the survey had recently been undertaken in the Caribbean Sea where the Dutch had covered astonishing distances submerged by running on diesel engines fed by a breathing tube called a 'Schnorkel'. Readings of the instruments could only be made submerged, when the submarine was free from pitch and roll.

The scientific results were to be sent to some government department presided over by an elderly retired sapper colonel and he came down to visit *Cachalot* at Portland. At the informal conference to which I was invited the colonel said to Conway, 'The place where I expect you to get significant readings is where you cross the precipice about a hundred miles west of Ushant on leaving the Continental Shelf for the deep Atlantic; now, when this occurs and your echo-sounder shows the moment of crossing the edge of the cliff, how accurately will you know your position, Commander?'

'To the nearest mile if the weather is fairly good,' replied Conway.

'Good God, sir!' said the sapper. 'When I was making gravity observations in the foothills of the Himalayas I knew my position within six inches!'

Cachalot carried out these surveys over the Continental Shelf, but with what result I don't know, nor do I know to what purpose.

It was shortly before or after Christmas 1938 that a significant visit was made to Portland. All ships in port were informed that the Minister of Defence would visit with a V.I.P. An A/S destroyer was to take them to sea to hunt an H class submarine from the Sixth Flotilla. The day was fine and the 'hunt' was I believe successful, and thus Admiral of the Fleet Lord Chatfield was able to show that inquisitive, but then powerless, politician, Winston Churchill, how effective 'asdic' was.

Two things I have always wondered about that visit. Firstly, did Chatfield say to Churchill, 'We are now about to hunt a submarine in an area of one hundred square miles,' or did he describe it as 'an area ten miles square'? Secondly, what would have happened if Churchill had said, 'And now, Minister, let's transfer to the submarine and see if they can catch us with me on board.'

I think it was in February 1939 – it was certainly after Munich – that I was ordered to carry out some practical experiments to find out how realistic it was to expect a submarine to observe international law in stopping, searching and placing prize crews on board merchantmen in accordance with the submarine treaty agreed between the maritime powers on 6 November 1936.

Porpoise was to be on submerged patrol about mid-channel and halfway between Portland and the Isle of Wight. A small fleet auxiliary tanker was to sail from Portland to the east in the forenoon and return westbound in the afternoon. *Porpoise* was to surface and train her gun on the tanker, who was then to stop engines and to broadcast an S.O.S. This alarm was responded to by the R.A.F. who sent an Anson aircraft to the rescue. In the meantime, the *Porpoise*'s crew were opening up the casing, pulling out the collapsible boat and trying to make it operative and sea-borne. So far as I recall we had two days of this farcical boating picnic, and in conditions of flat calm with all in favour of the boat. On the first occasion the boat did get seaborne and a few yards on her journey, on all subsequent occasions the very slow air-craft was always overhead before the collapsible boat was on deck and erected for launching. When war was declared the first action taken by submarines was to land all collapsible boats and clear the casings of all rope and other gear which might float as a result of depth-charging, or might foul propellers.

This particular exercise was carried out, I was told, on the orders of Admiral Raikes (Flag Officer Submarines). Although we thought it a waste of time it showed us the surprisingly quick response of the R.A.F. to a distress call. I do not know what official conclusion was drawn, but I suspect that in some quarters it was felt that the immunity of British shipping within a range of over a hundred miles of our coast was assured, because Germany was subject to procedures agreed to internationally.

In March 1939 Captain *S2* was busy changing his command at Devonport from the aged converted merchantman HMS *Lucia* to the brand new submarine depot ship HMS *Forth* and so it was that as senior submarine officer in the 2nd Flotilla I was told to lead the flotilla to Gibraltar for the combined Home Fleet and Mediterranean Fleet annual exercises. On arrival we moored close to HMS *Maidstone*, depot ship of the First Submarine Flotilla, under the command of Captain Philip Ruck-Keene, whom I had last seen during the Staff Course.

My opposite number in the First Flotilla was Commander William Banks. In the submarines assembled for these exercises there was a lot of experience amongst the older officers – Conway, Banks, 'Lofty' Power and others. There was also a radical deter-mined younger set, much encouraged in their thinking by Cap-tain Ruck Keene. Lieutenants Bickford, King and Bryant were full of ideas which were aired and discussed amongst the more junior officers. The First Lieutenants were mostly to make their mark in war, and in *Porpoise* I had the good fortune to have

73

Malcolm David Wanklyn as 'Number One'. Submarine participation was reserved for two exercises at the end of the manoeuvres.

As senior submarine officer afloat I was given the task of writing the orders for the first very simple exercise. This meant that an imaginary channel, about ten miles wide and eighty miles long and stretching to the south-west, was laid off on the chart about a hundred miles west of Gibraltar and that I was to dispose my submarines in it as I thought fit. Some hours after diving, but in daylight, an 'enemy fleet' escorted by every available destroyer would pass down the channel. Submarines were to attack without firing torpedoes, A/S destroyers were to attack submarines, who after they had been put deep were to indicate their position by smoke candle when ordered, so that the screening destroyers could assess whether their depth charges would have sunk the submarine.

The forces taking part were twelve submarines on one side, and five Glasgow class cruisers escorted by thirty-six destroyers on the other.

There was not much scope for originality on either side, but I varied things in this manner. I thought that Commander Power in the huge submarine *Thames* had little hope of escaping detection, so I put him in the centre at the beginning of the channel. I then left a blank for sixty miles and disposed the remaining eleven submarines at four mile intervals in two lines, with orders to keep in approximate station and avoid submerged collision by using asdic until the approaching enemy fleet could be heard, when asdic silence was to be observed.

On the day the sea conditons were about as adverse for detecting submarines as they could possibly have been. Power in *Thames* made a successful undetected attack. The Fleet pressed on for three and a half hours without anything happening and this I hoped would reduce the alertness of the asdic operators due to boredom. The result was that all submarines attacked and only one was located, held and sunk by the escort, the failure of the destroyer escorts being due chiefly to the adverse water conditions.

The last exercise was against the whole combined Fleet where attack on the surface at night was permitted. Commander Banks used some of his small S class for night attacks and Lieutenants Bryant, King and Bickford distinguished themselves. Red flares from Very pistols representing torpedo fire were fired from positions half-way between the destroyer screen and the battleships. In fact our smaller submarines were, on this one occasion, permitted to try out those tactics which Admiral Doenitz had been perfecting since September 1935.

The larger submarines were held back from this night attack as being too unhandy to avoid the dangers of collision, a sensible precaution. Next day fog robbed us of further opportunity and the manoeuvres were called off.

There was nothing whatever startling about the results to us submarine officers. The startling thing occurred at the Combined Fleet conference in the huge coal shed on Gibraltar Mole which was always used on such occasions as a theatre and as a conference hall. There were about one thousand officers present, who heard what was said. Before the 'wash up', as this post-exercise conference was called, the results had been quickly analysed. The submarine phase was discussed at the end, I was to expound about the day attacks in the eighty mile channel and Banks about the S class night attacks.

Before we set out for the conference Captain Ruck Keene (who was given no opportunity to speak or express an opinion) sent for me and said, 'At the end of your five-minute talk I want you to say, "The number of torpedoes fired theoretically was 200, the number of hits 44, so the submarines obtained twenty-two per cent hits." ' (The percentage I quote is accurate. I have guessed the other figures.) I knew that this was quite true and a very reasonable estimate, I also felt in my bones that it would have serious repercussions – to be candid I deliberately side-stepped this statement.

I replied, 'Yes, sir, but this would be more forceful if it came at the end of the submarine analysis. I suggest Willie Banks says it, and after all he belongs to your flotilla.'

'Quite right,' said Ruck Keene. 'Willie shall say it.'

After I had said my piece Rear-Admiral Tovey (Rear-Admiral Destroyers) said in the most forthright manner that although sea conditions may have been adverse on that day and in that area there was no excuse. The A/S screen's performance had been not only disappointing but rather alarming.

Commander Banks mounted the stage and made his commentary on the S class surface night attacks and then stated, 'Throughout the submarine phase of the exercise the number of theoretical hits by torpedo was twenty-two per cent,' and he stood, a lonely figure prepared to answer any questions, but none were allowed.

Up stood Admiral Sir Charles Forbes, Commander-in-Chief, Home Fleet. 'I wish to disabuse the mind of this young submarine officer who has just finished his statement,' he said in a tone of some annoyance. 'The sea-power that will win the next war will obtain three per cent of hits with the gun and his opponent will have scored two and a half per cent hits with the gun.'

Sitting beside Admiral Forbes was the Commander-in-Chief Mediterranean, Admiral Sir Dudley Pound, looking like a wise old owl and like a wise old owl he said nothing. I would like to know what in fact passed through his mind. It is on record that in December 1941 he held apparently views as unrealistic as those spoken by Forbes at this conference. He was on board the *Duke of York* with Churchill and Beaverbrook for their journey to America and, as Churchill wrote in *The Grand Alliance*, 'The great ship with her attendant destroyers plodded on. But we became impatient with her slow speed. On the second night we approached the U-boat stream. Admiral Pound who took the decision, said that *we were more likely to ram a U-boat than to be torpedoed by one ourselves.* The night was pitch black. So we cast off our destroyers and ran through alone at the best speed possible in the continuing rough weather.' (My italics).

7

By mid-August 1939 the 2nd Submarine Flotilla was based on Dundee and the submarines were on an exercise off the Norwegian Coast. My command, *Porpoise*, had hardly reached her patrol position within sight of the snow-capped mountains of Norway when all submarines were recalled to Dundee. On arrival the two minelayers *Cachalot* and *Porpoise* embarked torpedo warheads and were sailed for Portsmouth, where we again embarked our mines, left the previous October after Munich. We arrived at Portsmouth early afternoon and I was told to sail at midnight, with *Cachalot*, for Malta. I walked round to the Fort Blockhouse quarters of Captain S5 who would be giving me written sailing orders for my onward voyage.

C. G. B. Coltart was a very alert and unconventional officer, who had been in command of submarines throughout the First World War. He had also been my first commanding officer in the submarine service for a few months in 1922, before I had sailed for the China Station. I could never understand his slick cynicism and the light hearted and inconsequential way he met both success and failure. He obviously regarded both as impostors and he served in each and every rank with the same outward flippancy, but with much ability and shrewdness on paper.

I knocked on his cabin door and entered. 'Ah, Shrimp, how nice to see you, but I can't spare a moment now,' he said as he put on a sports jacket. 'I'm off to Bishop's Waltham. Since it is obvious that war is about to be declared I must deal with first things first, so I am off home to help my dear wife to "black out" our pet white rabbit, Alice; I had difficulty in finding the necessary black rinse, but I have it at last. I have written your sailing orders and I shall be back this evening. Come and see me at 10 pm.'

At ten I called back, I had my orders and both submarines were ready for sea. Captain Coltart welcomed me and offered me a chair. At once I sensed that I was talking to quite a different man, all that veneer of inconsequential jollity was gone and I was talking to a person I had never guessed existed.

'I want to help you with all those things that come to mind from my war experience. From the time you clear the Solent the war has started for you. The Germans may not wait for any declaration of war and you may be sure their submarines are already on patrol. You must assume you are already liable to attack. Off every focal point such as Ushant, Finisterre, Cape St Vincent, zigzag and be instantly ready to dive. Use your week on passage to Malta so that you feel confident that you can meet any situation you can think of and in particular defeat air attack by swift diving.' He talked on for about twenty minutes with practical, helpful advice, and after a pause he said, 'After the last war I swore that if there was ever to be another I would be the officer who said "And you might switch off the light." '

'What do you mean, sir?'

'Well, I suppose it applies to you too, for very shortly you will find yourself in command of a flotilla and so I beg you to take some trouble over giving your commanding officers that encouragement and sympathetic understanding that will give them confidence in you and in your interest in their affairs when they are out on patrol. I am sure you will as you are a submarine officer – but that brings me to "You might switch off the light." – a phrase that has stuck in my mind since the bitter winters of 1915, 1916 and 1917. For much of the time I was based on Blyth and we normally sailed after midnight so that no U-boat would see us leave. By dawn we would be far beyond the swept channel and in a suitable depth for diving. It was Commander S's orders that we were to report to him before sailing. I remember those interviews so well, in fact I wish I could forget them, but I can't.

'They went like this. I would go up to Shanks Willis's cabin in *Titania* and knock on the door, and knock at intervals of five seconds until there was a grunt of, "Come in, who's that?"

'"Coltart, sir."

'"What do you want?"

'"I'm sailing for patrol in ten minutes."

'"Oh – where to?"

'"Well, sir, you have told me to spend the next three weeks forty miles N.N.W. of Heligoland."

78

' "Oh, yes, an excellent patrol position – by the way what's the weather like?"

' "N.E. gale blowing, sir. It's snowing rather hard and the visibility is 200 yards."

' "Oh, yes, well plug into it. I say, you might switch off the light!" '

I understood his message very clearly.

I sailed with *Cachalot* in company at midnight (I suppose about 28 August) and arrived at Malta on 5 September to join the 1st Submarine Flotilla under the command of Captain Philip Ruck Keene, my old friend with whom I had served in China, Mediterranean and the Staff Course before this.

It was evident that the valuable new submarine depot ship *Maidstone* must not remain at Malta with Italy's pro-Nazi affiliations, and her fleet and air force which made Malta's future problematical. For these reasons Ruck Keene had established a submarine H.Q. on Manoel Island, a small peninsula close west of Valetta.

Two months with the 1st Submarine Flotilla at Malta commanded by Ruck Keene showed me a flotilla of the highest morale. I watched his methods. He had not been brought up as a naval cadet at Osborne and Dartmouth in the lap of tradition; he came from Haileybury and weighed up custom and tradition on their merits as the need arose. He had a flair for knowing what mattered, how much it mattered and putting things in their correct priority, and for cutting through time-wasting formality. He would tackle anybody or everybody who might be in a position to help, whilst rebuff or the annoyance of authority was flung off with a shrug. His boyish enthusiasm led him naturally to foster and encourage the young in his command. His four S class submarines, *Sealion*, *Salmon*, *Snapper* and *Shark* commanded by Bryant, Bickford, King and Buckley were full of ideas, discussion, initiative and confidence – qualities somewhat lacking in 1939.

As I was his senior submarine commander he would discuss his ideas with me and I would be the first to know war news that came in advance by cipher.

On 19 September Ruck Keene sent for me and said, 'Can you believe it? They sent *Courageous* out to hunt U-boats in Western Approaches and of course a U-boat got her!' He looked very tense, then added with a smile, 'Well, I suppose they have got to learn.' He and I did not know then that two days earlier *U39* had fired a salvo at *Ark Royal* and all torpedoes had failed due to faulty magnetic pistols. Because these torpedoes failed the four escorting destroyers were able to hunt *U39* and sink her, but if the torpedoes had exploded correctly the escort would have concentrated upon saving lives and the U-boat would have escaped.

On 15 October when I went to his office he said, 'A U-boat has just sunk *Royal Oak* in Scapa Flow!' He hesitated and added thoughtfully, 'I wonder if they will learn in time?' This news seemed particularly ominous from one particular point of view; I asked myself repeatedly, who are 'they' to whom he refers? Are 'they' truly representative of naval staff opinion or just one or two madmen who must be swept aside?

On 30 October *U56* fired three torpedoes at *Nelson;* all hit and all failed to explode. This we never heard about.

Early in October it became clear that Italy was sitting on the fence and the whole flotilla was ordered back to Britain. Because of my admiration for his go-getting enthusiasm, I was delighted, and indeed fortunate, to be appointed Ruck Keene's second in command of the 3rd Submarine Flotilla, now formed on the depot ship *Cyclops* and based on Harwich in early November 1939. The Flotilla was to be entirely S class. So *Sunfish*, J. E. Slaughter, and *Sterlet*, G. H. S. Haward joined the four S class from Malta. The first patrols off the Dutch coast and in the Heligoland Bight were unproductive, although not uneventful, but what concerned me mostly and taught me a lot was Ruck Keene's widespread projects as soon as we berthed at Parkeston Quay, Harwich.

The railway authorities helped in every way and we took over the two-deck concrete transit shed opposite the ship and the railway workshop. Next a telephone call to London and Thelma, his niece, a top flight shorthand stenographer, came to Harwich. Then a meeting in the Captain's cabin of heads of departments and commanding officers, which told us of the action to be taken to convert Parkeston Quay in about three weeks into a modern submarine base which was entirely self sufficient, except for a dry dock, and was to have the best amenities of any flotilla.

Ruck Keene explained, 'I have been told by the Director of Dockyards at the Admiralty that there is no skilled labour available in Britain to man the railway workshops for refitting war damage here. The Admiral Superintendent at Chatham says he has no labour available to make us self sufficient. It is intended that for any job beyond *Cyclop's* workshop capability our submarines must go to Sheerness. In other words we are expected to fight this war on a "steady does it" peacetime routine. So we will prove them wrong.

'I have a list here of the skilled civilian work force we need. We will advertise in the *Mail* and *Express* for a start.'

Next came various provisions and alternatives for the submarines to be kept operational in event of bombing and the many contingencies and hazards of war.

The submarine commanding officers who were present were there to be informed of what the flotilla officers were to do for their benefit. The submarines were to get the V.I.P. treatment which we depot ship officers and their Captain knew they deserved.

The activities allotted to me outside my service duties as second in command were typical of the wide ranging ideas and tasks that he handed out to all of us. I was to be responsible for local re-creation at Parkeston Quay and Harwich, in fact all those things for the entertainment of the submarine crews which occurred outside the depot ship but within the town boundary. When I learned that my particular task did not concern organised games, or sport or leave arrangements beyond Harwich, I could not imagine what was expected of me. However in a few minutes I was told to build a theatre on the first floor of the transit shed to accommodate an audience of 1,000; to equip the theatre with dressing rooms and amenities to satisfy a 'West End' company; to get some basic stage scenery and props, a couple of general purpose backdrops, and a stage curtain and surrounds painted; to obtain three full size billiard tables from Thurstons by persuading them to help a good cause; and to initiate a liaison with the proprietors of cinemas and public houses in Harwich so that submarine crews could have weekday leave until 11 pm while subject to recall at one hour's notice, their recall for emergency seagoing being my responsibility. On Sunday evenings the theatre would be available for stage celebrities from London – if they could be persuaded to come.

It was stimulating. We flotilla officers all had twice as much to do as we had before the meeting. The Captain's secretariat dealt with service matters as before while the beautiful Thelma dealt with the bright ideas just expounded.

There were 1,400 replies to the advertisements for skilled labour for service of national importance. Every letter was acknowledged, the hundred and twenty required were selected; the remainder of applications were classified, listed and posted to the Director of Dockyards, Admiralty – just in case he was short of labour. This work force arrived, settled down with excellent results, and became a permanent war asset to Harwich base.

I am explaining in some detail what occurred at Harwich because it was all quite new to me, and had I not experienced this common sense, straightforward method of convincing men who were running great danger that their service was truly appreciated, I would have failed a year later in Malta where conditions of service were at times quite desperate and men needed every encouragement.

The amphitheatre, stage and dressing rooms were soon constructed from railway materials by the *Cyclop's* shipwrights. Rowland Alston came from the Watts Galleries at Compton and painted stage effects. Thurstons sent us three excellent, full-size billiard tables and the experts to erect them for a total of £300. These proved so popular that the expenditure was soon recovered by charging sixpence an hour for play.

The London stage came generously to our help. Variety from the Coconut Grove night club gave two shows. Sidney Howard brought the complete cast of his revue down and finally, just before the phoney war ended, an entertainment was given us one Sunday evening, and amongst the stars were Peggy Ashcroft and Diana Wynyard. These kind folk would come all the way from London by motor coach, and back again after the show, on a Sunday, their only rest day in the week.

Boredom was prevented and appeciation expressed, the flotilla morale was kept at a high level.

On 2 December Flag Officer Submarines ordered one submarine to be sent to a patrol position about eighty miles west of Jutland. *Salmon* was due for patrol so I told Bickford that his submarine would be the test for my recall arrangements from Harwich town. At 10 pm the cinemas and main bars called on *Salmon's* crew to return on board immediately. In an hour all were aboard and *Salmon* sailed with some good humoured banter from Bickford about being used as a guinea pig.

On 4 December he had been dived on his patrol position for about half an hour when he sighted a northbound U-boat, fired a spread of torpedoes and sank *U36*. A few days later he sighted *Bremen* steaming south from Murmansk, surfaced and ordered her to stop and refrained from torpedoing her. *Salmon* was immediately forced to dive by escorting aircraft. On 13 December *Salmon* fired a salvo at three cruisers returning from minelaying off the Tyne and scored one hit on *Leipzig* and one on *Nürnberg* and returned to Harwich to a hero's welcome.

Two years together in *Thames* had made Bickford a firm friend of mine. He was awarded the D.S.O., promoted to Commander and ordered to go to London to lunch with the First Lord, Winston Churchill, the following Sunday. When he returned to *Cyclops* I naturally asked him about the lunch party. This he had enjoyed; several V.I.P.s were present including the First Sea Lord and Anthony Eden, but after lunch, when he went to thank his host and say goodbye, he was told to wait. After all the guests had left Bickford was given an armchair, a cigar and a brandy and two hours *tête-à-tête* with Churchill.

'When I found myself closeted with the First Lord, bursting with brains, inquisitiveness, ideas and searching inquiry it was damned difficult to know what to say, but you must answer his searching questions or naturally he thinks you either a fool or deliberately stalling. I answered his questions, but I am not sure that I answered correctly for submarines, I could only give my own opinion.'

'What is worrying you, Bick?' I asked.

'Well the specific question he wanted an answer to was this: "Did I find a war patrol in a submarine a great strain?" I replied truthfully, "Yes." So he followed this up with, "In that case what can be done to lessen the strain?" and having driven me into that corner encouraged me to suggest some easement of the strain; surely I could something? So I said, "Well, Sir, I suppose we could follow the German example and have two crews for each submarine." '

Here I interrupted and said, 'But Bick, are you sure the Germans do have two crews for each U-boat?'

'No, I am not sure, but I have been told that they have a pretty broad relief system, but it was this question and answer with the great man that worried me a bit, I did not expect to be cross questioned for two hours. I felt greatly honoured and rather squeezed dry.'

Later in the war, when I knew Admiral Sir Max Horton well he told me, 'Just after I took over as Flag Officer Submarines in early January 1940 Churchill sent for me at midnight. He said he thought I should have two crews for every submarine! Just imagine it! Suddenly to produce another sixty submarine crews! The dissolution of efficiency! The unacceptability to our service way of thinking! I argued back and was told that the Germans did it and that Bickford recommended it! It is naughty of him to pump young officers for bright ideas, but he always has and no doubt he always will, but I felt rather frustrated and angry when at 2 am I was able to leave, that his last remark to me should be "I remain far from convinced, Horton!" '

This question of crews changing submarines was to become a live issue in Malta and to prove Horton right.

The single meeting between Churchill and Bickford and its aftermath is a good example of the way this very great war leader sought out ideas, confronted authority with them and if they were not accepted 'remained far from convinced' and acted accordingly.

As a corollary to this, it was in February of this particularly severe winter that large areas of the eastern coastal waters of the North Sea were covered by ice. An R.A.F. reconnaissance reported in this sense 'German naval squadron including heavy ships at anchor fifteen miles north east of Heligoland.' Admiral Horton made a signal to *Sealion*, 'Investigate and attack.'

Bryant took his submarine in under the ice for a day's reconnaissance by asdic, but found nothing. The vessels were trawlers whose size and appearance were deceptive in snow conditions.

When Bryant was back and reported no success and the R.A.F. had amended their first report, Churchill telephoned Horton and said, 'I am not a religious man, Horton, but when I read your signal ordering *Sealion* to search under the ice I got down on my knees and prayed. I am indeed gratified by his safe return.'

When Admiral Horton told me this he observed, 'I much appreciated his keen interest but his knowledge of what was dangerous and what was not in submarine operations was naturally negligible.'

After the success of *Salmon's* December patrol and the loss of three submarines in January from other flotillas the phoney war continued without much activity in home waters or on the western front, but the Russians and Finns were locked in a winter campaign, which the Finns conducted brilliantly.

During the last week in February we received orders that our six S class submarines and six new T class were to prepare to enter the Baltic as soon as ice permitted. We would be based on Abo and assist the Finns in their war. Ruck Keene with his staff were to fly, while I was to sail from Cardiff to Trondheim with about 500 tons of flotilla stores and spare parts and travel to Stockholm by train. This really was a remarkable proposal, and to collect in two weeks all the stores, boxed, labelled and camouflaged as condensed milk or other commodity for a six months, unsupported campaign needed a 'round the clock' organisation. By 12 March all was assembled in our transit shed at Parkeston Quay. The next day the whole project was cancelled, since an armistice between Finland and the U.S.S.R., had been declared.

On 23 March the French 10th Submarine Flotilla joined us at Harwich and initially took over the Dutch coast patrols to allow our submarines to go further afield. This cooperation was short lived, being overtaken and erased by the blitzkreig, but I recall a remark from a conversation I had with one of the very few English speaking officers, who I found apprehensive and cynical.

'Do you consider your Prime Minister Daladier to be a determined fellow?' I asked.

'Ah, Daladier the bull!' he replied. 'The bull with the horns of a snail!'

I found his comment depressing.

In early February I carried out a ten-day patrol in command of *Sealion*, replacing Bryant who was on the sick list, and shortly afterwards I took *Sunfish* to sea for an anti-invasion alarm which only lasted three days. Nothing of note occurred except the discovery of a moored buoy with a green flashing light about twenty miles due west of Heligoland. *Sealion* kept near it for three days hoping it was a landfall buoy for U-boats or warships returning to Wilhelmshaven, but no enemy was seen in the low visibility caused by snow squalls. This war patrol was important to me; it made me realise the immense regard and trust that the members of a submarine's crew develop for their Captain after some months of war, and only second to that is the attachment they have for their submarine.

I felt that I was accepted in *Sealion* as an experienced and reliable substitute for their Captain, but I was under probation, my conduct in emergency was unknown. After two days off the Dutch coast we were ordered to patrol west of Heligoland and I laid off a course through the German declared mined area, which in my opinion, on German testimony, could be considered safe. We covered the sixty miles from west to east at four knots, submerged at seventy feet, and during this tedious passage I played a few games of Lotto with Hugo Newton, the First Lieutenant. Mr Reavill the capable Warrant Engineer, sat and watched the fortunes of the game for a while but he had something on his mind and finally exploded, 'I only hope Ben Bryant is too ill to realise that his *Sealion* is being driven about the North Sea without him on board, if he knew that I don't think he'd ever recover! No disrespect to you, sir, but she's his.' We all had a good laugh, nevertheless he meant and felt what he said – such was his intense loyalty. The same sentiments applied in varying degree to every man on board.

With the French 10th Submarine Flotilla assuming responsibility for the close reconnaissance of the Dutch coast our Harwich force could go further afield and on 1 April Admiral Horton summoned his Flotilla Captains to his London headquarters. He explained that the Home Fleet was about to undertake minelaying off the Norwegian coast to deter the constant heavy iron ore traffic from North Norway to Germany. A strong German naval reaction might be expected so he was already disposing submarines in anticipation of this. Those submarines returning from patrol were to be prepared for immediate re-deployment, a maximum effort was needed.

On that day 1 April 1940, Horton had at his disposal some twenty-four British submarines based on Dundee, Rosyth, Blyth and Harwich. Also at Dundee was the Polish submarine *Orzel* whose courageous escape from the Baltic was fresh in our memories.

By the time the British minelay took place on 8 April it was a matter of small consequence. The armed might of Hitler's Germany was committed to the invasion of Norway. The invasion is most thoroughly documented, but to us in submarines it appeared partly as a lost opportunity, and partly as an inexplicable let down on the part of our surface forces, which could not be explained away by Government indecision, although that was clearly in part to blame.

On the morning of 8 April our admiral had disposed nineteen submarines around the Isthmus of Denmark and off the south coast of Norway and that day he visited the Admiralty to confirm his dispositions.

He was ordered to withdraw *Triad* from Norwegian territorial waters at the narrow entrance to Oslo fiord, and to alter a few similar 'in shore' dispositions. *Triad* was withdrawn that evening and a few hours later the German Group 5, comprising *Lutzow*, *Blücher* and a large transport carrying the Army Commander-in-Chief, General Falkenhorst, and his staff passed the spot *Triad* had just vacated.

At noon on that same day the Polish submarine *Orzel* had stopped and having no gun had subsequently torpedoed a German north-bound merchantman off Kristiansand, which had proved to be full of German troops in uniform. This action by the *Orzel* was not known to all submarine officers at the time, but *Triad*'s change of position and lost opportunity was very apparent to us.

On the next day, 9 April, a Cabinet decision allowed our submarines to sink without warning German merchant shipping in the Skagerrak and Kattegat. This decision was received by submarines at 1700 that day and immediately acted upon. Two days later the area of attack was much enlarged and the submarines were at once informed.

The initial opportunity offered by Horton's dispositions and numbers had been lost but now was the chance to make up for lost time, which the submarines proceeded to do. Of course the German anti-submarine patrols and devices were intensified to the utmost in these waters, which were embarrassingly shallow except near the Norwegian coast. The direct route from the Baltic to Oslo was so intensely patrolled by air and surface craft that torpedo attack was becoming suicidal.

Ruck Keene appealed to Admiral Horton who repeatedly asked the Admiralty for sweeps by destroyers to be made into the eastern Skagerrak to eliminate the large number of enemy A/S vessels of the trawler type which were sweeping all day, and at night prevented our submarines from charging. Knowing Admiral Forbes' opinion of submarines, so publicly expressed a year before, was not encouraging and my Captain S would say to me daily, 'I wonder when he will have the guts to send a force east of longitude 5 East. It is surely impossible for him not to do so?' We awaited some action.

After several requests from Admiral Horton the Admiralty ordered a destroyer sweep of the Western Skagerrak. Horton pointed out that the important area was the eastern Skagerrak but without effect. The sweep was to be undertaken on the night of 17/18 April by four destroyers and air cover from dawn would be provided. The operation was then postponed twenty-four hours due to other commitments and was then cancelled by the Commander-in-Chief Home Fleet with the following message on the evening of 17 April: 'Although I have every sympathy with the extraordinarily hard times our submarines are having, and the good work they are doing, I do not consider this to be an operation of war, unless in fog, due to air attacks that the enemy can bring to bear.'

Finally on the night of 23/24 April the sweep was undertaken by three French *contretorpilleurs* (capable of 40 knots). They entered the Western Skagerrak, sank one trawler and two motor torpedo boats and retired. They were bombed by aircraft and undamaged. The refusal of help from the Commander-in-Chief and the final solution of calling on the French to pull our chestnuts out of the fire put Ruck Keene and me in a highly critical mood.

When the German occupation of Norway had become an established irrevocable fact and the submarines were mostly home to lick their wounds, three weeks had elapsed.

The scoreboard read

German losses (due to British submarines.)

Cruiser *Karlsruhe*, gunnery ship *Brummer*, U-boat *U-1* all sunk. The pocket battleship *Lutzow* had both propellers blown off and took a year to repair.
14 Transports sunk by torpedo.
4 Transports sunk by mine laid by the submarine *Narwhal*.
3 Transports damaged.

British losses (submarines only)

Thistle, *Tarpon* and *Sterlet* with all hands.

Analysis of attacks showed that out of 37 attacks 18 were known to have succeeded and three others were probably successful. The number of torpedo hits in our flotilla was about 25 per cent.

The crews of submarines, particularly those in the Kattegat, had run great risks while watching German shipping pass northwards in large numbers. In at least one instance the uniform field grey of the Wermacht massed on the upper deck was clearly seen. The submarines knew that their Government must rescind an international agreement obtained after years of patient negotiation before 'sink at sight' could be permitted; the reason was well understood however exasperating the experience. The signal timed at 1324 on 9 April allowing attacks was appreciated as quick work. The forbearance of the submarine captains under these circumstances was in marked contrast with the trigger-happy Captain of *U30* who sank the *Athenia* on the day war was declared in contravention of orders.

That forty-eight hours enforced delay was a lost opportunity – an exceptional opportunity due to Admiral Horton's dispositions to cover a different contingency. In brief the British had 250 torpedoes carried in twenty submarines disposed in restricted waters through which the Germans had to move their invasion fleet packed with troops. I do not think history shows many similar opportunities.

It so happened that Lieutenant-Commander Slaughter in *Sunfish*, about thirty miles north-east of the Skaw was keeping his eye in by doing a dummy attack on a northbound German merchantman at about 1650 on 9 April while the signal 1324/9 from Flag Officer Submarines was being deciphered, and as the directive unfolded he was given the message word by word at the periscope. As the deciphering task finished Slaughter said 'Fire' and the *Amasis*, of 7,129 tons, sank at 1700/9 April

I give details of this incident to show that the submarines wasted no time and at once became vulnerable to relentless hunting as soon as their position was established by their sinkings. Admiral Horton threw in all he had to exploit the attack on the invasion build up; for example he sent *Tetrarch* straight from her

89

building trials into the fray and on 23 April Lieutenant-Commander Mills attacked a large ship escorted by three destroyers and was subsequently hunted for forty-three hours before he could surface and make for home badly mauled.

The result of this three-week battle waged, entirely unsupported, by submarines was important but not crippling to the invasion. Each of the thirty-seven attacks brought concentrated retribution. The submarines had shown exemplary discipline before action was permitted and thereafter they showed guts and skill which earned from the First Lord of the Admiralty, Churchill, this commendation: 'Please convey to all ranks and ratings engaged in these brilliant and fruitful submarine operations the admiration and regard with which their fellow countrymen follow their exploits.'

I feel that Roskill in his admirable official history has on this occasion done less than justice in devoting only five lines to this prolonged struggle by our submarines, particularly when he omits to mention in this connection that throughout the most crucial phrase, from the invasion's start until 1700/9 April, our submarines were not allowed to sink merchantships on sight. On the subject of the use of surface forces at the critical moment Roskill writes

> But when the critical first days of the Norwegian campaign are reviewed it seems that the opportunity to inflict really serious injury on the enemy's expedition was, as is usual in such cases, a fleeting one and occurred during the night of the 7th–8th of April while the transports carrying his main forces were moving through the Skagerrak. Had the Home Fleet's flotillas, supported by cruisers, then been sent into those waters in strength the results might have been considerable. But the intelligence which indicated the need to adopt such bold and vigorous action was ignored or misinterpreted, and the opportunity was allowed to pass.

I cannot accept that without comment. Roskill is right in pointing out specifically the action that should have been taken, and perhaps that is as far as an official historian may offer opinion. A leader was needed to call for bold and vigorous action, and he was not there.

The loss of a specified number of cruisers and destroyers in exchange for several German divisions and their equipment, scores of enemy merchant ships, and the future use of Norwegian ports and airfields would have been an immense victory and one which our highly efficient light forces were particularly suited to achieve and due to the minelaying operation being undertaken were at sea off the Norwegian coast and suitably disposed to undertake offensive action. Any argument that such losses could not then be afforded is false since at that time the whole French Fleet was on our side and in any event our subsequent losses in the Norwegian campaign were considerable.

Roskill is a powerful protagonist of Admiral Forbes as Commander-in-Chief, Home Fleet. On each occasion of too little and too late, or no action at all, it is explained that intelligence was lacking or was not passed to the Commander-in-Chief, or some disability intervened outside his control. Roskill knows the whole story and I only know from intimate personal experience the submarine side, so I will concede that Admiral Forbes may have been an able Commander-in-Chief of surface forces, provided that is compatible with his actions, which include public derision of submarine power in April 1939 (despite its current demonstration), the employment of his aircraft carriers, in September 1939, to search for and kill U-boats (thus jeopardising *Ark Royal* and losing *Courageous*), and his signal of 17 April 1940 (which is nowhere mentioned by Roskill) refusing any support for our submarines by a night sweep with light forces, even in the Western Skagerrak.

Roskill's valedictory comment upon Admiral Forbes on hauling down his flag begins, 'Though the fifteen months of Admiral Forbes' war command brought no great sea victory in home waters such as might catch the public's imagination, they saw the steady application of the long established principles for the maintenance of the sea communications to these islands.'

They also saw the enemy take over the coastline from the Pyrenees to North Cape and the establishment of a continuous U-boat campaign in the Atlantic of far greater potential than that obtaining in 1917.

Not only were Britain's sea communications in greater peril than they had ever been in our whole history, but in place of clear direction and the exploitation of every offensive opportunity, there had been re-established the paramount importance of 'The

Fleet in Being', that god of the Grand Fleet and Jutland. How could it well be otherwise? Forbes had been Flag Commander in *Iron Duke* from October 1915 to January 1917. If however this apparent ineffectiveness was due to Admiralty intervention and interference, my criticism is unfair but the above summarises my opinion at the time and if it is wrong it is time it met authoritative rebuttal, for many submarine officers are of my opinion. If the Commander-in-Chief Home Fleet did not have freedom of action in exercising command over his fleet, then out of respect for his memory and reputation it is time someone in authority said so.

The reason why I doubt whether the C.-in-C. Home Fleet had effective command of his ships at this time, or any effective liaison with or assistance from the R.A.F., is because of the letter Admiral Horton wrote on 10 October 1941 (see Appendix 2) refusing the honour of following Forbes as C.-in-C. This letter was unknown until the publication of his biography in 1954. Max Horton certainly wrote from the heart when he penned that powerful letter.

Interestingly, at the end of the war I came to know Admiral Horton really well and discussed the war's progress widely with him. He was at times critical, but I never heard him make a criticism of Admiral Forbes, and I gained the impression that he considered Forbes had held command under severe operational handicaps. This may have been so, but I am still of the opinion that any member of the inter-war 'Establishment' had their own tradition, a modern and up to date tradition whose conception and birth occurred in the Grand Fleet, where the gun was the only gentleman's weapon and the 'Fleet in Being' the sacred object. I am today convinced that for Admiral Forbes the divine authority from whom tradition flowed was Jellicoe, not Nelson, and for this reason the word tradition had long been meaningless – throughout my service career anyway.

8

At Harwich our submarines, except for the gallant *Sterlet*, came back with their varied successes and experiences. *Sealion* had patrolled almost in sight of Copenhagen and had a ship to her credit. *Sunfish*, in a better billet with deep water, had sunk four, while *Snapper* had sunk a petrol carrier on 12 April and at dawn of 15 April in low visibility 'browned' a convoy with a full salvo, sinking at least two ships. *Shark*, west of Jutland was out of luck. Ruck Keene arranged enthusiastic receptions for them and on these occasions our civilian technicians recruited in November always left the railway workshop, having been invited on board by the Captain to see the return of the submarines they were maintaining. This simple act was important; our civilian technicians rightly considered themselves part of the flotilla.

On 10 May the 'blitzkreig' was launched and Churchill became Prime Minister.

After the invasion of Norway, five H class submarines taken from training duties at Portland and Portsmouth arrived at Harwich. Concurrently Ruck Keene in *Cyclops* and Captain Belot in *Jules Verne* were told to leave for Rosyth and Dundee respectively and sailed with their flotillas on 15 May, leaving me with a nucleus staff and a spare submarine crew on Parkestone Quay to organise the old H class into an anti-invasion force. We formed an officers' mess in the customs inspection room and office, and formed our sleeping quarters and mess decks by subdividing the baggage transit shed with tarpaulins and furnishings from local resources.

It was particularly important now to keep two submarines on patrol north and west of the Texel to give warning of invasion, and I sailed them forthwith only to find that this put them out of contact since their radios were First World War spark sets with a range of about sixty miles. I recalled them, and on arrival in misty weather they said how objectionable it was to approach

Harwich through the off shore shoals with a rating on the casing heaving a hand lead, since if air attack forced them to dive their leadsman would be drowned.

My base staff was now strengthened by the addition of two R.N.V.R. sub-lieutenants. I found them quite splendid. Paymaster sub-lieutenant Henderson, the son of the brilliant Controller, Admiral Sir Reginald Henderson who had died in office in 1938, looked after my correspondence and administration very adequately. Sub-lieutenant Penfold came as electrical officer, and he had some years practical and business experience. No problem seemed difficult to him; on hearing that we needed immediately new W/T sets and echo sounders for five submarines, he told me he thought he could arrange that all right and also fit everything with our own resources at Harwich. He contacted a chum in the Air Ministry who said that W/T equipment was ahead of Wellington bomber airframes and sent us six sets. The echo sounders came from naval stores and in three weeks all five submarines were modernised. All I had to do was to acknowledge Admiral Horton's congratulations with modesty. There is another important point; if these five submarines had had to go to Sheerness or Chatham dockyard the job would have taken longer and at that time I would have been most likely to lose one or more submarines through the constant aerial minelaying in the Thames estuary.

Each morning at 10 am I walked along Parkeston Quay and reported to Rear-Admiral Harwich on my submarine dispositions and to hear his news. On the morning of 21 May the newspapers showed the sword of the Panzer advance across France to have reached Abbeville and the coast. As I approached the Admiral's office the door opened and Commander Russell Grenfell came out. He had been senior lecturer at the Naval Staff College in 1934 and had returned from retirement to organise minesweeping from Yarmouth. I had not seen him for years and after our greetings I said, 'Until this morning I have not felt that the news from France was too bad, but surely, Russell, it is time that a counter-attack was made from the North and South to cut off all that German Armour?'

He looked at me with surprise and said, 'I certainly hope there is no fear of that! I would have expected that you might have been one of the pupils at Greenwich who would have assimilated the true exercise of sea power. If we are allowed to stay on the continent a series of eager generals will decimate our nation's manhood in this war as they did in the last. The only thing to do is to get out of Europe with as many men as we can pull out – but in any case we must get out. Then we must start the war again where it suits us. That is to say where the German is dependent upon sea communications, and then we must protect our naval bases and go out and slaughter him on the sea. I am disappointed that you didn't take all that in. Any recovery in France now would be most unfortunate.' I never saw him again.

He held his unusual theories fanatically, and who can say, in this extreme instance, that he was wrong? Who but Russell Grenfell would have seen so far, with such conviction?

Before the end of May, Dunkirk and the French collapse, Churchill found time to visit Felixstowe and Harwich. I was told he came to view the east coast defences, which were non-existent. We paraded on Parkeston Quay. It was a bitter cold afternoon and he walked round the two H boat crews in port, my base staff and of course the workshop civil staff, then the minesweeping trawlers; and a very motley crowd we were. Commodore Goolden had arranged a dais and the Prime Minister was asked to address us. He looked ill, with colourless cheeks and made a rotten speech without inspiration or spark of humour or even message. I reflected at the time that his health was failing. Within three weeks he was instilling hope and vigour into the whole nation with his speeches.

Our veteran H class patrolling the Dutch coast through the summer had an uneventful time; a minefield was located and a store ship sunk. However the main duty was to give the alarm in the event of invasion forces being at sea, and this warning patrol was faithfully performed despite the submarines being twenty-three years old.

In northern latitudes, as midsummer drew near depriving our submarines of darkness in which to surface and charge batteries, with constant enemy air patrols from the Norwegian coast and the Germans' active mine laying policy, our casualties assumed serious, and in July tragic, proportions. In May, *Orzel* was lost. In June, the Dutch submarine *O13*. In July, *Shark*, *Salmon*, *Narwhal*, *Thames*, and on 1 August, *Spearfish*. After being bombed and unable to dive *Shark* fought it out on the surface for two hours and shot down a German bomber, finally sinking with most of

the crew surviving as prisoners of war. From the six other submarines there was only one survivor, from *Spearfish*.

Besides the personal loss of friends we knew that the loss in
skill and experience was too heavy to sustain.

After the move northwards of the modern submarines from Harwich this small naval base supported escorts for east coast convoys,
minesweepers and established motor-torpedo boats (M.T.B.'s) at
Felixstowe. On the coast a balloon barrage took shape and up
river west of our quarters on the quay several dummy submarines
were moored. Base routine was deceptively quiet since outside the
harbour magnetic mines and air attack were an ever present threat.

The old coal burning minesweeper *Harrow* entered port about
1 June with some 300 soldiers on board, evacuated from Dunkirk.
I recall vividly their disciplined bearing as the ship berthed, and
when the gangway was down they made way for five nursing
sisters to step ashore first – five young women who despite their
appalling ordeal contrived to look neat and unshaken. A sergeant,
carrying all his equipment, said to me, 'It's hell over there, but
we'll be back.'

Occasionally an aircraft did a bombing run at night and one
pleased us by putting a stick of bombs beside our dummy submarines.

It was June that John Illingworth (now of yachting fame) was
recalled to his engineering responsibilities in *Cyclops*. Commander
Sam MacGregor succeeded him, and so started for me two and a
half years of work with a technical officer whose resource and
improvisation kept our submarines going under the gravest conditions.

MacGregor's first experience was unusual. A huge shipment
of rifles from America had allowed an issue to be made to 'organised service units' within the probable invasion area. One
afternoon a military lorry came to our shed and off-loaded 25
rifles and 1,000 rounds of ammunition, which were put in the
C.P.O.'s mess temporarily. Walking down the quay I was met by
MacGregor who said, 'There's been an accident, the military
brought us some rifles and ammunition an hour ago and during
"stand easy" a fool put a round in a rifle, "to see if it would fit,"
he tells me. The rifle went off horizontally and the bullet went
through the messes in the transit shed and through the arm of one

of our civilian workmen. I took him immediately to the surgery, no bone has been touched and he is all right, the amazing thing is that he told me, "You must expect this sort of thing in time of war," so I hope that's all we shall hear.' This proved correct. Due to the direct association established between the civilian work force and the submarines by Ruck Keene, this gallant fellow seemed to welcome a shot in the arm, instead of telling his union to sue the Admiralty for gross negligence.

As the air blitz developed during July and August, Admiral Horton warned that attempted invasion must be expected should the R.A.F. be overcome, and I was to make what arrangements I could to move all torpedoes, vital stores, and my staff and spare submarine crew at the shortest notice. When clear of the area I was to contact his headquarters to find out where to rejoin my submarines which would be sent north by him when they had expended all their torpedoes. The only solution was to commandeer a train and I found the railways most helpful.

At the end of August Admiral Horton suddenly arrived by car. I had not met him to speak to before and I don't think he knew me by sight. Horton, in plain clothes, moved around the base at speed and remarked, 'I see the Harwich base has not been ideal, have you made any arrangements in event of invasion?' I telephoned to a siding with a signal box some three miles down the line and in ten minutes a train arrived. We explained that the engine was kept with steam up and fires banked, the driver and fireman living in the signal box on the telephone. Next to the engine was a locked van with important technical stores, then three timber trucks with thirty spare torpedoes with warheads on, covered by tarpaulin. Then came a personnel carriage and restaurant car with ten days' provisions, and finally the guards van with a portion having sand-bagged protection, and within this area a Wellington bomber radio set to keep us in touch continuously with his headquarters in London.

'I like that,' said Admiral Horton. 'It's good because it works.'

So the 'MacGregor – Penfold express' largely decided my future. Shortly after this I was told to report at his headquarters on 7 September, when he told me I would go to Malta to command the submarines he hoped to have there at the beginning of 1941.

It was not a good day to visit London, which was heavily

bombed that afternoon. I boarded the 7.30 pm train from Liverpool Street for Harwich and as the train pulled out the air raid sirens wailed and the train stopped on top of a high embankment. A mile to the south the docks still burned and waves of bombers aimed at the flames to stoke the fires. It was midnight before the train moved me from my enforced grandstand view of that scene of destruction, which seemed literally to 'set the Thames on fire'.

From this time until the end of the war I served either directly under Sir Max Horton or in direct correspondence with him on personnel and material needs. He was the most important man I have ever got to know well. He was a 'lone wolf' and the reason for our friendship was in part due to my never serving on his staff; I could not have stuck the pace. During his last week on the active list in August 1945 I stayed as his guest at his Western Approaches Headquarters – Derby House Liverpool – and we both knew that we had been through so much together that his regard for me was frankly paternal. His valedictory words to me on that occasion were, 'Remember that in future I am not between you and the Admiralty to support your views and to moderate your written word. To get what you want from bureaucracy needs vision and patience. Uncompromising demands will never get you anywhere, particularly if you imply that the seat of authority is foolish!'

His father was an Englishman and a stockbroker, his mother a Jewess from a well known banking family. Thick set with a big head and mobile expression dominated by ever alert eyes, his whole being expressed obvious physical and mental power far above the normal. People either cared deeply for Sir Max or hated him. He was, I noticed, so strongly influenced by first impressions that he seldom, if ever, changed his opinion of a man's character and ability, and this was occasionally unfair. During the war the vast majority of his subordinates formed a deep affection for him though many feared his ruthlessness. He worked quickly and decentralised fully.

So far as war events permitted he played golf every day from 2 pm to 5 pm, and to compensate for this worked after dinner until about midnight. He was a good golfer playing off a 9 handicap, which more correctly should have been 4, his ability being in his concentration and his determination to win which made his short game very accurate. This daily exercise refreshed and invigorated him marvellously.

His favourite quotation was from Proverbs Chapter 29 verse 18. 'Where there is no vision, the people perish', but I also remember his 'What were the first things I did on hearing that war was declared? Why, to buy a gross of golf balls and a gross of whisky, of course!' His views on promotion were equally strong, 'You are wasting your energy putting X at the top of your promotion list, Simpson. I will support you in any award for gallantry you may make, but a man who consistently shields his subordinates and takes the blame for their errors is unfit for higher command.'

The few times I played him at golf we played for half a crown and he gave me a stroke a hole: this usually resulted in a close match with me winning. He would then say without a smile, 'We will now play the bye without any strokes for five shillings.' He always won. He would then go to the club house and buy me a drink.

Leaving Harwich in late September I called at the Ministry of Sea Transport to arrange my passage to Alexandria where I was to report before Christmas Day. I was told to join a six knot convoy round the Cape leaving in about a week and due at Suez 20 December, and that there was no alternative. This news appalled me. How could I, a submarine officer, sit in a six knot ship for twelve weeks with U-boat sinkings steadily increasing, and arrive at Alexandria sane? It was the one thing I had no intention of doing if there was any way out. Unmarried, without home ties, and with savings in the bank, there was an obvious alternative, which was to pay my own fare round the world.

As I went by tube to Admiral Horton's headquarters to get my final briefing, I decided to ask him, and to make sure the matter was not sprung on him in an annoying way I asked the Chief of Staff to tell him what was in my mind, and that I wished to visit friends in the U.S.A. As the Battle of Britain was still being fought out this now seems to me an outrageous request, but Admiral Horton did not think so.

He first discussed my future job in Malta, which was all rather tentative, but it seemed probable that three Unity class submarines would arrive Malta in January and by sending me all the new construction of that class of slow small submarines, he hoped for a steady build up.

'You are to report to Admiral Cunningham before Christmas Day, otherwise your time is your own. Take this note to the Ministry of Shipping and get a new itinerary, which I must know. Get a civilian passport as you will be visiting a neutral country and take this note to the Bank of England yourself and wait for the reply. You must have some cash visiting the U.S.A. and I have asked for £100. Goodbye and good luck.'

Who but Sir Max Horton would, or even could have treated me so handsomely in September 1940? Nobody I've ever met.

9

SUBMARINE experience within the Mediterranean, since Italy had declared war on 10 June 1940, had in general been one of bitter loss and small success. The balance sheet at the end of 1940 showed nine Italian merchant ships, one U-boat and one torpedo boat totalling 37,000 tons sunk for the loss of nine submarines. Furthermore half the enemy tonnage sunk had been accounted for by *Truant* (Hugh Haggard), one of four T class submarines sent from the North Sea to strengthen the Mediterranean Fleet after the disastrous loss of five submarines in June and July.

The Italian experience was similar, since fourteen of their U-boats were sunk in the Mediterranean during the same period. Captain Raw gave it as his opinion that our heavy losses were due to mining, but in fact the first six were sunk by Italian destroyers and torpedo boats on anti-submarine sweeps.

I was taken to a conference with the Commander-in-Chief, Admiral Cunningham. Commander Power, his Staff Officer (operations), who was a submarine officer, was present besides Raw and myself. I was told all I needed to know and I was given great freedom of action. My directive was

(a) The Malta based submarines were operationally under Admiral Cunningham and my operational reports and requirements were to be passed through Captain Raw (*S1*)

(b) In the event of enemy attack on Malta I automatically came under the operational control of the Vice Admiral Malta.

(c) I was at all times under the administrative control of V. A. Malta.

(d) The object of the Malta based flotilla was to deprive the Italian army in Libya of supplies by sinking southbound shipping. Regarding northbound shipping this should not in general be attacked because of torpedo shortage unless the target was a warship, a tanker, or a large transport.

Those were my brief specific orders.

Admiral Cunningham then commented in a general way: 'I think our initial submarine losses have been due to mining, so my advice is to keep outside the 100 fathom line, but you must do what you yourself think in this matter. I warn you that my old friend Admiral Ford [Vice Admiral Malta] will want to tell you what to do with your submarines and this you are to resist. If you don't get results and don't dispose your forces to suit me I will very soon let you know. Until then you have a free hand to act as you think best to achieve your object.'

I had several days to think about the heavy losses, read the 1st Flotilla patrol reports, talk to submarine officers and look at charts. The conclusions I came to were that if the losses were due to mines, this was merely coincidental; there were so many other good reasons for casualties that mines were liable to be exaggerated. For example the O, P and R class submarines were all between eight and twelve years old, built for Pacific patrol, large and unhandy. They had been ordered from Hongkong and Colombo to Alexandria and after nearly ten thousand miles running on the surface were called upon to undertake war patrols in the clear water and bright night conditions of the Mediterranean. The submarines were unsuitable and the long passage immediately prior to war patrol was unfortunate for men and material. On these grounds I decided to disregard the threat of mines except off ports and in the Cape Bon – Sicilian channel. I did not think shallow water had anything to do with the mine threat, there was too much of it.

On 5 January naval forces left Alexandria and Gibraltar to pass shipping to Malta and to Greece. I took passage in the destroyer *Janus* arriving at Malta, which I knew so well, on 8 January 1941.

Malta and Gozo had come under the protection of the British crown in 1800, when they were captured from Napoleon, and the position was confirmed by the Congress of Vienna in 1815.

At the outbreak of war the islands had a population of about 300,000 people who depended upon imports of almost every commodity, except water and vegetables; indeed earth had been a regular import in peacetime. Since all timber, also, had to be imported it was extremely expensive and it was only used for rafters and window frames in the construction of their houses. The walls were made of massive blocks of the local limestone – each averaging about two hundredweight – while flat roofs and floors were made of more flat limestone slabs about four inches thick but of a similar weight.

The local limestone is tough, resilient and not liable to splinter; it is easily workable and the Maltese are adept at working it. Its main advantage at this time, however, was its resistance to high explosives and large numbers of temporary dwellings were cut into the limestone which makes up the islands by its embattled inhabitants.

The people of Malta are of two distinct types. In general the aristocracy and intelligentsia of the island are of Latin origin and Italian speaking, and like the Church have Italian affiliations, although at the beginning of the war they had an uncompromising dislike of fascism. On the other hand, Malta's working class and peasants are, like their language, of semitic origin. They are, it seemed to me, not at all volatile – in contrast to their Latin compatriots – but rather unimaginative, determined and dour. They became increasingly loyal to Britain, and angrier and angrier with the Luftwaffe, the worse the conditions became.

The Navy had long had a base here since it formed one of the finest natural harbours in the world. To the south-east of the finger of limestone three hundred feet high on which Valetta is built lies the Grand Harbour, two miles long and eighty feet deep with four large inlets striking to the south-east with a modern dockyard around the two central ones, French Creek and Dockyard Creek. Each creek has a graving dock at the head of it. Also in the harbour were a floating dock and floating crane for the largest capital ship repairs. Oil fuel storage was in tanks cut deep under rock. To the north-west of Valetta was Marsamxett Harbour, averaging seventy feet in depth and a mile and a half long. This long strip of water separated the capital city from its 'West End', which Sliema with its good class dwellings might be termed. Within Marsamxett Harbour lies the fifty acres of rock called Manoel Island on which was the submarine base. In many places in these outstanding natural harbours the limestone seawalls are vertical, so that cruisers, destroyers and submarines could lie alongside. The Mediterranean is a tideless sea, but all harbours are subject to a heavy swell when the seasonal wind, the 'Gregale', is blowing.

All these features were as well known to the British Government on 10 June 1940 as they are today. To enemy governments these vital statistics were available from Admiralty charts, 'Sailing Directions' and *Whitaker's Almanack.*

The facts, properly interpreted, meant that Malta, if *defended* from air attack, could support a fast surface force of cruisers and destroyers which must have caused the Axis to abandon the North African campaign virtually at British dictation. Malta was a unique weapon for killing Italian and German troops, which was the one essential for winning the war, while conversely it was extremely difficult for the German and Italian airforces to kill people in Malta. They could knock it flat but they could not kill people.

Figures explain best. There were altogether 3,343 alerts on Malta and it is believed that some 16,000 tons of bombs were dropped. These destroyed about 35,000 buildings of all kinds. The total number of civilians killed by this policy of 'suppression' was 1,540.

This should be compared with the 60,500 civilians killed by air attack on Britain, despite an all-out defence and much of the attack being concentrated on airfields, or the enemy being forced to jettison bombs, whereas in Malta there was no effective air defence until mid-1942. These figures show the importance of limestone and house construction in Malta, and the effectiveness of deep shelters.

During the Battle of Britain attacks on great towns were spasmodic, devasting, inflammatory, deadly and resisted by every means known to science and the courage and skill of the R.A.F. During the battle of Malta the attack was prolonged for two years, being turned on and off at the will of the enemy. Kesselring's elimination of Malta went on and on for twenty months; with the population half starving the whole scene was one of attrition. The orders (much publicised since the war) of the British A.O.C. were, both from the Air Ministry and Middle East, to attack. Not to defend the island and its unique qualifications as a sally port for slaughtering the enemy fully committed in North Africa by fast surface gunships supplemented by submarines. The Air Marshal had no option – he had no aircraft suitable for defence.

The Air Battle of Malta was an unnecessary ordeal by blast and rubble suffered by a half-starved population until their capital city and its suburbs were slowly demolished as they sat under rock and listened to the fury, whilst the means to fight back gradually died. It was not a glorious victory but eventually a long overdue recovery from a stupid policy.

Except for the brief, highly rewarding, visits of surface ships in mid-April and mid-October 1941 the naval force to be based at Malta was to be our smallest and slowest submarines. That was the best that could be done until air defence for Malta could be established, which we confidently expected in a few months.

Geographically, Malta was ideally situated for intercepting shipping from Italy bound for Tripoli but in other respects special difficulties were apparent. The enemy commanded the entire northern coastline of the Mediterranean except Greece and Crete which were shortly to fall to him. Britain held Gibraltar and the Egyptian and Palestinian coasts. The enemy therefore dominated the skies.

In 1943 and 1944 when Allied forces had recovered North Africa and the foot of Italy only, Admiral Doenitz has this to say about campaigning conditions for his U-boats:

> The conditions under which our U-boats fought in the Mediterranean were particularly arduous. In these narrow waters the enemy was able to give air cover to the whole of his sea traffic. Shipping from the Suez Canal and Alexandria to Tobruk and Malta sailed the whole time in immediate proximity to the coast. It was therefore easy to protect it from the land. Thus from the very outset the U-boats in the Mediterranean found themselves confronted with very strong defensive forces. Furthermore thanks to fair weather conditions nearly all the year round the sea remained for the most part calm and smooth. This made it easier for the enemy to locate and hunt our U-boats and at the same time made it more difficult for the latter to deliver any surprise attack. All the greater, therefore, must be the credit given to the U-boats for their achievements.

I welcome this unsolicited testimonial to my submarines who

fought throughout 1941 and 1942 under aerial bombardment at sea and in port with the enemy in command of the whole seaboard except Gibraltar and the Egyptian and Palestinian coasts. It is indeed a compliment from the highest authority and certainly borne out by his experience. Of sixty-two German U-boats which entered the Mediterranean in 1941–45 no less than forty-eight were sunk.

The submarine base on Manoel Island in Marsamxett Harbour had moved to the Lazaretto, a fine extensive building in which persons arriving in Malta had been quarantined in the days of bubonic plague. An isolation hospital for infectious diseases had formed another wing, but the building had long been empty. The whole structure was of limestone blocks and slabs quarried on the site and was about 500 feet long and 100 feet deep, facing south. The harbour's water to a depth of forty feet lapped the front of the building which, in two storeys, was protected on the north by the sheer rock face from which the stone for its building has been cut. The one long building was subdivided into four by three courtyards. The rooms running north and south were spacious and high, making good barracks.

The eastern end had rooms for isolation quarters, making suitable officers' cabins, surrounding a central mess. Between the dwelling rooms and the harbour's edge a wide corridor ran the length of the building at both ground and first floor levels. The main entrance was the west end of this corridor and ground level, the back door was at roof level in the centre of the building on the northern side leading to a stone staircase.

An important feature was that a bomb had to make a direct hit to cause damage, for otherwise it would fall into deep water or on to solid rock above roof level. There was a great deal to commend Lazaretto for a wartime shore base. It was spacious, strongly built, submarines could lie alongside it and behind the building was thirty feet of vertical limestone rock, at present forming the back wall, into which we could burrow to make bomb shelters.

The government department loaning Lazaretto to the Navy had stipulated that we were to respect and preserve the names of the illustrious who had recorded their tenancy by carving upon the limestone blocks over the past 200 years. On the front of the building at roof level was a verandah connected to the back door over the roof. This central high area gave a sunny sheltered and quiet viewpoint over the harbour and towards Valetta. It was here that most inmates whiled away their days of quarantine and carved their names on the walls. The names such as Borg, Mifsue, Smith and Jones with dates, all seemed common-place enough; the term illustrious seemed out of place, but on one stone carved in sloping script was 'Byron'. So this was the tedious experience he so much resented and this was where he stood and pondered before writing his unkind commentary on Malta on 26 May 1811,

> Adieu thou damnedest quarantine
> That gave me fever and the spleen.

When I left over two years later, the heavy blocks with the names of 'the illustrious' still stood, while every ceiling and most of the other structure was demolished.

The maintenance of these buildings was presided over by an ancient mariner, Lieutenant-Commander R. Giddings, who had been recalled to naval service from being Manager of the Malta Wine and Spirit Company. He was nearly twenty years my senior and was affectionately referred to as 'Pop'. He had a 'ship's company' of some thirty Maltese sailors whose assorted skills served the 'ship's' needs.

In the same age group as Giddings was our doctor, Surgeon Captain Cheeseman who was living in retirement with his wife at St Julian's Bay. Very fit and active, he filled the post well and would walk or bicycle daily to his work.

An old friend, Lieutenant-Commander Bob Tanner, who had left submarines due to his eyesight becoming defective, was my Staff Officer (Operations); an officer of precise mind and habits with an unruffled temperament and droll sense of humour, he was well cast for his job. On my first day he explained that at present only one submarine was operating from Malta. The Free French Submarine *Narval* was on patrol and should be returning from the Tobruk direction; in fact *Narval* had already been sunk off Derna by the Italian torpedo boat *Clio* on 7 January.

It was particularly sad that the only French submarine in the Mediterranean that rallied to the Allied cause was at once lost and it seemed to augur ill that my first report to the C.-in-C. should be, 'Regret to report *Narval* now three days overdue and must be considered lost' – that matter of fact phrasing with its load of doom, so often repeated in the two years ahead, which on each occasion seemed to increase in my mind the searching self-criticism which responsibility brings.

10

On my second day I visited Admiral Ford in his remarkable operations warren of rooms and tunnels cut out of rock about half way up the sheer facade of limestone, some 200 feet high on the Valetta side of the Grand Harbour. Sir Wilbraham Ford was a big man in every way, full of resource and confidence; his foresight in preparing net defences and under-rock oil tanks amongst many other precautions during the phoney war were now making Malta a viable naval base. It was good to meet his Staff Officer (Operations), Martin Evans, a friend from China days, for I would be constantly working with him and other members of his versatile staff.

It was on this day, 10 January, that it all started. The first dive bombing attack of the German Air Force. An impressive sight indeed, and as the attack was chiefly on the aerodromes some five miles away we had a grandstand view. Concurrently about fifty miles to the west the aircraft carrier *Illustrious* was the centre of attack receiving six bomb hits and was fortunate to reach port.

The Gibraltar half of 'Operation Excess' was arriving and during the afternoon Sam MacGregor, whom I had left in Harwich, joined Lazaretto to continue to exert his resourcefulness. In his engineering duties he was helped by Mr Creed, a commissioned engineer of similar staunch ability. There was one other officer at Lazaretto, Mr Warne, a torpedo gunner who as an able seaman in 1925 had been stuck at the bottom of the China Sea with me in *L7*. Warne's job was to supervise torpedo maintenance and availability in the rock-shelter torpedo depot. I was lucky to have him.

That evening I was writing in my office when a kilted officer entered, saluted and handed me an envelope. The letter read:

The Officer Commanding Submarines,   Paignton,
Malta.   Devon
                                      December, 1940

Sir,

Captain Taylor of the Liverpool Scottish is directed to report to you. He has with him three officers and sixty other ranks. They are ordered to cooperate with you for the purpose of executing 'Schedule B'. They have approximately one ton of special stores.

Welcoming this athletic looking, cheerful officer I said, 'Please give me the other envelope about Schedule B.'

Taylor replied, 'I only brought one envelope, sir. I have never heard of Schedule B.'

'What is in this ton of special stores?'

'Collapsible rubber canoes, tommy guns, and their ammunition, hand grenades, demolition stores and several hundredweight of plastic explosive.'

I went out with Taylor and met his commando, and in welcoming them to Lazaretto assured them that a hammock made a comfortable bed. In the mess Taylor introduced me to his officers – Lieutenant Walker, an Essex farmer in his middle thirties, Lieutenant Broome, rather younger, a midlands business man, and Dudley Schofield, not long from school, a subaltern in the Royal Fusiliers. Taylor, who was a timber merchant in private life, explained that they had left Paignton in a hurry to catch this convoy from Britain and were trained and keen to attack any shore targets. I was then told of the dive bomber attack on the aircraft carrier and that the commando had taken passage divided between destroyers and that they had entered harbour before *Illustrious* who was then limping into port.

The submarines *Triumph* (Lieutenant-Commander W. J. Woods) and *Upholder* (Lieutenant M. D. Wanklyn) were the first arrivals on 14 January. *Triumph* was on passage to join the 1st Flotilla at Alexandria; taking passage was Commander James Fife, United States Navy, a submarine officer who was embarked as an observer to see and report upon the war. This officer was to become Admiral Submarines in the Pacific theatre in 1944–45 and all British submarines in the Far East operated under his command in the war against Japan.

Apprehension hung heavily over Valetta. We had seen *Illustrious* limp into port with six hits from heavy bombs, and she was now alongside the south wall at French Creek where every effort was being made to make her seaworthy. On 16 January I took Commander Fife to call on Admiral Ford and while we were overlooking the Grand Harbour a total of sixty bombers attacked, in formation, from the east.

Looking up, the bombers were in flights of five like arrowheads in a straight line, at precise intervals of about 800 yards as far as the eye could see. Silver flashes around and above them indicated their fighter escorts glinting in the sun on this cloudless afternoon. The formation was at about 15,000 feet, approaching relentlessly and, seemingly, quite slowly.

The meagre Valetta A.A. defences opened fire and *Illustrious*'s guns joined them. Then as the foremost German flight reached its attack positon the leader swung on his nose and plummetted downwards, his consorts following at precise intervals of about five seconds. The leader, aiming his plane at *Illustrious*, released the bomb at about one thousand feet and flattened out to swerve away a few hundred feet above the sea, then home to Sicily. This meant that when one bomber was releasing its bomb the next one had just started its dive, while the next flight of bombers came forward to the point of delivery.

There seemed to be gaps in time of half a minute between flights, so that the whole bombardment lasted about ten minutes. That was my impression, but I did not watch it all. I could not bear to see the 'inevitable' catastrophe of *Illustrious* either blowing up or sinking alongside the wall. I said to Jim Fife, 'I'm taking shelter' and turned into the tunnel, although I had nothing to shelter from since the target was a mile away. The sound subsided and I emerged to see the worst, but a cloud of dust had risen to 1,000 ft around French Creek. This slowly subsided and there lay *Illustrious*, apparently untouched with her pom-pom crews moving behind their guns.

This 'miracle' should have given us the clue to a large measure of safety, for it was the dust cloud that must have saved the ship, which had received only one superficial hit doing little damage. Just seventeen months later smoke canisters lit around the harbour proved most effective in frustrating bomb attack, but nobody had the vision to learn the lesson from this vivid demonstration.

On 18 January the bombers returned and decided to go for the airfields, using a proportion of the twin engined Ju 88s, which were glide bombers rather than dive bombers and carried a heavier load. This change of target seemed inexplicable. At sunset on 23 January *Illustrious* left harbour and arrived safely at Alexandria two days later. This episode, a clear omen for the future, was not all one way. The few Hurricanes and the A.A. defences had accounted for sixteen of the enemy.

On 17 January *Usk* arrived, having been ordered to proceed direct from the west of Scotland to Malta, a distance of about 2,500 miles, immediately after completing working up after building. This long voyage made it necessary to change over to the reserve lubricating oil tank, which led to serious engine trouble that was eventually traced to a bucket full of carborundum dust having been put into the tank. *Usk* limped into Malta on five cylinders of one engine, the other eleven cylinders having run main bearings. This was my second personal experience of sabotage and since it was about five months before the attack on Russia I do not doubt that it was politically inspired.

Other arrivals during this tense period were *Unique* (Lieutenant A. F. Collett), and *Upright* (Lieutenant E. D. Norman) and the fitting out of messdecks, sleeping quarters, sick bay and administrative offices was going smoothly. Sam MacGregor had planned the layout for repair shops and periscope shop and was meeting stiff resistance from the dockyard, who in reply to his request for machine tools and stores was told that 'Dispersal is against dockyard policy.'

As I walked around Lazaretto I rejoiced that its design was so suitable, since the British Treasury had turned down D'Oyly Hughes's shelter plan put forward in 1934 at an estimated cost of £340,000. I wondered what my greatest difficulties would be, and oddly enough I thought on precisely the same lines as Max Horton, when for reasons of personal efficiency he had laid in a supply of whisky and golf balls. It seemed clear that we must live in constant fear of starvation, and that my submarine crews returning from patrol would get neither rest nor recreation which would be bound to react upon morale. Returning from my contemplative stroll I entered the ground floor gallery only to be confronted by a mule drawing a cart with a driver sitting amongst ten-gallon drums full of 'gash' from the messdecks, and followed by a prosperous looking Maltese merchant. I made inquiries and he explained that he had an arrangement with the canteen committee to remove all gash and pay the committee thirty shillings a week. I congratulated him and passed on, arranging a canteen committee meeting next morning.

A commanding officer cannot, or certainly should not, interfere with the decisions of a lower deck canteen committee which were legal, normal and, in fact, common practice. So I had to make a persuasive speech, not pointing out any fear of starvation, but the fact that we had outbuildings on Manoel Island suitable for pigsties, we had Maltese seamen amongst whom were undoubtedly skilled pig farmers, and since we were so lacking in any form of amusement or variety in diet I thought that pig keeping should supplement both needs.

Finally, having so successfully recovered the £300 which I had invested in billiard tables at Harwich, I promised to finance the project with a sum of up to £300. This suggestion was not welcomed with any enthusiasm and obviously aroused a good deal of suspicion. If I was willing to invest £300, concurrently depriving them of £78 a year canteen fund income, what was the real answer? What was this new C.O., who had just arrived, going to make out of it? Or, if he was not going to make money, what exactly was he up to? A searching argument ensued and I offered to leave the room if they wished it, but finally Chief Writer Lyons told me that fortunately there was no signed contract over the gash and I could have it and good luck.

Pop Giddings found pig keepers and prepared sties. I set off with Commander James Fife, U.S.N. to the weekly market in a country district where a sale of 'middle whites' was due. We purchased two magnificent 'gilts in pig' as I was told they were, and some feeding concentrates as a pick me up after farrowing. The sows were settled in sumptuous quarters. A notice on the ship's company board announced the 'arrival of your pigs' and they immediately aroused widespread interest. Sam MacGregor inquired, 'I see both pigs are twelve cylinder jobs, what occurs if they give birth to fourteen pistons?'

Towards the end of the month day and night bombing of Malta was routine. Morning raids were usually 'recces' with the real hardware arriving in the afternoon in quantity, and at night from small flights. It was convenient for me that the aerodromes and the dockyard were the targets, we only got 'night casuals'. I sent my three U class submarines on patrol off the Tunisian coast, and near Cape Bon which had not previously been investigated; they saw some shipping but had no luck. *Triumph* was told to remain at Malta for the present and our American friend James Fife moved on to Alexandria having learned something of 'dive bombing' and 'hog husbandry'.

Early in February Lieutenant-Commander Hubert Marsham arrived to become my deputy. He had just left the submarine *Rover* and active Mediterranean patrols, so knew the score from experience. Throughout the next two years he loyally and imperturbably played his part with a great deal of sense, and removed from my ken all petty worries and details of which I never heard a whisper. So my team was completed. I could not have found a better one.

I was working at my desk with my cabin blacked out one evening about 1 February, when Bob Tanner brought in a young military officer, saying 'Lieutenant Deane-Drummond, sir.'

This young officer, fair haired, lean and of medium height had an intense dedicated look and immediately rather annoyed me. He said, 'I am the officer sent ahead of the main body in Britain for operation "Colossus". I am looking for suitable quarters for our accommodation from which to mount this most secret operation and I think, sir, that this place will do quite well. It is big enough and it is isolated and could be made secure.' I asked him just how it was that he knew so much about my base before coming to see me, but it was soon explained that he had arrived at the end of the day and Bob took him around the place while it was still light.

'Well, tell me about operation "Colossus",' I said.

'It will be the first parachute operation of the British Army,' Deane-Drummond continued. 'The setting is this; the heel of Italy has a natural and adequate water supply but it happens to be highly charged with magnesium. To relieve the inhabitants of Brindisi and the countryside, some two million in all, of endemic diarrhoea an aqueduct brings their supply from the Apennines and it is our object to destroy the aqueduct.'

'Ah,' I said, becoming interested, 'and so closet two million

114

Italians for the duration of the war. I bet Winston Churchill thought this one up.'

'That is our object,' said my visitor, without a flicker of a smile.

'What do you want me to do?'

'Provide accommodation for from two to seven days for forty parachutists and our equipment and explosives, and also for the aircrews for eight Whitley bombers. Four of these drop us at the demolition site and four continue to Foggia to bomb the aerodrome as a diversion.'

'When do you start?'

'Our first date is full moon, the night of 10–11 April; we need the best moonlight conditions but any night up to the sixteenth would just do; we need an early moon-rise and a good light. I believe, sir, that you have a big submarine here to pick us up after the operation. I was told to discuss this with you.'

The fate of Operation 'Colossus' is fully recorded in Deane-Drummond's book *Return Ticket*, which gives a good account of this, and other, remarkable adventures and escapes of this resourceful warrior, but certain aspects of this operation which was not at all plain sailing for me deserve comment. Before such dull though important details I will state that the operation took place in ideal weather conditions on the night of full moon.

All things considered the drop was successful but the explosives were rather scattered. The real snag was that the aqueduct supports were not of masonry but of ferro-concrete and very much stronger. I understand that the result was that no support collapsed, although the main pipe was breached and the water cascaded into the valley, and in addition a railway bridge was completely demolished. Because no support collapsed the damage was made good by the Italians with little inconvenience.

After two days marching to the west coast through the Apennines the forty parachutists were captured. However, had this gallant band been blessed by every fortune they would not have been rescued since circumstances prevented *Triumph* going to their aid.

Next day Woods (*Triumph*), Tanner, Deane-Drummond and I held a meeting to decide on the precise date, time, method and geographical position of the recovery of the parachutists. I made it quite clear that dropping by parachute was a very simple matter compared with rescue by submarine and that if there was any leak of information regarding the rendezvous the whole rescue must be abandoned since *Triumph* would be a sitting duck for any enemy snare.

We decided that the parachutists would be recovered by rubber canoes from the shore on the southern bank of the Sele river (where there were high reeds) two hours before moon-rise on the fifth night after the drop. That was a clear cut decision, but we had to know a lot more. Were there patrols or sentry boxes by this apparently swampy river mouth? Had the peasants harvested the reeds for thatching? In fact, an air photograph was essential.

I went over to Chief Staff Officer (Operations) at air H.Q. Valetta. I asked if he knew of 'Colossus' and he said, 'Yes, it has been approved that the eight Whitley crews are to be accommodated and victualled by you.' So I went ahead and asked for an east coast of Italy photo recce. I explained the critical circumstances of submarine recovery and therefore the precise need for absolute secrecy. Having put all this over to my colleague I said, 'How can we assure that nobody but you can possibly know where this recovery is to take place?'

'That's easy, I'll merely say I want a photographic reconnaissance of the coastline from Cetrana for a hundred miles north to Salerno, and I won't even say what it is for.'

I left well satisfied and on about 6 February went to the same office to collect my photos. A very long and clear coastline photo was given to me confirming that our recovery site was well chosen.

About 8 February the parachutists arrived under the command of Major Pritchard, Royal Welch Fusiliers, a fine keen team of adventurers who I believe would willingly agree with me that their expedition and its humorous objective was a 'glorious lark' except for one very brave man who really stood little chance of survival while under cruel stress. Major Pritchard asked me to meet his men before they left and this I did, promising them so far as I was concerned safe recovery, but knowing all too well the immense difficulties. Pritchard then called forward Sergeant Picchi and I shook hands with him. Pritchard said, 'We are very grateful to Sergeant Picchi for being with us. He knows the country well although for many years he has been at the Savoy Hotel, London.' They stepped into buses and were off to the aerodrome.

116

Some years ago I called at the Savoy to enquire the true story and drama of this mild man's devotion to Britain. I am indebted to *Meet me at the Savoy* by Jean Nicol for the story. Fortunato Picchi worked in Britain for twenty years, the last fourteen at the Savoy where he was the deputy ball room manager. His hero was Garibaldi and he carried in his pocket a quotation from Garibaldi. 'England is a great and powerful nation, foremost in human progress, enemy to despotism, the only safe refuge for the exile, friend of the oppressed. If ever England should be so circumstanced as to require the help of an ally, cursed be the Italian who would not step forward in her defence!'

When war was declared it was inevitable that a manhunt ensued in the hotels and restaurants of the West End. Britain was not to blame for that and Picchi found himself interned in the Isle of Man. From this position of complete safety Picchi volunteered to parachute to his boyhood countryside in response to his hero's call. After some months in captivity in Italy he was recognised by an interrogator and was shot.

The Whitleys were due back at Malta between 3 and 5 am, four having dropped the parachutists immediately south of Calitri and four having bombed Foggia airport. In the middle of the night we got a signal from one Whitley bomber. 'Port engine cut out, slowly losing height crew will rendezvous in marsh south of Sele river.' The signal was encoded by a quick coding machine with a security estimated at twenty-four hours. I naturally thought that the Whitley was returning from dropping parachutists and there had been some loose talk on passage, but I was wrong, the plane was coming back from Foggia.

Next morning I sailed *Triumph* for the recovery, promising Woods I would inform the Admiralty at once, which I did and added, 'I consider that any attempt at recovery must now be abandoned.' I shortly received the order '*Triumph* is to return to Malta.'

I have related this incident, of how the rescue arrangements were compromised and therefore abandoned, because of its importance. Throughout this book I have aimed to avoid petty criticism or controversy but, in this instance, my confidence in the standards of security recognised by the service with which I was in almost daily consultation and cooperation was badly shaken. Was it just a fluke that this bomber's crew, finding a forced landing inevitable, had selected this rendezvous by chance because it was a near point on the coast from where they were forced to crash land, which had cover and could be quickly and precisely described? Or had this secret rendezvous been broadcast throughout all eight bombers before the operation?

The more I thought about it the more I attributed the disaster (for so this seemed to me) to sheer coincidence. My argument was that if the crew knew the rendezvous the signal would have read, 'Making forced landing, see you soon,' but to have made 'Proceeding to rendezvous on coast south of Sele river' on an insecure cipher was sheer madness. Why not just go there? I decided I could not confront the staff officer who had arranged the photo recce, since that would jeopardise all future cooperation. I never got a clue to the facts.

This made me aware of the difficulty airmen had in understanding, or perhaps in troubling to understand, the hazards confronting their brothers-in-arms who moved a hundred times slower than they did. In this case infantry in the mountains struggling at ten miles a day, with a highly vulnerable submarine coming to the rescue at three miles an hour during daylight and ten miles an hour at night.

It was not until the war was over that I found out that the parachutists were all captured on their way to the coast, so that this episode had not prevented their rescue.

Another 'military' matter intruded during February. I had informed Admiral Cunningham of the arrival of the commando company under Captain Taylor and suggested certain targets, particularly the vulnerable railways which hug the Italian coastline. One morning a brigadier called and explained that his visit was on behalf of the general who considered the commando should be under his orders. I showed my letter consigning these troops specifically to me.

'But,' objected the brigadier, 'how can you deal with men subject to Army regulations and not to King's Regulations and Admiralty Instructions?'

'That is not a difficulty at all,' I replied. 'I will check on this point today and if there are objectors I will hand them over and I will inform my Commander-in-Chief. If, however, every man wishes to stay under my command I will keep them.'

The whole commando paraded that afternoon and I explained

the predicament and added, 'I hope very much that you will remain with me and that you have settled in with the Navy and do not object to sleeping in a hammock. The point at issue is this: in the Navy we only resort to courtmartial for the most serious offences, and in case of disciplinary troubles you must accept summary punishment from me. Alternatively you can join the Army today and lose a free issue of rum daily and duty free tobacco and cigarettes. All those who wish to revert to the military command – one pace forward – march!'

Nobody moved, so the commando stayed at Lazaretto.

It seemed a remarkable coincidence, and one that I have been inclined to hold against Captain Taylor's aggressive humour, that throughout the next two years the only case brought before me was that of Corporal G. Simpson, charged with calling his sergeant a bastard (which neither denied). I disrated the accused to private and was delighted to note that when I finally left Malta he was a sergeant, not due to nepotism either.

During this military activity the submarine war was slowly developing. Following the three unfruitful patrols in late January five submarines patrolled between Cape Bon and Tripoli during February. Starting to operate in the wake of catastrophic losses and a minimum of result, it was necessary to feel one's way. Initially the patrols were short with good reason; I wished to glean every bit of information from returning submarines, and avoid losses with vital opinions and data on board on how to prosecute the submarine offensive from Malta. Having started in this way we found in general it was the most suited to our central position; a short patrol followed by a comparably short rest period. Another factor was that submarines were in zones of possible contact with the enemy within fifty miles of Malta. There was no respite on passage to or from port; so it was that the short patrols varying from four to twelve days continued as permanent practice, dependant upon torpedoes remaining, and other reasons considered on their merits.

Throughout the following two years (excepting May, June and July 1942) the number of Malta based submarines at sea at any given moment averaged between three and four. The maximum flotilla strength reached twelve in late 1941 for a short while. Submarines on patrol might average sixty per cent of the flotilla strength, but under the stress of harbour bombing fell well below fifty per cent.

While experiences quoted from patrol reports will sometimes be given there are several autobiographies written by submarine commanders which explain the tension, the tedium, the dangers and thrills of submarine patrol. My purpose is more generally to give the setting and the events of the Malta campaign as a whole.

During February five submarines completed seven patrols. Some useful information on enemy traffic was gathered but without material success except in the case of *Upright*. Lieutenant E. D. Norman, who was my most experienced commanding officer at that time, took with him for this patrol Lieutenant Schofield, Royal Fusiliers, and four Commando N.C.O.s just to get their 'sea legs'.

Norman told me on return that he was on the conning tower with the Officer of the Watch and Schofield as a look out, charging batteries on a very dark night not far from the island of Lampedusa. The asdic operator reported high speed propellers closing rapidly from the North on the Cape Bon Tripoli route. Norman turned *Upright* towards the sound, which appeared to be on an almost steady bearing, indicating that the target was steering almost at the submarine. Norman sighted two dark objects fine on his bow, shortly to cross from starboard to port at very close range. He said 'Fire,' then 'Dive.' The targets were uncomfortably close when the first was hit on a very fine angle of impact.

Norman continued, 'I am sure they were warships by their speed and silhouette and I do believe they were bigger than destroyers.' We had only a few days to wait when a report was received from a Tunisian source that naval caps had been washed ashore with *Armando Diaz* on their ribbons. This success was really important; it not only did the flotilla good but also warned the Italians that their cruisers could not use this route with impunity even at high speed at night.

Throughout February the Luftwaffe had maintained a heavy bombardment of Malta, concentrating primarily upon the air fields and the dockyard. In the case of the latter a direct hit was scored on the Naval Store Officers' records. Sam MacGregor and I were watching this attack from our verandah outside the mess and noted how upon an easterly breeze the suburbs of first Floriana and then Hamrun were gently smothered by an infinity of paper forms. Sam remarked, 'It is not the policy of this Dockyard to resort to dispersal, I quote, but I reckon that must have loosened things up a bit.' It had, and thereafter we were invited to help ourselves. A balanced repair workshop with necessary stores was quickly established.

It was apparent that sustained air bombardment must be expected and at night we had direct hits on Manoel Island which made me appreciate our extreme vulnerability, particularly to casualties in personnel. Supposing for instance we were to receive a direct hit on the officers' or the Engine Room Artificers Mess, the whole flotilla's activities would cease. Following the experience of Britain in the blitz the value of rooftop lookouts, or 'Jim Crows' as Churchill had named them, became apparent, and volunteers at once came forward from the Maltese Boy Scouts. Two fine lads joined us at Lazaretto and served with courage and complete reliability throughout the siege.

The air defence routine was that when enemy aircraft were showing on the radar screen a red flag was hoisted on the Castille flagpole, the highest point in Valetta. When the enemy formations had assembled and were on their way, perhaps ten minutes later, the air raid warning sirens would sound. At this moment the duty scout would go to his post on the roof, armed with a hand operated klaxon horn, and would watch the bombers as they approached. If it became obvious that the target was the Valetta area the scout would leave his roof top and run the length of the verandah sounding his horn. In this manner normal work could continue undisturbed if the enemy's target was the airfields, and we only 'went to ground' when the attack was on us or the dockyard.

In these early days the alarms and actual air raids became so constant that men became casual and a direct hit demolished our sick quarters, killing the C.P.O. Sick Berth Attendant who having cleared everybody else out had himself returned to the dispensary. After this casualty I issued an order that when our air raid klaxon sounded everyone was to run for shelter. At this same time we asked Mr Watson, the Admiralty Civil Engineer, for the construction of permanent under rock sleeping quarters, sick quarters and dentistry, and general workshop for all submarine running repairs. These works were all put in hand at once, about twenty Maltese quarrymen working through the year, so that when our very existence depended upon them in January 1942 we were able to survive.

A near miss by our pigsties in the middle of the night did not prevent the successful arrival of two litters and the quick fattening of ten weaners I had bought to eat the waste food.

During the first three weeks of March two south-bound enemy ships were sunk, one being the troopship *Capo Vita*. It was on 1 March that I was persuaded to let one of my submarines carry out an operation about which I knew nothing, a very stupid act on my part. Military intelligence told me that a submarine was required for a certain very important operation to be successful, and added that success depended upon the minimum number of people knowing of this operation, which it was hoped would be kept to three military staff and the submarine's commander. I told Dick Cayley to report and to agree only if he felt there was no abnormal danger. Cayley sailed with *Utmost* and did the job without trouble. I never learned what it was, but I never again allowed myself to be left out of the picture, which was just as well as things turned out.

The incidents recorded in this chapter took place against a background of relentless bombardment by the Luftwaffe of the airfields and the naval dockyard. Despite submarines lying alongside or in the Lazaretto creek our base was not singled out for attack during this four months 'blitz', which lasted from 8 January to 11 May 1941, when suddenly attacks ceased as the Luftwaffe were redisposed for the attack on Russia to commence on 22 June.

On maps recovered from the wreckage of a German bomber in mid-April the southern arm of Marsamxett Harbour, called Msida Creek, was marked 'U-boathausen'. This was half a mile from Lazaretto. So it appeared that due to the enemy's disregard of us we escaped this first blitz, except for some bombs on Manoel Island during night 'terror' attacks against the Valetta district, and the one direct hit we received which demolished our sick quarters.

The R.A.F. under the command of Air Vice Marshal Maynard contrived to expand their airfields and dispersal areas, despite daily attack. The restrictions on fighter retaliation were crippling, since the Hurricane had insufficient performance advantage over the Ju 87 and Ju 88 bomber at the altitude of the enemy's approach, which was about 15,000 feet, so the normal proceedure seemed to be to attack the bombers as they retired after dropping their bombs. However, there were so few fighters that no serious opposition could be mounted.

On 16 January when *Illustrious* was attacked in the dockyard six Hurricanes were operational. On 11 March Admiral Cunningham writing to the First Sea Lord says, 'I have just seen the Air Vice Marshal from Malta who is here to report. He has only eight serviceable Hurricanes left. He is being sent six from the shortage here.' He explains in this letter that in the Western Desert the R.A.F. had thirty fighters to the German and Italian 'over 200'. This was the situation immediately before Rommel struck. These two sets of figures show the desperate air situation of the Mediterranean.

Our team of about twenty Maltese masons and labourers made good progress with the rock-shelter installations. We were working against time now. Had the Treasury approved the rock shelter scheme under Valetta proposed in 1934 at a cost of £350,000 (the cost of one medium sized submarine), which had received the Commander-in-Chief's and the Board of Admiralty's support, we would have started the war with docking facilities, maintenance, supply and living quarters for six submarines under 200 feet of rock.

Currently it was quite unacceptable to have submarine crews in port from patrol and for rest having to huddle into inadequate shelters at all hours of the night. Owing to the war almost all the splendid residential flats of Sliema were empty and the landlords very willing to let them at greatly reduced rentals. These flats were mostly ten to fifteen minutes walk from Lazaretto, but far enough away to be outside any genuine target area.

I told my submarine C.O.s to encourage syndicates from their entire crews to rent flats, these flats to be officially recorded at Lazaretto for emergency recall purposes and for occasional inspection by the Chaplain, who seemed a suitable person to check on a proper standard of cleanliness and maintenance. This move to flat dwelling was greatly appreciated by the submarine crews. It provided dispersal and gave the men real rest, and a higher standard of living than they had ever experienced before. It is with pride that I record that in two years I never had one complaint, and these could come from a wide field such as rent over-due, or damage to property, disorderly behaviour or complaints from neighbours, but the sailor's appreciation was shown in his response.

11

WHILE the submarines permanently based at Malta were all of the small 600 ton Unity class, the larger T class on passage to or from Captain S1 at Alexandria were at times diverted to Malta for some special purpose, also the many large submarines employed in store carrying called two or three times a month from June 1941 onwards.

Triumph's part in the intended recovery of the paratroopers was the first occasion of a T class visit, then *Truant* called in February and we at Lazaretto were grateful to discuss night attacks with Haggard, who had up to then sunk single-handed a tonnage equalling all other submarines in the Mediterranean.

On 22 March *Rorqual*, a minelayer of the *Porpoise* class arrived from Alexandria to embark mines for a projected lay near Palermo. During General Wavell's final advance across Cyrenaica from Benghazi to El Agheila a ginger-bearded Italian, General Bergonzoli, received much publicity through his nickname in the press of 'Electric Whiskers'. It seemed to us at Lazaretto that Hugh Dewhurst, the C.O. of *Rorqual* had Bergonzoli beaten except for colour. Dewhurst was thick set, and of medium height and had grown a 'full set' with such success that his moustachios (well greased to hold them horizontal) measured nine and a half inches from tip to tip. His thick side whiskers and pointed beard added to a formidable appearance. He had a large head and not the least interesting feature of his hirsute extravagance was to observe from behind how a full inch of moustache protruded horizontally port and starboard on a level with the lobes of his ears.

In January, Dewhurst had laid mines off Pola and while retiring submerged had sighted an armed tug towing a large barge carrying a battery of field artillery. He correctly judged that seaborne field artillery in a slight roll would be helpless, so boldly surfaced and opened fire on the tug and knocked out its two guns, then switched to the six guns on the barge and silenced them, leaving the whole eight gun array a shambles by the deft use of *Rorqual*'s single four inch gun.

I suggested that after laying his mines he might find a trip along the north coast of Sicily and a short wait north of Messina fruitful before his return to Malta.

Dewhurst set off by the middle course through the Sicily – Cape Bon Italian mine barrage, and laid his mines off Palermo on 25 March – which five days later sank a 1,500 ton tanker. He torpedoed and sank a tanker of similar size on leaving the Palermo area, and then on 30 March torpedoed the tanker *Laura Corrano* of 3,700 tons; she did not sink, so he surfaced and sank her with his gun. Continuing eastward towards Messina, as he approached the Messina – Naples route he sighted the Italian U-boat *Capponi* approaching from the south. To quote his own words when he returned to Malta, 'Thanks for the tip to go north of Messina. I was steering east submerged, at about three knots in broad daylight and maximum visibility when I saw this U-boat approaching from starboard to port on a steady course. I gave no order for alteration of course or speed; I only had to say "fire" when the sights came on and blow it out of the water.' Dewhurst's martial progress continued for a few months, and I believe he was the first officer in the Second World War to earn three D.S.O.s, which he uncompromisingly accomplished by July 1941.

At this particular time enemy convoys were carrying the vital build up for Rommel's *Deutsch Afrika Korps* (D.A.K.). I had only five U class submarines. Norman, who had sunk *Armando Diaz* so brilliantly, became ill and returned to Britain, and his relief, Wraith, had not got his eye in. Nor had Wanklyn in *Upholder*, whose torpedo expenditure without result was actually making me wonder whether such a poor shot could be kept in command. Collett in *Unique* had sunk one ship; he was a plodder without that flair for making opportunity. Cayley in *Utmost* was my best C.O., with two ships to his credit and robust confidence. From 1 March I kept him at sea for thirty days out of thirty-eight – that is the danger in moments of crisis. Was I asking too much and as a result would he be lost due to overstrain? Lastly *Ursula*, Lieutenant A. J. Mackenzie, had done some useful reconnaissance off Cape Bon but no sinkings. We needed more submarines and just a slight respite from the bombing of the dockyard, but that was not to be.

Usk had arrived from Britain, sabotaged in January but the Commanding Officer's nerve had gone and I had to send him on to Alexandria and put the spare C.O. in command.

At this moment we seemed to be ineffectual when most needed. Admiral Cunningham sent four destroyers under the command of Captain P. J. Mack to operate from Malta. Acting on air reconnaissance they intercepted and sank an entire convoy of five ships off Kerkenah Bank, on the night of 19 April, for the loss of HMS *Mohawk*. This fine example seemed to remove our temporary difficulties. Enemy convoys were thereafter hit regularly and in Wanklyn's case the change was one from never hitting to seldom missing.

In retrospect it is easy to judge which incidents are of vital importance and which are not, but at the time it takes experience and daily visits to intelligence to select the targets or projects that matter. If the flotilla commander tries to drive his submarines too hard he will suffer heavy casualties and loss of confidence. An important matter in my position was to recognise which signals were made by Admiral Cunningham himself, which came from his Chief of Staff or the S.O.O., and which came from the duty staff officer. The last type were always the most pressing, the most dangerous and the least fruitful. I will give examples.

From C.-in-C.   *To* Submarines Malta.
Enemy convoy position X steering for Benghazi reported by aircraft at 2335. It is vitally important this convoy be attacked by every available submarine. Convoy expected Benghazi noon.
Time of origin 0110

A signal made in the middle watch telling me to disregard everything for a 'vital' target would obviously be an overstatement and I need do no more than move the nearest submarine if its chances were good. Such a signal can only have been made by the duty staff officer.

From C.-in-C.   *To* Submarines Malta.
While maintaining your existing anti-convoy patrols endeavour to place submarine for interception in event of fleet movement Taranto to Naples after sixteenth.

1530

This is the Chief of Staff, or the S.O.O., looking ahead and perhaps acting on intelligence or a practical reason, and it is dispatched in time to make arrangements, and for the submarine to move to position submerged by day and so get there undetected. It is an important signal to be carried out with precision.

From C.-in-C.   *To* Submarines Malta.
Kesselring has established his H.Q. at the Miramar Hotel Taormina. Eliminate him.

2130

This is made by the Commander-in-Chief himself. It is obviously made by Admiral Cunningham – it is brief, unexpected and absolutely unambiguous, and must be carried out. In fact that is exactly the signal that I got from him towards the end of April 1941, so I sent for Captain Taylor of the Commandos.

The Miramar Hotel, Taormina, on the east coast of Sicily had the following broad characteristics so far as I recall from the Baedeker tourist guide. About 200 yards from a rocky coast and 200 feet above sea level, the surrounding country being an olive grove, the hotel site appeared to be cut into the hillside, so it seemed that the back door would lead on to the first floor. We guessed that the bridal suite would be over the main entrance, because the photograph of the hotel gave that impression. We guessed the hotel's size to be between 100 and 200 bedrooms. We estimated that Kesselring's entourage, staff and security troops would number 200 and that four sentries were likely to be on guard duty simultaneously at night. We hoped Kesselring would sleep in the bridal suite.

Tanner brought David Wanklyn to the conference. He had spent his honeymoon at Taormina just three years before. 'There is the rock where we lay and sunbathed, and it has over twenty feet of water right up to it. I could take *Upholder* right in and put her bows against that rounded rock, which is ideal for landing from, and it is the nearest point to the hotel.' Unfortunately he had not stayed at the hotel or ever entered it.

Except for an excellent detailed chart with accurate depths, contours and the hotel's position and a poor photograph we knew nothing, which made planning easier. It was decided to fit *Upholder* immediately with a large pudding fender round the bow, and to embark Captain Taylor, Lieutenants Walker and Broom and twenty troops, all wearing rubber soled shoes. They were to land at 0100 on a night when moonset was about 0200. This meant that the moon would be behind the hill but for the first hour the gloaming, and thereafter the darkness, would help.

The officers were armed with tommy guns and a few hand grenades. The four silent sentry killers had knives and hand grenades. Two men each carried 30lbs of plastic explosive and pencil fuses in order to blow in the front door, and blow up the bridal suite. The remaining fourteen commandos were to work in pairs, one with a tommy gun and spare magazines and his mate with as many hand grenades as he could efficiently carry. The tommy gunner was to shoot anyone who put his head out of a window, and the grenadier to fling a grenade in through the window. The dispositions around the hotel were to be arranged by Captain Taylor, as were all these special arms.

For withdrawal, the broad idea was that the attempted silent killing of the sentries would occur thirty minutes after landing, the explosions and firing would take less than ten minutes and embarkation under cover of *Upholder*'s Lewis guns would be completed about moonset, which would assist *Upholder*'s escape.

I signalled the C.-in-C. to say *Upholder* and twenty-three commandos would attack in nine days' time. The pudding fender was built onto *Upholder*'s bow, while all the best cricketers in Taylor's team were busy throwing dummy grenades through window frames hung in a cutting on Manoel Island. I felt sure they would make a big impression, although the venture seemed suicidal.

There were four days to go when I was told the Governor wished to see me in his office. General Sir William Dobbie fixed me with his intense blue eyes and said, 'I am told, Simpson, that you are mounting a special operation in which military personnel called commandos are involved, tell me about it.'

I told him and he replied, 'Is this a naval operation or a military operation?'

'Well, sir, surely it is a typical example of a combined operation.'

'I hope very much that it is not,' retorted Sir William. 'You know, Simpson, I abhor butchery.'

'I know, sir, that they have a very slender chance of getting away alive, but they are brave men and I have been watching the enthusiasm they are putting into their training. I think it is the best we can do with our meagre resources.'

'You misunderstand me, Simpson. If your commandos were training to bring Field Marshal Kesselring before me unharmed as a prisoner of war through a well thought-out, cutting-out operation I would approve, but if you intend to persist in this butchery I must insist that it be called a naval operation.'

'Very good, sir, it is a naval operation.'

As I walked down that broad sweeping marble staircase, suits of armour with metalled gloves grasping embossed shields flanked my progress. I walked over to the nearest and tapping his cuirass I said, 'The days of chivalry are over, chum. You might tell the boss.' Then I felt rather ashamed that I should have sunk so low. I must attribute my fall to progress.

The day before *Upholder* was to sail, a signal came from the C.-in-C. 'Special operation with *Upholder* to be postponed until next suitable moon. Convoys loading at Naples likely to sail tonight and all submarines should be disposed to intercept.'

Two weeks later a further signal came 'Kesselring has left Taormina' so the outcome of this 'butchery' was never tested.

During April three submarines joined from Britain – *Union* (Lieutenant R. M. Galloway), *Unbeaten* (Lieutenant E. A. Woodward), and *Urge* (Lieutenant E. P. Tomkinson). On the passage across Biscay *Urge* had identified and sunk the Axis tanker *Franco Martelli* of 10,500 tons, on passage to Brest with a cargo of oil for the U-boat base.

Military Intelligence (M.I.6), who had been helped by *Utmost* in early March, came to me twice in April for jobs to be done. Colonel Bertram Ede ran this department; a debonair cavalryman with a very impressive chain around his middle supporting a vast bunch of keys. His office in the Castille employed a number of pretty girls who took their duties very seriously, as of course they should, but there were times when I wondered what there was to be serious about, except the dangers the submarines were called upon to run. Ede's deputy, a major, was 'the man who fixed things' and submarines were his vehicle of trade. He too was a cavalryman but of the horse-and-hay élite rather than the horsepower-and-petrol mob. He had a persuasive manner, a charming smile and a droll sense of humour.

Intelligence is of particular importance to submarines, since they are so slow and circumscribed in their movements. There were two useful sources, air reconnaissance and enemy intercepted signals, if they are capable of being deciphered. Nothing else in my experience was of any assistance, but we tried hard to help 'Military Intelligence' which benefited from Lord Gort's re-organisation in mid-1942.

The first problem in April 1941 was that a British army officer was in Tunis having escaped from France, could we pick him up? I consulted Cayley (*Utmost*) and suggested that the officer be instructed to take a rowing boat at Hammamet, row out two miles south off the town and clear of other boats, and start fishing during the afternoon of a certain day. An hour before sunset, if all was well for the recovery, he should tie a shirt to an oar and hold it up as if drying in the wind. If it was not safe for the submarine to surface and rescue after sunset in the dark a pair of trousers were to be tied to the oar. In either event this officer must be alone in the boat. This worked well, and Cayley had no problems.

The lieutenant from a territorial infantry battalion had found himself south of Rommel's thrust through France of the previous year. His French was not good and his accent atrocious, but he understood the language. He acquired plain clothes, a rather threadbare blue serge suit and grey felt hat. He had walked from the Cambrai district the whole way to Marseilles; he told me he dared not risk asking for a lift. At Marseilles he contacted the criminal world in dockland; it was before any rescue route had been thought of, the reigning head of the underworld shipping him through to Tunis where he managed to contact Malta. This officer, so full of determination and resource had one thing much in his favour, he was just about the most ordinary looking man imaginable, there was nothing whatever remarkable about his average height, his rather pallid complexion, or his expressionless and bored eyes. A faceless man, he stayed in our mess two weeks, became a sort of mascot and I cannot remember his name or regiment.

During the war the Germans recruited and trained volunteer Irishmen to be parachuted into Eire where they were to become spies. I was told in 1944 by the Chief of Police in Ulster, who had an excellent understanding with his colleague across the border, that only about six were parachuted into Eire and that only one of these had any hostile intention to Britain. The others were pleased to be parachuted home with £100 in cash in their pockets.

The same technique was employed by the British. Italians and Arabs were recruited from the Abyssinian campaign prisoners of war, and after training were sent to Malta to be 'planted' in Italy or North Africa. So far as I recall we landed seven agents by folbot from submarines, three singles and two pairs, between April 1941 and October 1942. The first was a Tunisian lawyer who did not come from Egypt but was evidently an enemy 'plant' on us. He came to Malta direct from Bizerta I was told, presumably by arrangement with Military Intelligence. In late April 1941 we landed him as requested near Castellammare, about thirty miles west of Palermo, in Western Sicily. I met all seven of these so called agents and he was the only one who looked a crafty professional.

The major would tell me at intervals how valuable this spy was proving. In late September he asked me to send a bag to him containing Italian currency and new codes and instructions. I refused and said that this was within range of a Hurricane, so the R.A.F. could drop the bag at night at a prearranged place on the beach, having identified his position in the usual way by coloured torch or some prearranged signal. The major insisted that this was no good because he would lack positive proof that his agent had actually received the bag, in which case the agent might be telling the truth if he said he had failed to recover it, or he might be trying to get double pay and allowances. In the end I was talked round to undertaking this supposedly important mission. I felt confident that arrangements could be made to side-step any treachery so far as the submarine was concerned, but I did not regard the landing of the bag with the money as dangerous; I foolishly thought all would be well because the agent must need the money.

In August two young sub-lieutenants had joined the spare crew at Lazaretto. September had been spectacularly successful for the flotilla, and when *Urge* was briefed to undertake this patrol both these young officers applied to man the folbot. In a moment of thoughtless overconfidence I agreed that one could carry out this mission and B. N. T. Lloyd was chosen.

In briefing Lieutenant Tomkinson I explained that he had two opportunities to land the money and that a dim blue light would be shown from the agent ashore in the small sheltered cove where the bag was to be landed. I emphasised the possibility of being double-crossed and recommended the second night as the safest for the operation.

On the first night Tomkinson was stopped and listening on asdic a mile to seaward of the cove when approaching propeller noises were heard. Just before 2 am, the time the landing was supposed to occur, an Italian E-boat swept into the cove and stopped. After half an hour the enemy started engines and disappeared towards Palermo. Tomkinson was of course convinced that the E-boat had been sent for him but was not sure that the agent had betrayed him. Because there was the possibility that the agent might wish to return to Malta Sub-lieutenant Lloyd was dispatched the following night from outside the cove as it was calm and no enemy propeller noises could be heard. When his folbot reached the beach he was met by bursts of tommy gun fire and killed instantly. Tomkinson watched this through night binoculars.

I reported this dangerous episode to the major who did not seem at all surprised and said that a double agent was very useful provided one was sure of his duplicity, which was now established. I got a well earned reprimand from Admiral Horton who stated, 'We are desperately short of trained submarine officers and a man of Lloyd's stamp could be in command in two years at the present rate of casualties. You have commando troops provided for this type of work, so use them.'

I should here explain that all submarine patrol reports went from me with my comments to Captain S1 at Alexandria, thence to the Commander-in-Chief Mediterranean and thence to the Admiralty and Admiral Submarines. This meant that Horton got information by this route anything from six to ten weeks after it occurred. Since the Admiral Submarines was responsible for supplying me with all replacement personnel, spare gear and material and submarine torpedoes, he had to know our needs as they arose; for this reason I sent Horton a monthly letter which was a précis of all operations and a full statement of our personnel and material needs direct by air with the Island's official correspondence to London.

At the beginning of May I sent *Usk* with Lieutenant Darling in command, to patrol north-east of Cape Bon, in deep water but in sight of the Cape. I chose this position as reasonably safe, likely to be rewarded by targets and success to redress the balance of her past experience of sabotaged engines. She was never heard of again.

At the time we assessed the cause of loss as Italian mines and this remains the probable cause. By mid-May when I knew she was overdue, the treacherous agent had already been landed west of Palermo and there was no call for routine passage between Sicily and Cape Bon, so the area was for the time avoided and patrols south and east of Sicily paid rich dividends.

After the armistice with Italy in September 1943 my successor, Captain G. C. Phillips, then Captain *S10*, received Italian naval information from the Italian Admiralty, and this included the charted positions of all Italian minefields. The result is quoted in the Admiralty publication *Submarines. Operations in the Mediterranean.*

Captain *S10* reported in his monthly letter for September 1943 that an embarrassing amount of intelligence became available from Italian sources, the positions of their minefields being the most useful and interesting. These were so numerous and widespread that it is difficult to see how our submarines could have been operated had the positions of these fields been known previously.

The Sicilian channel, on paper, was certainly impassable on the routes we used regularly for twenty-four months and the concentrated activity off Brindisi and Bari was carried out with no fewer than thirteen separate minefields enclosed in areas of fifteen miles radius from each port. The remarkable thing is that out of thirteen British submarines lost up to that date in the Mediterranean due to unknown causes, only three can have been casualties in the Sicilian Channel – *Usk* (May 1941), *Tetrarch*, (October 1941), and *Talisman*, (September 1942).

On this point, I remember vividly a conversation I had with Lieutenant Maydon in the early desperate days of 1942. He commanded the submarine *Umbra* and I was sending him to the convoy route south of Cape Bon. Before he left I added, 'So far as I know the area is free of Italian mines, and regarding present German minelaying operations off Malta I will try to ensure you are routed clear of all trouble.' Maydon replied, 'Yes, sir, I know you will, but of course I never give mines a thought; if submarine C.O.s allowed mines to be considered we would soon go daft.'

The loss of *Usk* which we assessed as due to this cause made me spend many hours considering a solution to the problem which must soon arise, how to circumvent the Sicilian Channel minefields with such consistent reliability that my C.O.s would regard dispatch to the Tyrrhenian Sea north of Sicily without any added tension to their hazardous life. I thought then that the threat of Italian moored mines was exaggerated and I am sure that the impression of Captain *S10* in September 1943 was too pessimistic. To lay moored mines in deep water presents special difficulties due to the length of the mooring wire and its fouling by marine growth. To lay moored mines in shallow water is simpler but the mines are more subject to the effects of swell and storm. In either case I did not consider an Italian moored mine-field to be an effective hazard after six months from the time of laying. That was my opinion at that time, which I think was a common-sense assessment.

Shortly after the loss of *Usk* the irrepressible Dick Cayley in *Utmost* returned from a southern patrol and reported, 'Coming up to periscope depth for a periodic all round look I found we were passing a domed object, it seemed like the top of a mine just buoyant and with no horns showing. I put the stick up another three feet and took an all round look. To my horror I counted about twenty within a hundred yards of me. Wondering what was my best way out of this danger from every quarter, the mine I was looking at grew a horn, opened an eye and winked. They were Mediterranean terrapins and at that moment I knew the full meaning of the term "mock turtle".'

Occasional reference to mines occurs in the flotilla's patrol reports; as an example *Upright*, Lieutenant Wraith, nonchalantly stated on 23 October 1941, 'Proceeded at periscope depth to cross 100 fathom line. Two heavy bumps felt and a loud scraping noise down the ship's side. Nothing could be seen astern through the periscope. It was thought that this might have been a mine, so course was altered to the northward and *Upright* kept outside the 100 fathom line in this vicinity for the remainder of the patrol.'

The great difference between Italian and German methods in the Mediterranean was that the Italians sowed contact mines over large areas, by the thousand, to restrict our movements or guard port entrances. The Germans sowed, either by parachute air drop or from fast motor boat, individual very large antennae mines,

E*

either in the harbours, or on the towns, or in the approaches to the Grand Harbour and Marsamxett Harbour. While the German effort was quantitively small, and restricted to rather shallow water, the individual antennae mines were hideously lethal.

In July 1941 I was ordered to provide protection north west of Sicily from Italian fleet interference during the passage of operation 'Substance' (a convoy to Malta). I chose my best team and briefed *Upholder* (Wanklyn), *Urge* (Tomkinson), and *Utmost* (Cayley). I disclosed that my plan was that in future all submarines should use the same route and that the route should be precisely used by shore fixes. The following routine for passage through the Sicilian Channel would be invariably followed, except in emergency: 'Submarines leaving Malta would make night passage so as to arrive ten miles S.W. of Cape St Marcos (close west of Sciacca) at dawn. Dive to 150 feet and steer course 300° blind for 55 miles, thus surfacing with Marettimo Island to the N.E. ten to twelve miles distant. Return journeys to be made in the reverse direction during a day's diving in a similar manner, speed being adjusted to suit the hours of daylight. This route, I explained, was unlikely to be heavily mined, being so near the enemy coast, so it would be under shore observation and also would be used by their coastal and fishing craft. I continued, 'The question now is who will go first, for I will sail you at twenty-four hour intervals, each submarine on arriving south of Marettimo is to report his arrival.' 'I will,' said Cayley, urgently. So *Utmost* sailed and two days later I received the signal, 'Utmost to S10. Next Please.'

We kept to that route for the next two years and had no further casualty on it. I do not believe *Tetrarch* and *Talisman* were mined here, there was another reason for the former's loss. My U class submarines came to regard this passage as a matter of ordinary routine.

Our daily life at Lazaretto throughout April 1941 and early May was one of apprehension. Our survival as a base was likely to come to an abrupt end at any moment. The Luftwaffe, having made their debut in January, followed up with increasing vigour. There were 107 air raids in February and 105 in March. In April the bomb weight of raids increased dramatically whilst the method became more lethal. Attack both by day and by night contained an increasing percentage of parachute mines.

I had seen the effect of these mines dropped in residential suburbs of London, where each explosion had razed to the ground about one acre of dwellings. In Malta the solid masonry restricted the damage to one or two complete dwellings, leaving in their place a heap of huge stone blocks which remained a jagged obstacle for years. The main purpose, however, was to mine the entrance to the Grand Harbour in particular and to Marsamxett Harbour also, which was achieved with good effect by the enemy. Since the harbour entrances were the true target it followed that the seaward residential area of Sliema suffered as did St Elmo and Bighi.

There was no minesweeper at Malta capable of detonating these mines so it was essential to mark accurately by cross bearings the position of each mine as it fell in the harbour, which became the duty of the spare submarine officers under the spare C.O. They were remarkably successful. Our submarines crept in and out of harbour hugging the Valetta side of the channel without loss and without curtailing or cancelling a submarine patrol.

I was so preoccupied at this time with out local problems that I made no routine calls on Admiral Ford and his staff and the R.A.F. operations room, and I did not realise that the Grand Harbour situation was critical. The large number of mines had made marking their positions valueless. There were between thirty and forty in and around the entrance.

After his successful sortie and sinking of the five-ship south-bound convoy, Captain Mack and his destroyers were recalled on 19 April to Alexandria and at the end of the month his place was taken by Captain Lord Louis Mountbatten in *Kelly* with five destroyers newly arrived from England. I got a telephone call from H.Q. 'The Fifth Destroyer Flotilla arrived this morning and Admiral Ford wants you to go over with your charts at 1400 today to tell Mountbatten where the best hunting grounds are.' This led to a slight pantomine which contrasted our respective ways of looking at the same problem. I prepared my chart, rolled it up, tied it to the front handlebars of my push bike, and an hour before our meeting set out on a sweltering cloudless day to pedal the nine miles round the heads of the harbours to visit *Kelly* at Parlatorio Wharf. When I entered the dockyard the air-raid sirens blared and as I boarded *Kelly* the quatermaster said, 'Captain's compliments, sir! Will you please go down to his cabin and make yourself at home, the captain will join you as soon as he has satisfied himself that we are all ready for this air-raid, sir.'

I went aft to the captain's cabin and sat down but I wasn't a bit comfortable. Ten minutes had gone since the warning, there might be a further ten minutes, but probably less. What the hell was I doing here anyway? What possible use could I be to my submarines when dead? I got up and walked around the cabin, which was modern and plainly furnished, and detected a few touches which were not standard fittings. I looked at the silver framed signed photographs from royal relatives and was interested that he agreed that in war one should enjoy personal possessions and treasures for just as long as one could.

I could stand this wait no longer, there remained three minutes at the outside and this raid was obviously directed against these new arrivals which the morning's recce would have announced. I went on deck and said to the quartermaster. 'Tell your captain that I have gone to that rock shelter over there,' (about sixty yards distant), and walked over the gangway. At that moment Mountbatten, coming from the bridge, came over the gangway and greeted me. 'They tell me over the telephone that the raid is "seventy plus", what exactly does that mean?'

'It means that at least seventy bombers and accompanying fighters are on their way.'

'Well, Simpson, you've had a few months of this, what do you do under these circumstances?'

'As soon as we know the raid is heading for us we all run into the shelters under forty feet of rock. It is my order that everyone is to run; but then we have no guns to man. I suggest you and I take shelter now, sir. The whole of this flotilla depends upon you.'

But I could not shift him one inch. We stood there, just half way between the shelter and his ship while high up over St Elmo were the wedges of bombers coming in.

'Our problems are different – you see *Kelly* is mine,' and we stood looking admiringly at her.

To the practised and tuned-in ear there is a detectable sound as of rushing air for about two seconds before bombs strike the ground close to, and I heard just this. 'Look out,' I yelled and we ducked. A stick of medium bombs fell into a store beside us on the wharf, and just over *Kelly*. Some intervening stone block walls protected us. As the dust cleared we walked to the shelter and I gave my chart and explanation, mounted my immediate command, a bicycle, and pedalled home. Time and time again I was to thank God that I had no ship to look after in addition to my flotilla command.

My advice did not bear fruit. The 5th Flotilla carried out one sweep to the south west of Malta but found nothing and on return the destroyer *Jersey* was mined and lost near the entrance. In fact intensive mining stopped all surface ship movements until a channel was blasted through by depth charges.

On 9 May convoys with fleet protection from both east and west converged on Malta (Operation 'Tiger') in very favourable weather with low cloud, and the minesweeper *Gloxinia* with the latest magnetic sweep had accompanied the fleet from the east. She streamed her sweep, a flexible pipe about 100 yards long with a powerful electric pulsator in the tail. About fifteen magnetic mines were detonated inside and outside the Grand Harbour breakwater and then *Gloxinia* came round to us and in half an hour had detonated all eight mines and 'swept our stables clean'; what a relief that was.

The 5th Destroyer Flotilla returned to Malta on 11 May to continue operations from this base after parting company with the fleet returning to Alexandria. A week later it was ordered east to join in the battle for Crete.

These were the circumstances accompanying Malta's loss of the last surface striking force to operate from there for five whole months, until Force 'K' arrived in October 1941.

At this time the scene at Malta was one of considerable urban damage due to four full months of aerial bombardment from the Eighth Fliegerkorps. The people of Malta with rare determination were everywhere cutting safe homes into the rock by hand picks. The island had just been reinforced by supply ships and tankers on passage to Alexandria.

The aerodromes and the dockyard had born the brunt of this attack, yet the former had expanded and the latter managed to keep operational in all essential repair departments.

Inexplicably Lazaretto remained virtually unscathed; was it possibly because the German intelligence officers discounted our using an old hospital for bubonic plague and isolation purposes as a submarine base? My flotilla then numbered eight U class submarines and the young C.O.s had settled down to sink ships.

At this time the tempo of air attacks reduced appreciably, and although nuisance raids and recces persisted the inconvenience seemed small. Life returned to near normal. The German Air Force were pulling out for the invasion of Russia on 22 June.

12

It was my practice to allocate patrol positions in my sailing orders somewhat precisely in a formula of the type, 'You are to establish patrol in southern approaches to Messina in vicinity of Lat. *X* and Long. *Y*. If it is necessary to leave this position you should withdraw southward on course *Z* a distance of up to forty miles.' By using this formula I knew where the submarine was fairly accurately, and if the captain had been forced to quit his position due to a torpedoing or other reason I would know that the enemy convoy route, which I had given him to retire along, was still patrolled. The captain also knew that I expected him to equate the risks he took with the probable reward.

It seemed sense that if we could with experience maintain a high dividend without high losses this should be done, and the effect would snowball as the flotilla grew in strength. Lastly I forbade the use of challenge and reply identification signals, nor were these cumbersome lights to be carried in Malta submarines. The question of whether a submarine sighted on patrol was to be attacked was always my decision. In this way we had no misunderstandings, and a responsibility was removed from the C.O. We sank seven U-boats and only missed one or two possible opportunities. In his sailing orders the C.O. would read, 'Submarines encountered are (or *are not*) to be attacked.' In addition to increasing the security of our own submarines it was obvious that no U-boat challenged at night was going to continue on the surface, the enemy would dive immediately and so escape.

The welcome return to more normal life as the air attack eased may have been reflected in our mounting successes. On 20 May *Urge* torpedoed two large supply ships, one of which sank, and *Upholder* torpedoed a large tanker, which was eventually towed into Messina. The heavy depth charging put *Upholder*'s asdic out of action beyond repair at sea. Wanklyn withdrew southward down the East Sicilian coast. He had two torpedoes left.

Just after sunset on 24 May he came to periscope depth and sighted three heavily escorted liners, fired his two torpedoes from inside the screening destroyers and sank the liner *Conte Rosso* (18,000 tons) which had 3,000 Italian troops on board, more than half of whom perished. An accurate depth charging followed and it seems likely that the large number of troops in the sinking *Conte Rosso* saved *Upholder*, since Wanklyn was unable to take any informed avoiding action. Over forty depth charges came at intervals and so close that they could be heard moving through the water. All that Wanklyn could do was to creep away as deep as possible. During this manoeuvre the signalman's nerve snapped and he suddenly dashed at the lower conning tower hatch and started unclipping it; he had to be manhandled and held down.

When back in Malta Wanklyn recommended that the signalman be returned to general service as unsuited to submarines. The poor fellow was really distressed and requested to have the matter adjudged by me. Of course, I upheld Wanklyn's decision but I reassured the signalman that it was nothing for him to be ashamed of.

During that last week of May the Battle of Crete was being fought out. Life in submarines was an easy ride compared with the critical casualties suffered by the Mediterranean Fleet in rescuing the Army, when operating without R.A.F. help. The R.A.F.'s Cyrenaican bases had just been over-run by Rommel, and the R.A.F. had insufficient resources to cover even the African campaign effectively.

This terrible trial of strength between the XIth Flieger and parachute battalions on the German side and the Mediterranean Fleet endeavouring to support or to evacuate the Army's rear-guard in Crete was devasting to both contenders. Our fleet losses were: Sunk, Cruisers, *Gloucester, Fiji, Calcutta*. Destroyers, *Juno, Greyhound, Kashmir, Kelly, Hereward* and *Imperial*. Damaged beyond repair on the Mediterranean station, 2 battleships, 2 cruisers, 2 destroyers. Damaged and repairable at Alexandria, 3 cruisers, 6 destroyers. The personnel casualties were over 2,000 killed, comparable to losses in a major fleet action.

The Commander-in-Chief makes these points in his covering despatch on the gruelling nature of that battle:

'The cumulative effect of prolonged seagoing over extended

periods without the inspiration of battle with the enemy. Instead, the unceasing anxiety of the task of trying to bring away in safety thousands of their own countrymen.

'More than once I felt that the stage had been reached when no more could be asked of officers and men, physically and mentally exhausted by their efforts and by the events of these fateful days. It is perhaps even now not realised how nearly the breaking point was reached, but that these men struggled through is the measure of their achievement, and I trust that they will not lightly be forgotten.'

Finally Admiral Cunningham ends his despatch with, 'It may be that the Admiralty would like a change in command of the Fleet out here. If this is so I shall not feel in any way annoyed, more especially as it may be that the happenings of the last few days may have shaken the faith of the personnel of the fleet in my handling of affairs.' (From *A Sailor's Odyssey* by Admiral of the Fleet Lord Cunningham of Hyndhope.)

Although these critical events happened far to the east of us and outside my personal experience I refer to them because I feel that these events have already been forgotten to such an extent that young people have never heard of this national example of human endurance.

Other points deserve note. In April 1940 it was not considered expedient by the Home Fleet to risk any surface forces attacking an invasion of Norway, which comprised eight enemy divisions, in excess of 150,000 troops by the time it was finished, the Commander-in-Chief commenting that to risk surface ships without air support was not 'an operation of war, unless in fog, due to air attacks the enemy can bring to bear.'

In May 1941 the Mediterranean Fleet suffered these casualties unflinchingly to save our rear guard of 25,000 troops of the highest quality, the Commander-in-Chief Mediterranean commenting, 'We cannot let the Army down.' Were circumstances so different that both were right?

Lastly the Minister of Defence and Chiefs of Staff had experienced Norway, Dunkirk and now Crete. By the end of June the invasion of Russia had been launched by Hitler which precluded the simultaneous invasion of Britain. Yet the fighter build up in Britain continued whilst the ineffective defence of Malta persisted without Spitfires, to the point where our possession of a fine defendable port and experienced fast surface forces to work from it was virtually ignored.

With this heavy loss Admiral Cunningham had to continue active support for the Army in capturing Syria; the supply of Tobruk and the ever persistent problem of the supply of Malta. It was grand to feel that at this moment we were proving effective and despite his anxieties he found time to signal to me. 'I wish to express my appreciation of the successes which have been achieved in the last few weeks by you and your command in attacks against the Tripoli convoys. In these times of adversity this work is more than ever important to the Empire's effort. Well done and carry on!'

Since I was a commander, and so a wardroom officer, the question of my messing alone had never arisen, and thereafter was never considered, which was as well, since the time was not so far away when everyone from A.B. and stoker up to and including the captain were to mess in the same disused storeroom with its roof kicked in, wide open to the rain and skies.

This arrangement of commanding the flotilla and living in the wardroom suited me well; I not only had the chance to discuss events in the relaxed atmosphere of the smoke room but also to listen to ideas from every quarter, and if I overheard an idea which I thought a good one I did not pretend it was mine. We would have a C.O.s and staff conference and use our combined experience to assess it and if we thought it worth while I would report to the authority concerned what our opinion was.

I recall a typical example; some young officer in the mess said, 'The way this island should be supplied is by submarine, and since that huge white elephant, the Free French submarine *Surcouf*, is now in America she should be converted to store carrying. She could really make a difference.' The more I thought of this idea the more I liked it. On inquiry I found that *Surcouf* had been based at Halifax since February and was about to start a long refit in U.S.A. We know she had a surface displacement of over 2,800 tons. She carried a very heavy armament of over 20 torpedo tubes and twin 8 inch guns in a turret, a hangar for one aircraft and had a surface speed of 18 knots.

Our conclusions were that if this submarine was immediately converted to cargo carrying she could make two trips a month

144

from Alexandria, discharging 4,000 tons a month provided a large proportion of her main ballast tanks could carry fuel oils.

The supply of Malta was the main preoccupation of Admiral Ford, so I took our suggestion to him and he welcomed it as well worth forwarding to the Admiralty. Some months later he told me that the proposal had been turned down immediately by the head of the Free French Navy, Admiral Muselier, who had stated that *Surcouf* was his most important unit. So *Surcouf* refitted and eventually put to sea for trials, was rammed at periscope depth by a merchant ship off the U.S.A. and lost with all hands. I believe she could have handled one-quarter of Malta's basic needs.

To supplement our convoy sinkings we were now beginning to land train wrecking parties and to see the spectacular results of these demolitions. A glance at the map of Italy and Sicily shows how vulnerable the rail system is to sea attack.

During 1941 and 1942 a total of twelve train wrecking sorties were staged from Malta. In addition to this both trains and power lines were successfully demolished by gunfire on two occasions, when eventually *Unbroken* arrived with a 3 inch gun and proper sights in place of the useless twelve pounder fitted in the earlier U class. It was in June 1941 that our commandos began to get results and I quote a typical example.

Urge with a folbot party onboard was on patrol in the southern approaches to Messina and noted that five miles north of Taormina there was a tunnel a few hundred yards long cutting through Cape San Alassio. Just before midnight on 27 June Tomkinson landed his commando. Forty pounds of plastic explosive was placed about fifty paces inside the northern entrance, to be detonated by a pressure switch attached to a rail and operated by the weight of the train.

The party returned and had been on board a short while. The submarine lay surfaced charging batteries on a dark night. It was nearly two o'clock when an electric train, winding north from Catania to Messina, entered the tunnel. Then a vivid blue flash belched out of the north end of the tunnel followed by uncanny silence. Tomkinson remained patrolling the vicinity for the next three days and nights and the tunnel was alight with arc cutting and demolition lights.

This was butchery of the worst type. It was a direct assault on the civil population for the inconvenience of the military, which was exactly what we had suffered in London and in Malta; I had no qualms and arranged such activities at every opportunity until the Commander-in-Chief signalled to me a mild reprimand when a submarine was away train wrecking when a convoy passed, 'Convoys are your primary target.'

The reason why I wished to attack the railways to a substantial degree over a widely dispersed area was due to the Italian reaction. We noticed that after a few attacks the railways were constantly patrolled day and night by men either singly or in pairs at intervals of about two miles, and of course at tunnel entrances, over a distance of possibly 800 miles, since we struck occasionally between Palermo via Messina to Syracuse on the Sicilian coast, and from Salerno round the toe to Crotone on the mainland. Thus for a negligible effort we estimated that up to 2,500 Italian men were fully employed doing nothing.

On 30 June Bob Tanner came into the mess about supper time. 'You're promoted to captain, sir. Congratulations.'

A much more important local event had happened earlier in the month; our first porkers were despatched via the abattoir to the Naval Victualling Yard deep freeze, and from now on about twelve good porkers were put on hooks every month awaiting the day when we should really need them.

The three summer months of 1941 covered were a time of marked success and also of good cooperation with the R.A.F., whose Maryland aircraft gave us splendid reconnaissance service. The R.A.F.'s fighter position had improved from thirty in mid May to a hundred in July, due to four reinforcing flights, and this was to be the strongest fighter position for over a year.

Reconnaissance by experts, such as Warburton in the Marylands so well suited to the task, was adequate to cover the important enemy ports only, but this gave good results because if a convoy had sailed from one of the only three Italian departure points, Taranto, Messina or via Cape Bon, the routes used for Tripoli or Benghazi were infrequently changed and interception by Blenheim bombers by day and Swordfish by night was usually achieved.

The first Blenheims arrived in late April and were reinforced in June, July and August so that towards the end of that month there were for a short time 32 Blenheims; also 12 Swordfish, 7 Marylands and 15 Wellingtons.

The Blenheim technique was for a flight to set out at an altitude of about a hundred feet and, on sighting a convoy, go in at mast-head level releasing a stick of bombs with an eleven second delay fuse. This gallant point blank tactic was effective but led to crippling losses, usually from enemy light flak but sometimes, if the target had been an ammunition ship, it would blow up with such force that it would bring down the attacking Blenheim, despite the eleven seconds delay which should give the Blenheim over 500 yards clearance.

When I was told this I was frankly sceptical, until a year later an enemy ship had been stopped by R.A.F. action near Lampedusa Island and I sent *United* (Lieutenant T. E. Barlow) to sink it economically. Barlow fired one torpedo from just over 1,000 yards. The ship blew up with a mighty detonation. A solid girder, presumably part of the ship, struck *United* on the front of the conning tower and crushed in the casing around it, the sea bubbled with falling debris and some object struck the pressure hull with such force that a circular hole about four inches in diameter was made in it over the steering compartment. A wood plug was driven in and *United* returned to Malta unable to dive. I realised then the fate that overtook several of the Blenheims.

The Swordfish torpedo-carrying strike aircraft were manned and maintained by the Navy under Commander Howie and stationed at Halfar. They were under the operational command of the A.O.C. Malta and I know that Air Vice Marshal Lloyd held them in high regard. I bicycled over to see my old friend Howie and had an interesting talk with him. The Swordfish, nicknamed 'stringbags' due to their untidy and out-of-date appearance were biplanes, with pilot and observer and armed with one 18 inch torpedo. Their maximum speed was about 74 knots. They were used exclusively for night attack and were remarkably successful. I asked Howie why they were not shot out of the sky, since at 75 knots they appeared almost stationary. Howie replied, 'Enemy flak is always bursting far ahead of us. I don't think the Axis has an A.A. gunsight that can allow for speeds of under 100 knots.' There were other reasons for the Swordfish successes; the slow speed gave time for careful assessment of enemy course and speed and correct attack course, while the naval officers and ratings who flew them had specialised in this task.

The Wellington bomber's special niche in the air offensive picture was for night radar location and flare dropping, for which they were very suitable, but they were not suitable for launching a torpedo since they flew too fast for accurate attack, and this practice was a waste of valuable and scarce aerial torpedoes.

Before midnight on 25 July I was told to report to naval H.Q. where I was warned that something suspicious was occurring about six miles north east of Valetta and I must not allow any submarines to sail or to arrive until the mystery was resolved. Something had appeared on the radar screen which seemed to be a stationary ship.

At dawn gun fire woke me and I dashed up to Fort Manoel for a good view. Fast motorboats were approaching and zigzagging as they skimmed the smooth sea at about forty knots. The multiple Hotchkiss guns at Fort St Elmo guarding the entrance let them come within effective range and then mowed them down, and as each one sank it exploded.

The intention had been that these fast, one-man boats, driven by Isotta Frascini engines, were to dash into harbour through gaps made in the boom defences by midget submarines. The boatmen having passed through the boom were to point their boat at one of the six ships of the newly arrived convoy (operation 'Substance') and about fifty yards before collision the crewman was to jump over the stern. On contact the explosive bow fell off and sank and exploded at a set depth to blow the ship's side in below the waterline.

In the event one midget submarine was lost at the harbour entrance, while two attacked at wrong places, so the boom was not breached. This was of no importance since the St Elmo gunners sank all boats well out to sea, except one or two prematurely abandoned which were finally brought into harbour for inspection. On the horizon the Italian vessel *Diana* from whom they had been launched was retreating whilst two large E-boats, which I believed towed the explosive boats from *Diana* for the first few miles towards the harbour, were now attacked by Hurricanes and were gutted. Nothing but *Diana* got away.

The surface warning radar proved its value for without it the guns would not have been manned and ready.

During July Lieutenant Colonel Stone of the New Zealand Division who had fought against the German paratroopers in Crete visited Malta and gave a series of talks on his experience. He emphasised the supreme importance of every person carrying a rifle so that the greatest possible number of parachutists could be killed in the air. As a result rifles and ammunition from the Naval Armament Depot arrived in large quantities at Lazaretto. They were stored centrally but we did not begin rifle drill to repel boarders. The fact was that the base staff were very fully occupied keeping the flotilla fit to fight.

I held a theory then which was comforting and I am sure wholly wrong. I felt certain that Italian heavy warships would approach Malta and knock out the four 9.2 inch coastal batteries before the main assault, which I thought would be by both paratroops and surface assault simultaneously. Holding this theory with conviction I said to my staff that an attempt by the enemy to capture Malta seemed highly probable, but I was sure that we would have adequate notice so rifle training was only to apply to persons without previous experience and submarine work must not suffer.

In late July *Union* became overdue, and it is now known that she was sunk by the Italian torpedo boat *Circe*. In mid-August the submarines *P32* and *P33*, which I had sent to the northern and eastern approaches to Tripoli did not return, both were lost by mine and both were very recent arrivals on the station. The loss of three submarines in four weeks was a bitter set-back. It again raised the important question in my mind: what was the best way to introduce a newly arrived submarine to the dangers of these mid Mediterranean patrols? The patrol positions allocated to *P32* and *P33* were quiet numbers. I needed to know if these two channels through the minefield off Tripoli were still used, so stationed them well clear and sailed *Unique*, an experienced submarine, to guard the western approach to Tripoli, and she exchanged messages with *P32* by asdic on 18 August. It seems that both submarines (*P32* and *P33*) during the course of their patrols may have closed Tripoli somewhat for reconnaisance and that the minefields had been refreshed and extended.

On the morning of 20 August Lieutenant Hezlet, temporarily in command of *Unique*, carried out a brilliant attack on a convoy of four liners with heavy sea and air escort, which had already been reinforced from Tripoli by fast coastal motor boats. Hezlet sank the liner *Esperia* (11,400 tons) and put so many troops into the sea that he was able to retire without any serious depth charging. To add to this success *Urge* torpedoed, but did not sink, the liner *Duilio* (23,000 tons).

This submarine blitz against the Italian liners was carried decisively into the next month, and so it suitably 'christened' the formation of the 10th Submarine Flotilla, under my command, with my Captain's pennant to fly from the Lazaretto oil barge, which was named HMS *Talbot* without ceremony.

What a lot of nonsense this seemed to me. It made no difference whatsoever whether I was 'Commander Submarines Malta' 'Captain Submarines Malta', or 'Captain *S10* of Malta' flying his broad-pennant from an oil barge. I was still on paper 'operationally under the control of Captain *S1* Alexandria', who fortunately for both of us never once in two years interfered with my operational independence. There was a very good reason for this chain of command; it assured that *S1* 'devilled' all my paperwork instead of this chore falling to the Commander-in-Chief's staff.

I mention this apparently petty personal matter because I remember so vividly my reaction at the time. On 30 June when I was promoted to captain I was grateful but I felt it was detrimental, or could be, to the very important position I held in the wardroom of being an accepted member of the mess in my own right, and not the 'captain' who should only enter the wardroom when invited, but had to be tolerated because of the conditions of service.

The formation of my submarines into a flotilla, on paper, with the attendant rigmarole I thought unnecessary. It was evidently thought that we hoisted colours in the morning and hauled them down in the evening with due ceremony. In fact no white ensign flew from Lazaretto. We had not been deliberately bombed yet and were not advertising ourselves. Perhaps it was not understood that Ju87 dive bombers, after pulling out of their dives on the dockyards, would often come over Lazaretto at a height where the pilot's goggled helmet and hand gestures could be seen clearly, so the one thing we must not look like was a naval establishment, which was an added reason for having all men in uniform in rock shelters during raids.

At 1.30 pm on 17 September Bob Tanner brought me 'hot' news from an air recce of Taranto and an intelligence forecast. The sum total of this was precise and indicated that any submarines I could sail in the next ninety minutes could probably intercept a troop convoy of three liners who were then with steam up in Taranto.

This route had been used before with the troops arriving at Tripoli about 9 am and a landfall being made at Homs about 6 am. It seemed well worth working on such an informed guess. I sent for all the C.O.s in harbour to confer in my cabin immediately. Woodward, Wanklyn, Wraith, Hezlet and Tomkinson were present. I put forward my plan, which was that the five submarines should sail in two groups, three to form a line some sixty miles north east of Homs to attack in the dark about 4 am, two to make a landfall at Homs and attack by daylight at about 7 am. The night attackers to be *Upholder, Unbeaten* and *Upright* with Wanklyn in centre position as senior officer, who was to lead his force to his billet and then spread them accurately from there and maintain relative positions by asdic ranging. *Urge* and *Ursula* were to spread and attack five miles north east of Homs.

I was well aware that this was a sudden call and affected some submarines which had only just returned from patrol, so I added, 'After this operation you will all return to Malta, which means you will be away about forty hours. Everyone will need to sail an hour from now and if there is anyone who doesn't feel up to it please say now.'

Tomkinson replied, 'Quite frankly, sir, I don't care about these sudden schemes devised on a signal just received. I would ask you to count me out.'

'All right, Tommo, then *Urge* won't go and Arthur Hezlet can take long stop at Homs alone in his *Ursula*.'

I tell this to explain two things. Firstly I did not want any C.O. on this short and probably hectic operation who did not feel up to it, or was even critical of it. There was no time for long discussion and consideration of alternatives. I thought my plan safe and effective so it was to stand. I knew very well that Tomkinson and his *Urge* would be the first to volunteer if he were feeling rested and relaxed; obviously he was tired and on edge and had the guts to say so. It was just this relationship between myself as a member of the wardroom and a brother officer which was so invaluable to me in assessing the possible. Secondly, it will be noted that Lieutenant Hezlet, who sank the liner *Esperia* in *Unique* on 20 August, was a month later commanding *Ursula*. Hezlet was spare commanding officer and alternated from one submarine to another so as to give each C.O. one complete patrol off duty every six months, or in case of sickness to be available to assume command. The C.O.s needed to be studied and their idiosyncrasies respected.

The result of this sortie was that *Upholder*, from a range of about 3,000 yards, with gyro compass out of action and firing from the surface at night with the submarine yawing heavily, sank the *Neptunia* and *Oceania*, each of 19,500 tons, loaded troopships going south, drowning 5,000 troops. Shortly after dawn, and coming from the rays of the rising sun, *Ursula* heard the propeller beat of a fast vessel. It happened that of these three liners, *Vulcania* was four knots faster than the others, so a combination of the rising sun, a speed error and a long distance shot made *Ursula's* salvo miss astern.

At the site where the liners had been sunk four destroyers were moving around picking the soldiers out of the sea. Wanklyn set course for Malta submerged, he had two torpedoes remaining. Woodward (*Unbeaten*) closed the scene with all his torpedoes and left the destroyers to their rescue work. Wraith (*Upright*) watched these destroyers also, but as he happened to have torpedoes in his tubes whose depth setting could not be altered without withdrawing them (they were destroyer torpedoes) he could not reset his depth to hit them. So it was that four destroyers packed with troops got away. I thought about this quite a lot, I knew that to be merciful was something we were in no position to afford.

This raises an important point. On this occasion and again when the cruiser *Trento* was sunk by *P35* on 15 June 1942, there were Italian destroyers, important units of nearly 2,000 tons displacement, virtually defenceless, while picking up survivors within sight of two or three of my flotilla submarines with torpedoes ready to fire who, on both occasions, withdrew without attempting to attack them.

I thought this quite wrong, but I said nothing because I felt that my commanding officers had enough to contend with, without my urging them to do something which revolted them and would lower their opinion of me. Also it was unlikely that any order I gave them in this regard would be observed, since the commanding officer alone used the periscope during an attack and he could blandly deny that targets were offering. This would engender a lack of frankness between us which would be disastrous, because it would create two schools of thought in what was a united team.

To me it seemed that fully viable ships of war must be sunk under any conditions and the troops on board them who were shortly to confront our own army must be drowned, because casualties largely decided the war militarily, so this was our duty. About half my commanding officers were exerting all their skill and determination in the pursuit of their profession whilst accepting the transfer from peace as the natural consequence of political failure and the war as their opportunity, and since it was a foul business they had no intention of making it fouler by sinking ships rescuing helpless drowning men, even if those ships were destroyers, and those men armed combatants.

On return to harbour on 19 September John Wraith, commanding *Upright*, said to me, 'It was most unfortunate that I had only destroyer torpedoes on board, set to 24 feet since there was no time to withdraw them and set to ten feet. I would have had a good chance of sinking all four destroyers.' Similarly it was fortunate for the enemy that Tomkinson in *Urge* was not present.

I know what Admiral Cunningham's opinion would have been since at the close of the Tunisian campaign he made this signal to his fleet, 'Sink burn and destroy, let nothing pass.'

The immediate enemy reaction to our June sabotage forays against the railways encouraged us to plan something that would cut a main line for many months. This ambition was quite beyond our resources which any civil engineer could have told us had we consulted one.

I sent a proposal to Captain *S1* that my commando should make a major attack on the railway viaduct over the steep valley of the Torrente Furiano, where a lengthy rail bridge is supported on six masonry piers. This bridge, some thirty miles west of Messina on the Palermo line, had been studied through the periscope by a submarine who reported a quiet district with the bridge very close to the shore and the watercourse usually dry. The Commander-in-Chief approved and also sent *Triumph* for the job as we needed a large submarine. I was delighted to see W. J. Woods again, (now a commander) who was to undertake this task, which I cheerfully thought would isolate Palermo and make that considerable town and shipyard a liability rather than an asset.

The party for landing comprised Second Lieutenant Schofield, Royal Fusiliers, in command, and ten commando troops and a seaman petty officer from *Triumph* whose particular responsibility was securing the plastic explosive to the piers by rope in the positions required by Schofield.

The landing party, about eight folbots and stores, which included five hundredweight of explosive was a bulky liability to have on board for at least four nights each way if there were no delays, so the torpedo compartment was made into a military mess and store room, and to do this only two torpedoes were kept in the forward salvo.

Triumph sailed on 19 August and reconnoitred the area of attack on the 22nd but could not land that night due to a heavy swell. Next morning the Commander-in-Chief ordered *Triumph* to patrol the northern entrance to Messina as Italian main fleet units were known to be at sea.

Having established patrol on the enemy's front doorstep Woods found that not only was he limited to two torpedoes, and with the landing party using up the submarine's oxygen, but also the asdic motor was burnt out and his bifocal periscope fogged up. In effect the submarine was deaf, partly blind and cluttered up with military. On the night of the 25–26 August an enemy destroyer patrol put *Triumph* down in a hurry and next morning at 6 am distant depth charging heralded the approach of important units.

There was one battleship and two cruisers escorted by numerous destroyers, the visibility was poor. In the event Woods fired at the rear cruiser, which offered the best chance, and he hit her in the propellers with one torpedo. Following that the depth charge counterattack persisted until 7 pm but the enemy never gained contact nor were dangerously close. The 8 inch cruiser *Bolzano* reached Messina where she was many months in dockyard hands.

When able to do so *Triumph* returned to the Torrente Furioso viaduct but right in the position Woods wished to launch his party a fishing boat cruised back and forth. *Triumph* chased it, took the crew of three men on board and sank the fishing boat, but this delayed the landing a further twenty-four hours. On the next night the landing was made and demolitions went according to plan on a rather reduced scale. In loading the many folbots in a swell in the dark some were damaged and the landing party was reduced to eight.

Triumph moved to seaward charging and then returned submerged at dawn. Looking up at the bridge there were two trains, one on either end of the bridge with the engines looking at one another; and in the centre was one pier blown up and two spans collapsed. This was certainly excellent, but where were the four canoes with the eight canoeists? They were to be all together and two miles off shore for a rapid pick up before air patrols intervened. Woods searched in every direction with his one good periscope but saw nothing. He had to withdraw when the alarm was raised. Continuing the search at dawn the next day without result he returned sadly to Malta after an adventurous and highly successful patrol which had seriously damaged a heavy cruiser.

The viaduct was, I believe, repaired within two weeks, with all materials brought by rail and the outstanding engineering ability shown by the Italians in repair, salvage and practical engineering. This particular foray was hardly worth the effort and loss of men.

Schofield and his party were made prisoners that first morning, shortly after *Triumph* had withdrawn. The reason why Woods could not locate them through the periscope was due to an early morning fog lying on a calm sea to a depth of two or three feet. Schofield told me after the war that the canoes waiting out at sea for *Triumph* to surface beside them could see one another's heads sticking out of the mist, their bodies and the canoes being invisible at short range.

While *Triumph* was resting for a few days at Lazaretto I saw an old friend coming out of her fore hatch. Able Seaman Harrison had served in *Thames* with me nine years earlier, and during that commission Mrs Harrison had presented him with triplet sons. A.B. Harrison was now a three badge rating and his heavy frame propelled by a seaman's lethargic gait was surmounted by his usual self-assured cheerful expression. 'How nice to see you and how are Mrs Harrison and the three boys?—They must be fine lads now!'

'Well, sir, it was just bad luck. A bomb got the lot of them at night in that blitz on Devonport.'

Five months later Harrison was lost in *Triumph* in the Aegean. His type were the salt of the earth.

13

ENEMY air-raids in August and September fell to an average of one every twenty-four hours. A fair proportion were night raids which in my opinion were of exceptional entertainment value and good for morale. The casualties resulting from them were negligible. The air-raid sirens would blare and we would get the radar report over the telephone that 'four bandits' were approaching. No klaxon sounded for this. It was exciting to stand at night on our front gallery, with overhead protection from shrapnel, to watch what the Army's new radar-controlled searchlights and the R.A.F.'s Beaufighters would lay on for our entertainment. The drone of the enemy's engines, which was quite easily distinguished from the note of our own, would pervade the upper air at about 18,000 feet like a bad smell; one could only guess the general direction. Then the fingers of light would pierce the night, then more, until about twelve were searching. Then a shout from a messmate, 'That one behind Floriana is on to something!' then, 'Yes, by Jove and it's holding it!' At once two or three other searchlight beams would lock onto the enemy and all other searchlights go out on that instant. When that occurred one knew there was only one result. I am sure I never saw a failure.

Suddenly from behind the enemy a Beaufighter would open up with a burst of cannon fire for perhaps three seconds, tracer and hits would make an impressive display but no sound of this gun encounter would be heard by us, only the steady drone of the engines of this enemy and his three consorts. Then there would be explosions and fireworks on the ground as the enemy bombers now all under threat jettisoned their bombs which were ill aimed and the damage unimportant compared with day Stuka attacks. Then the Beaufighter, after a pause of ten seconds, would pump in another burst. 'There they go!' would be the shout, 'One, two, and there's three, parachutes open now, good God! that bomber is tough, who's flying her anyway?' Then another burst from the

Beaufighter and suddenly the whole aircraft was a mass of flame and came 'catherine-wheeling' to earth.

I don't think two bombers were ever snatched from the skies in one of these night raids, but one was almost routine. As it fell you could hear the cheer go up throughout Valetta, Floriana, Pieta, Hamrun, and around to Sliema behind us. A great solid yell of Maltese appreciation and defiance.

On the broad estimate of one-third night raids, one-third recces and one-third well-conducted powerful daylight thrusts we were getting about two serious raids a week, compared with two or three a day in the January to May blitz. The monthly raid score had fallen to thirty compared with over 100 during the blitz. At this time a convoy with 65,000 tons of supplies arrived in July and another with 85,000 tons followed in September.

These spectacular successes of the R.A.F. fighters with the new precision of the army's searchlights were self evident. The submarines advertised their successes by flying a 'Jolly Roger' when entering harbour if they had sunk an enemy ship. Each success was recorded by a white chevron for a supply ship or a red one for a warship stitched on to this large flag by the signalman, and if the Jolly Roger was flying a submarine was cheered into harbour by crowds on both sides of the entrance.

So in this pleasant respite of August and September life was jolly. Malta was world news and apparently Malta was winning, we were not alone now, and the attack on Russia had drained off the venom of the Luftwaffe. However, this recovery was based as anyone could see on the enemy's initiative and could be dissipated at his decision. The Defence Cabinet did not use the pause to strengthen fighter protection with Spitfires. It was clear that our obliteration remained an enemy option.

At Lazaretto the Maltese labour force continued energetically to put all our essential services under rock. Commander MacGregor installed a full size cinema projector under rock and we had made a chapel and cinema with excellent acoustics in a stone store-room. MacGregor kept in touch with the Gibraltar film distributor for the R.N. Cinema Service, which Lord Mountbatten had initiated before the war. Under the circumstances we felt very privileged and selfish to have a private viewing of the latest American films, but there was an absolute prohibition on our loaning films outside the R.N. In 1941 we saw Walt Disney's *Dumbo,* and Adolphe Menjou and Ginger Rogers in *Roxy Hart.* For exercise there was hockey on Manoel Island and sea bathing at Sliema.

Fresh water for all purposes at Lazaretto was never rationed. The huge caverns hewn in the limestone in the higher centre of the island by past generations allowed water-bearing fissures to collect and channel excellent water into adequate reservoirs. Hot baths for crews in from patrol were essential, and were assured by MacGregor acquiring a large domestic boiler. He fitted an electric fan on the front, acquired a few tons of sawdust from the dockyard joinery shop and then fixed a drip feed, supplying submarine main-engine, dirty lubricating oil on to the sawdust. This was lit with diesel and when the fire had raised the temperature the sump oil was turned on. So throughout the siege we had unlimited hot water for 600 people (except when the water mains were cut) without encroaching on our electricity ration.

For the sailors' interest the farming was diversified. Sailors could keep rabbits in hutches, which could be fed with Manoel Island weeds and bought lucerne. Chickens were impossible for lack of grain but one turkey stalked the yard.

Service establishments kept very much to themselves as there was no petrol for passenger transport, so social life tended to reach only walking distance from home. Crossing harbours by boat was unpopular since on a prolonged raid people could be cut off until the all clear. Lieutenant Collett, the captain of *Unique,* bought a well-groomed pony and dog-cart and became quite a feature of the Malta scene; a large man in naval uniform with a pitch black beard driving his gig at a spanking pace with a friend beside him. This alone shows that conditions were near normal through these summer months.

My particular friends were Wingrave Tench and his wife Greta who lived at St Julian's bay, three miles on a bicycle from Lazaretto. Gravy and Greta with their adorable nine-year-old daughter, Susan, kept open house for us submariners. Gravy was managing director of a large firm and had been appointed by the Governor to undertake the dual task of head of censorship and in charge of the distribution of food; the civil administration decided the ration, or how much of available foodstuffs could be issued daily. It was Gravy Tench's task to organise the soup kitchens and ration carts and that distribution was equitable and

F

effective without waste or black marketing. In this he was assisted by energetic and able Maltese civil servants who in their turn co-opted local authorities such as school teachers to assist. How ration distribution and food kitchens were organised in this over populated hungry island I really do not understand and I can find no written record of its secret. I shall refer again to this miracle which seemed to me to show loyalty, discipline and security in a most remarkable degree, for I never heard of misunderstandings leading to blows, or hunger and frayed tempers causing disturbances. This is to me the most remarkable feature of the whole siege. It was as if the Maltese people recognised this threat as part of a proud history, as if they said, 'We've met these conditions before and we've always won our sieges.'

The Tench house was a haven of normality and charm. It was also a meeting place for Major Francis Gerard, the mercurial and talented Information Officer, and occasionally Andrew Cohen the Deputy Civil Administrator, a brilliant substantial person with a permanently puzzled expression, whose droll histories of his daily problems contrasted with Gerard's flamboyant wit and gestures. In good times and in critical ones I knew that I was welcome at St Julian's Bay, and would come away refreshed.

That universally known slogan of the Windmill Theatre, Piccadilly, 'We never closed', was equally applicable under tougher conditions to our one and only *Times of Malta*, the daily paper edited by the indefatigable Mabel Strickland. She somehow managed to obtain newsprint and never failed to print the paper in the heart of Valetta. Under siege conditions a newspaper has added responsibilities, it is important to morale and its 'Letters to the editor' are a remarkable barometer of this vital human quality, but perhaps this was more apparent at Malta than elsewhere.

Rather more precise a barometer was set for human physical achievement. Commander MacGregor would watch with close attention the progress of his under-rock workshop, a beautiful arched-roofed vault, of 120 feet by 60 feet, by 20 feet high. The amount of rock removed weekly varied directly with the calories in the workmen's ration, which in 1942 fell to 900 a day from the 3,000 which is normal.

Radio receivers were privately owned by many people who could tune into any station within the orbit of their receiver, but there was also the local Malta broadcast which used the island's telephone system. The Information Office would relay by telephone to loudspeakers in village street centres the B.B.C. news followed by local news, which normally commented on enemy air activity. So no agency whatever outside Malta could listen in to an island broadcast.

In Lazaretto we were all fans of 'Lord Haw Haw' and the wardroom loudspeaker was always tuned in to receive 'Jairmany calling! Jairmany Calling!' which was considered good entertainment value. Lieutenant Poole, the First Lieutenant of *Urge*, was an inspired mimic and occasionally gave his version of these enemy broadcasts.

About one-third of my officers and men had served in Malta before, and in my case I had visited five times in twenty years. So many of us had our own particular friends, particularly amongst the Maltese trading community in Valetta. I could call in at Palace Square to talk with my friends, the brothers Marich, whose business comprised a small cigarette factory with their own blend of Turkish tobacco and a homely shop 'The Smoking Divan' where seats and ashtrays on either side invited the visitor to stop and talk, and try one of the cocktails for which their barman was renowned. In 1920 Marich's was practically a gunroom club, full of life and chatter but in 1941, virtually deserted and with cracked walls and their business ruined, I half expected some sign of sullen recrimination. Instead I always received a warm smiling welcome from both brothers who seemed not a day older than at our first meeting.

Down Strada Reale on the left as I walked towards the steps to naval H.Q. I would pass Carmella Cassar's lace shop and step in for a chat. The regally ageless Carmella was perhaps sixty at the time, a tall well-built woman whose youthful beauty was still reflected in her distinguished bearing and self assurance. Carmella was almost an institution, she knew all the Flag Officers of the Royal Navy and their wives back to 1900. Because she was Carmella Cassar who knew everyone she was a great source of information, not in petty scandal but in good solid opinion.

When Carmella heard about the submarines entering harbour flying the Jolly Roger after a successful patrol the idea appealed to her. The Maltese lace and other articles of exquisite needlework which was her stock in trade came from the convents, so Carmella had a series of Jolly Rogers made by the nuns in black silk about twelve inches by eight inches with the white skull and crossbones realistically embroidered on them. One of these was presented to each submarine commander, and of course this officer after his latest success would take his silk flag back to Carmella for the nuns to embroider the new chevron on to it. Thus it was that Carmella became an encyclopaedia of submarine operations and could speak with authority on the subject.

It was, I am sure, another powerful cause of high morale that the people were kept informed of our air and our sea successes, there was no need in this 'tight little island' for slogans such as 'Careless talk costs lives' or 'Walls have ears'. On the contrary, when naval surface ships had a success this was broadcast by the Information Office as a special announcement, with the comment that, 'The force will be entering harbour in two hours, so turn out and give it a cheer!' Thus military successes were Malta's successes and an achievement in which each individual could take credit.

Throughout 1941 the Union Club, a well-appointed fine building, comparable in service and amenities with a London West End club, was kept open. It was supported intermittently by serving officers who thought such an institution, which certainly needed support, was worth joining, but the backbone of its members were those service officers long retired, whose permanent home was now Malta, and who lived within cycling distance. These veterans were to be met, propping up the bar in uniform. They held *ad hoc* posts which were not sinecures, since casualties from illness or enemy action occurred and replacements took a long time to arrive. It was during this quiet period in the summer of 1941 that I called in at about noon on my return journey to Lazaretto. A venerable Paymaster Captain in full regalia was 'taking the waters' alone, so I joined him and as we were chatting an air raid warning sounded.

In support of my own regulations I excused myself and told him that I must keep to my own rule, which was to be in Lazaretto and under rock during raids. I had walked as far as Palace Square when it became obvious that this was not a bomber raid but a dog fight occurring between fighters, and I moved out into the square to have a look. At about this time one of our fighters attacked an ME 109 and slew the German pilot. The aircraft, with its engine at full throttle, plummeted from 20,000 feet in an uncontrolled roar. It descended, apparently vertically, straight into the town and I am surprised that under the circumstances the Messerschmitt was not the first plane to break the sound barrier: it must have been close to it. This Me 109 went through the roof and four floors of the house next to the Union Club bar, and ended as pulverised metal in the basement. I never met my friend again to offer him the other half; he quit the Union Club for years.

The sailors with their syndicate flats seemed well satisfied to spend their leaves with a minimum of interference, but when they were duty watch at Lazaretto their quarters were comfortable and spacious. In the wardroom, although each submarine had an officer's flat in Sliema, the mess was preferred when the bombing was light; my officers really enjoyed one another's company. I never noticed any jealousy or unfriendly rivalry between submarine C.O.s or their subordinates. When Wanklyn drew into the ascendant as the most successful submarine captain nobody grudged him this hard-earned honour and this was in sharp contrast with the rivalries which I know existed in flotillas during the First World War.

At Lazaretto there were many vital questions to be dealt with constantly, but they were not allowed to obsess people or monopolise conversation. Sam MacGregor had a great antidote for the worrier over material defects which were being repaired. He treated the whole flotilla as a sort of extension course from 'Pamela's First Term at St Cuthberts'. I often heard in the mess this type of conversation in reply to an anxious enquiry from an officer about repairs to machinery.

'The job will be finished today and will be stronger than before.'

'But, Sam, are you sure?'

'Of course I am, there's no shoddy work at St Cuthberts, and if you doubt me you'll have to go and blub to the matron!'

That always fixed things and in the office of matron I never heard further doubts.

It is generally accepted that the commanding officers of submarines, by the nature of their work and the fact that only one man at a time can look through a periscope, have exceptional responsibilities and also exceptional opportunities. Admiral Horton's instructions that C.O.s were to be treated 'as Derby winners' because of their unique value to the country was the assessment of a tough realist. So it was that the characters of these C.O.s set the tone of the flotilla. It would be tedious if I wrote thumbnail sketches on the twenty-five or more C.O.s who operated from Malta during the siege, but I will remark upon five who served in the first year. Four were killed in action and one survived but they were all successful in command. Each one possessed that ability to make instant decisions which reaps reward in submarine warfare. It is lacking in some officers who, though they know their job, only go for certainties and therefore miss the opportunities seized so quickly by the best.

The officers I have chosen were all in their first commands in 1941 and so aged between twenty-eight and thirty; by the end of 1942 my youngest C.O. was Lieutenant Roxburgh, who got his command aged 23. Such were the dictates of our heavy casualties.

Richard D. Cayley, always appeared light-hearted, and almost flippant, when in harbour. He carried a mouth organ in his uniform coat pocket and he could play extremely well. He was a great asset to the mess and behind his cheerful appearance was a shrewd, tough, and brave man who volunteered for special duties and undertook them with a sound balance of caution and determination. At sea he was the only one of my C.O.s who slept at night on the conning tower, where he slung a short and broad hammock under the chart table and curled up in it. During daylight when the submarine was submerged he would relax in the wardroom either reading, or doing gros point needlework. His outlook was entirely unselfish and for the flotilla.

It was Dick Cayley whom I had called on to patrol for thirty out of thirty-eight consecutive days in March and April 1941, when he seemed to be the only officer with the experience and ability to hit the enemy. It was he who immediately volunteered to blaze the route through the Sicilian channel minefields which we were to use continuously and successfully for the rest of the war. In Cayley, experience and skill were nicely balanced with gaiety and resolution.

M. David Wanklyn stood about six feet one inch, with handsome aquiline features. As he had been my First Lieutenant in *Porpoise* immediately before the war, I felt very close to him in his problems and his war. He was an enthusiastic games player for the sake of exercise, but he had not got an exceptional eye for ball games, certainly no better than average. The pursuit at which I

164

thought he excelled was dry fly-fishing; he was in fact a precise person with a good brain. Wanklyn made such a poor start in February, March and early April 1941, by which time he had expended about twenty torpedoes without result, that I feared he might never make the grade. I have heard it said in submarine circles that to be a good submarine attacker it is necessary to be a good mathematician. My experience does not corroborate this, although a quick calculating brain must be of value. Wanklyn was a case in point, although he was an excellent mathematician he could not hit his targets for three months. Then suddenly he got the knack, which was not all cool calculation. His two outstanding attacks were when he sank the liners *Neptunia* and *Oceania*, entirely by eye, with his instruments broken down, and secondly when he sank the U-boat *Almirante St Bon* at night with only one torpedo at 1,200 yards range by judgement born of experience. He was not a better attacker than many others in normal circumstances but two things happened. Wherever Wanklyn was sent the enemy appeared, and noteworthy targets too, this gave him much practice and increasing confidence, which made him turn fleeting opportunities into complete success. His modesty made him loved and respected by all.

The Board of Admiralty published an appreciation of his, and of *Upholder*'s, services, a very singular honour, which reads

It is seldom proper for Their Lordships to draw distinctions between different services rendered in the course of naval duty, but they take this opportunity of singling out those of HMS *Upholder*, under the command of Lieutenant-Commander Wanklyn, for special mention. She was long employed against enemy communications in the Central Mediterranean, and she became noted for the uniformly high quality of her services in that arduous and dangerous duty. Such was the standard of skill and daring that the ship and her officers and men became an inspiration not only to their own flotilla but to the fleet of which it was a part, and Malta, where for so long HMS *Upholder* was based. The ship and her company are gone, but the example and the inspiration remain.

E. P. Tomkinson, about six feet two inches tall, and powerfully built, had been for two years the R.N. golf champion. At this game he was in a class by himself so far as the Navy was concerned, and the qualities of concentration, a strong will and tenacity demanded by it were plain in his character. With an impressive black beard he looked formidable when serious, but he was a gay personality with a gentle nature who hated the war and despised its 'rewards'. When his great friend and companion, Wanklyn, was awarded the Victoria Cross at the end of 1941, Tomkinson, whose skill was comparable and whose successes were not much less, said to me, 'I'm glad Wanks has got the V.C. He's earned it, it suits him and it makes him so happy; but, sir, if you want to know what medal would make me most happy, it's one they haven't struck yet. It's the end of war medal.' He meant that with all his heart.

Since he was in this war he was firmly of the opinion that our duty was to kill the largest possible number of the enemy in the shortest possible time, because that was what would ultimately settle the matter and allow us all to return to normal lives and to home, which to him meant everything. So, although he hated war he had a particular loathing for the regimes that we blamed for it and regarded the enemy with contempt.

Like Wanklyn, his ability, presence and intelligence made him a born leader, but unlike Wanklyn (who had served with me before) Tomkinson did not accept all my ideas as either good or even reasonable ones. When some deep-rooted conviction on his part was in danger of being disregarded by me, he would come and see me and state his case from which he knew he could not move. This quality of his was of value to me, partly because I knew his mature criticism was always checking over my problems, and that his loyalty was complete.

Lieutenant John S. Wraith appeared, on first acquaintance, to be an average, rather shy, officer, who seemed self-deprecating and possibly lacking in self-confidence. This was the veneer to a very modest man with a great sense of humour who in action was entirely self confident. I well remember how in the early hours of 13 December 1941, in command of *Upright*, Wraith carried out a night attack on an escorted convoy in the Gulf of Taranto. He sank two new sister ships, only a few months from the builder's yard, on their first laden voyage, both of 6,335 tons. His typical explanation was, 'They simply committed suicide, sir. Just ran into my torpedoes!'

After taking *Upright* back to Britain in March 1942 Wraith was sent on a lecture tour of British factories to boost morale. I always wish I had heard one of them, I fear he would have painted an odd picture to the factory worker of the ease with which he just said, 'Fire' and the enemy did the rest in self destruction. Johnnie Wraith was lost in the Aegean in *Trooper* in October 1943.

Lieutenant Edward A. Woodward was a young officer of exceptional physical stamina. He was probably the best middle distance swimmer in the Navy. He had a particularly good eye for periscope attack while, at the same time, his theory and mathematical ability put him in the top flight of those who relied chiefly on instruments when time allowed such lethargic assessment. In fact when he returned to Britain in May 1942 he was posted ashore to design and supervise the building of a complicated new submarine attack teacher embodying the many new hazards this war had introduced.

At Malta in 1941–42 Teddy Woodward found that it suited him best to play the game of war in reverse. The pace he set himself during rest periods in Malta would have put most men in hospital. He would arrive at Lazaretto from the rigours of holiday in Malta's 'watering resorts', which seemed never closed to Woodward, looking pale and in need of complete rest. He would climb to the conning tower and say, 'Let go everything. Slow ahead port,' and would escape from the dangers of a social 'sea lion' amongst the mermaids of Malta's coastline into the refuge of wartime submarine patrol.

Once clear of harbour his grand First Lieutenant (A.D. Piper, R.N.R.) would take over and direct *Unbeaten* to her patrol position. By the time the submarine arrived Teddy was not thinking about the dangers ahead, but fresh as a daisy he could reflect with satisfaction at the dangers so recently surmounted while on leave, and apply his fully revived talent to sinking the enemy.

Woodward sank the German *U374* and the Italian submarine *Guglielmotti*, and about four supply ships and four schooners were either sunk or torpedoed. While this is a highly creditable score Woodward did not have his share of good fortune regarding enemy major war-vessels and liners. It seemed that I usually had him stationed in the wrong billet in a patrol line.

On return to port, usually with the Jolly Roger flying, Woodward, bursting with health, would confide to me an address where he could be found on leave and then set out bravely to meet the dangers and demands of yet another holiday.

F*

Woodward alone survived the war.

Arriving at Malta with the September 1941 convoy from Britain was Bill King, who had commanded *Snapper* in the Harwich days, now in command of *Trusty*. He was on his way to Alexandria and thence to Singapore and grim adventure. In company with *Trusty* was O.R.P. *Sokol* (Polish submarine *Falcon*) commanded by Commander Boris Karnicki, who had come to join the 10th Flotilla. O.R.P. *Sokol* was British built and originally HMS *Urchin*, so belonged to the small U class which made up the Flotilla.

Commander Karnicki and his fine ship's company were an important addition to our flotilla for reasons beyond their fighting value. They brought comradehip, variety and an irrepressible sense of humour to our isolation.

On meeting Boris Karnicki I felt I should make this handsome, deep-voiced Polish officer feel at home in his new surroundings. I said to him, 'We are very isolated here and I expect you and your men will find Malta under these conditions rather strange. Please come and see me at any time and with any problem that may crop up.' This was I thought polite and friendly of me but I never heard of a situation that Boris could not cope with and on this very first meeting I was to receive my first surprise.

Boris replied, 'Thank you, captain, I shall remember that. I must report, sir, that *Sokol* is here for your full operational use. The situation is no longer in doubt because, when we had passed Gibraltar and were submerged one morning and all was quiet, I summoned my entire ship's company to the control room and I said very clearly so that all could hear, "I, Boris Karnicki commanding O.R.P. *Sokol* declare war on you, Benito Mussolini!" So now everything is quite all right, that is, sir, so far as I am concerned.'

I was not sure whether Boris was being amusing or not and said, 'I am sure your government will take over details like the declaration of war.' But Boris replied, 'I do not think so, sir, they have not done so yet. Italy and Poland have always before been friends, since Poland is strongly Roman Catholic. So I believe this rudeness will be avoided.'

I liked Boris's personal declaration of hostilities aimed at Mussolini and avoiding the Italian nation. I was to learn that he was not being amusing but just being 'Boris'.

168

Boris and his four officers took a flat on the Sliema front, which was the top one in a four-storey building. They at once acquired an upright piano which was much used since all played a bit, and in particular 'The Polish Grand March', so I was assured. His sailors also rented flats and fitted in with Lazaretto life quite splendidly. There was an extra officer and a few ratings who were available to replace any cases of sickness, sub-lieutenant Tailor R.N.V.R. served on board for liaison or ciphering duties, although *Sokol*'s officers were all competent English speakers.

Boris was a renowned raconteur, and it was on these occasions that his complete grasp of English was apparent. Stories of his early life fell into two main categories the 'mainly military' and the 'somewhat blue'. The first always concerned 'My father' and the second 'My oncle'. I only remember two brief examples of these remarkable histories which were eagerly awaited and solemnly delivered in the wardroom.

'It was about 1918 that my father was in command of about two thousand sabres fighting the Bolsheviki and suddenly my father was confronted by twenty thousand sabres under Marshal Budenny. Now my father was a very great military leader and skilled tactician, so what do you think my father did?' The whole mess was tense with expectation. 'What did your father do, Boris?' 'What the hell of a situation!'

'My father turned his two thousand sabres right about, and rode like hell.'

Secondly, 'When my oncle was keeping his brothel in Harbin' – interruptions – 'You mean harem, Boris, your uncle would not keep a brothel.'

'Ah, well, it does not matter to this story, but I think it was a brothel all the same.'

O.R.P. *Sokol* went on patrol in the Gulf of Sfax which I had selected as a quiet spot for a first venture. Nothing was seen but, in one considerable area, the submarine could not be properly controlled submerged due to a dense growth of sea weed. Late in October *Sokol* patrolled off Ischia and torpedoed the escorted passenger ship *Citta di Palermo* and was heavily counter-attacked. Other torpedo attacks were made and when returning to Malta only one torpedo was on board. This was fired at a 2,500 ton ship north of Palermo at night but the torpedo missed. *Sokol* closed on the surface with the 12-pounder gun manned, and fired at the ship's waterline from point-blank range, eventually sinking the ship just as all ammunition was expended. These 12-pounders were almost useless.

After breakfast on 3 November Government House telephoned me to say that General Sikorski, Prime Minister of Poland, with a staff of about three had flown into Malta after dawn and wished to visit *Sokol*. I had just received *Sokol*'s arrival signal for noon and suggested that General Sikorski should be at Lazaretto at 11.30 am to see the arrival of his submarine, which I explained had met with success.

General Sikorski arrived and watched *Sokol* enter harbour, flying a Jolly Roger with two chevrons sewn on to it. He had previously questioned me about the patrol, and also on how *Sokol* suited the flotilla, and he was delighted to be on the Lazaretto gallery as his submarine came alongside after a marked success. It so happened that Sikorski was an old friend of the Karnicki family, about whom we submariners had heard so many improbable reminiscences, and Boris was thrilled to meet his Prime Minister, who spent much of that day with us and met all the crew members. Next day I gave the General the patrol report and expressed my genuine pride at *Sokol*'s ability and performance, and before he left in a small ceremony attended only by the Poles General Sikorski took the *Virtuti Militari* medal off his own chest and pinned it on to Boris. On 5 November Sikorski flew to Alexandria *en route* for Moscow.

14

As we entered the last quarter of 1941 the position in the Mediterranean was becoming highly critical for the Axis; the cause of this reversal of fortune was quite clearly due to the anti-shipping offensive staged by the R.A.F. and the submarines based on Malta. These facts and figures can be studied in detail in the official histories, so a round figure for June to September 1941 inclusive will suffice. Within the whole Mediterranean the Axis supply ship losses were 101 ships of 270,000 tons.

Indeed, the shipping casualties inflicted on the Axis up to the end of August, had caused the German staff in the Mediterranean to report on 9 September:

> Now, as formerly, the most dangerous British weapon in the Mediterranean is the submarine, especially those operating from Malta. In the period covered (11 July to 31 August) there were 36 submarine attacks in the Mediterranean of which 19 were successful.

> In spite of improved harbour defences, submarines lurking in or just outside the harbours have sunk or damaged eight ships.

> A very severe supply crisis must occur relatively soon. This is because Italian freight space which is sunk cannot be adequately replaced and also because air transport can never be a complete substitute for sea transport.

In reply Admiral Raeder wrote on 14 September:

> The naval staff agrees entirely with the evaluation of the situation. . . .

> The situation as described is untenable. Italian naval and air forces are incapable of providing adequate cover for the convoys. . . . The Naval Staff considers radical changes and immediate measures to remedy the situation imperative, otherwise not only our offensive but the entire Italo-German position in North Africa will be lost.

These pessimistic but realistic reports were passed to Hitler in full at the Fuehrer Naval Conference at Wolfsschanze on 17 September. Hitler's reaction was to order six U-boats to the Mediterranean in October and a further ten in November. This decision is strongly criticised by Admiral Doenitz as being a dissipation of effort from the vital U-boat area, the Atlantic. This may be so, but the impact of the German U-boat in the length of the Mediterranean cannot be denied; before Christmas the aircraft carrier *Ark Royal*, the battleship *Barham* and the cruiser *Galatea* were all sunk from this cause and more sinkings were inexorably to follow.

In mid-November Hitler approved the transfer to the central Mediterranean of German technicians with asdic and other anti-submarine devices. The sea war was being intensified against us, and the loss of *Ark Royal* on 14 November was, in many ways, a fatal blow because it precluded a large reinforcement of aircraft being flown to Malta from British carriers, since only the small *Eagle* and *Argus* were then operational and in home waters.

On 5 December Hitler ordered the return of a Fliegerkorps from the Russian front to Sicily. The pressure was on. Two days later the Japanese struck at Pearl Harbour, which had one effect on Malta. It meant that an Allied aircraft carrier could now do for us what we had so long not done for ourselves – fly Spitfires to Malta.

It was on 21 October that Force K arrived at Malta from home waters, consisting of the two six inch cruisers *Aurora* and *Penelope*, and the two destroyers *Lance* and *Lively*. On 8 November, acting on an air reconnaissance report, the force sailed on an ENE course to intercept a convoy of seven merchant ships escorted by six destroyers and a distant escort of two heavy cruisers with four destroyers.

Force K sank the entire convoy and one destroyer and returned to Malta unscathed.

Following this annihilation of Axis supplies, Force K repeated the performance on 24 November, sinking two escorted petrol carriers to the north of Benghazi. The result of having fast gunships based at Malta was the reason why in November only 8,400 tons of Axis supplies reached Africa. It was their most disastrous month.

On 1 December, to open the new month's account, Force K made a high speed sortie and sank all there was on the sea – a tanker with troops on board, a supply ship and the destroyer escort.

Supplies in general but fuel in particular had to be got through somehow, so the Italians decided to take petrol through as deck cargo in cruisers. Two six inch cruisers of 5,000 tons were taking petrol from Palermo to Tripoli on the night of 12–13 December. These cruisers turned north about midnight to avoid aircraft from Malta who were dropping flares. Commander Stokes, leading a division of four destroyers from Gibraltar to Malta, hugged the coast off the cliffs of Cape Bon and at reduced speed kept out of sight of the cruisers whose silhouettes were clearly visible to the destroyers. As the forces were drawing abeam all destroyers fired torpedoes, later opening fire with guns. Both cruisers were sunk immediately at about 2.30 am.

Next morning, about 10 am, having heard nothing of this victory I was walking to naval H.Q. via Strada Reale. I called in at the Office of the *Times of Malta* and was talking to Mabel Strickland when her telephone went and she said to me, putting down the phone, 'We had better get up on the Baracca and give them a cheer, they are just entering harbour.'

In this way I heard for the first time of this further victory – a remarkable achievement which underlined again and again the true value of fast, radar-fitted gunships with a few torpedoes for 'big game hunting', in order to isolate completely the Axis forces in North Africa. Radar was our secret weapon against which the Italian Navy was powerless, the priceless weapon which assured complete night fighting domination.

As Commander-in-Chief Mediterranean in the early 1930s, Admiral Sir W. W. Fisher had given his fleet a new confidence in night fighting which permeated the Royal Navy, but it was the invention and adaptation of radar, which was by this time effective, combined with flashless cordite, that made it possible to accept any odds with confidence in a night surface mêlée. There was another feature to this new technique of night fighting, the speed of the action as well as its devastation. During 1941 in the Mediterranean, British surface forces fought four night actions.

From these brief encounters, chiefly by light forces, the enemy lost three heavy and two light cruisers, two destroyers and twelve supply ships for the loss of one destroyer. The only enemy ships to escape were some of the escorting destroyers.

From June 1941 until November 1942 submarines were in constant use as store and personnel carriers to Malta. From Alexandria the large minelayer *Cachalot* and some of the O, P and R class from the pre-war Far East Flotilla were used. From Gibraltar new submarines on passage to join the 1st and 10th Flotillas brought personnel and mail. The *Olympus* was used continuously for store carrying from Gibraltar and from February 1942, the large and fast *Clyde*.

During March 1942 *Clyde* was converted in Britain for bulk dry store carrying, one of her three battery sections being removed, which allowed an additional internal cargo weight of 120 tons. This enabled vital supplies of ammunition for Malta's A/A batteries to be landed during the crisis of April 1942.

Unless (as in *Clyde*) special arrangements had been made for store carrying, the additional dry load carried internally in a 1,500 ton submarine was only about twelve to fifteen tons. The 'wet', external cargo in tanks was very much larger and could well be over 100 tons.

The freighting of dehydrated vegetables was not a success. For example with *Cachalot*'s second store trip, arriving Malta in mid-July 1941, Lieutenant Commander Newton brought five tons of dehydrated cabbage compressed into bricks about 2 × 1 × 1 feet, wrapped in canvas. These were stowed from the forward bulkhead of the torpedo stowage compartment right through the living quarters and over the batteries to the engine-room bulkhead, covering the entire internal deck.

The 900 miles from Alexandria took about six days and the temperature on board was high, rising during each daylight dive until the submarine surfaced after dark and the diesel engines drew in the fresh night air.

Half-way through the second day's dive the crew noticed midges appearing in very large numbers. It was found that the Nile Delta cabbages were hatching out. By the evening a fog of midges darkened the submarine's lights. After coming to the surface and going ahead they were sucked through the main engines and the air cleared. The intensity of the hatch increased each day as the cabbage bricks warmed up. However, on arrival at

Malta this cargo went into refrigeration and quietened down again. I believe that it maintained its calorific value for use in the communal soup kitchens.

It was on the return journey to Alexandria that *Cachalot*, with about twenty-five passengers on board was told to be on the lookout for an escorted enemy tanker on passage from Taranto to Benghazi. A vessel was sighted at night in poor visibility and was followed for a while. From this stern view with the surface ship making some smoke it was thought to be the tanker and Newton decided to attack it with his 4 inch gun. The vessel was the Italian torpedo boat *Papa* and as a result *Cachalot* was sunk. The Italian captain withheld fire at point-blank range allowing *Cachalot*'s entire company and passengers (some ninety in all) to abandon ship and be taken prisoner, and *Cachalot* sank with only one casualty. This humane and chivalrous act was so out of keeping with the ruthless trend of the war that it deserves to be recorded with gratitude.

From early June until the end of 1941 sixteen submarine store trips were run to Malta giving an average of one arrival every twelve days.

In mid-November 1941 an incident on one of these store trips showed the eccentric behaviour of a competent individual under stress; or perhaps it only showed how ridiculous and obstinate a fanatical trade unionist can be. It caused me later to disregard regulations.

On 13 November 1941 *Regent*, on passage to refit in Britain, arrived at Malta with a full load of stores. I met the commanding officer, Lieutenant Knox, at the discharge berth and found him to be a worried man; an event which he could not possibly overlook had upset his ship's company and the general regard for discipline on board.

The previous month *Regent* had spent five days off Benghazi. This patrol position had been in uncomfortably shallow water and where enemy naval activity had persisted; in fact Knox had watched five minelayers for five days and plotted what he thought was a new minefield being laid. Throughout this prolonged reconnaissance in the presence of the enemy he had more than once got into difficulties by striking the sea bed and upsetting the submarine's submerged control. He had been much assisted by the cool efficiency of the 'Outside E.R.A.' Indeed, so impressed was Knox that on return to Alexandria he had put this man's name forward for recognition.

The engine-room artificer who is called the 'Outside E.R.A.' in a submarine is the man responsible for the maintenance and working efficiency of all machinery outside the engine-room. That is to say the high pressure air system and the pumping system – in short, the diving mechanism. The man in question was a technician from a factory in the midlands who had joined up for the war and had been given the temporary rate of E.R.A.- 2nd class, for which his age, experience and trade qualifications entitled him. He was a man of average height with flaming red hair, beard and whiskers, aged about thirty.

On this November store trip to Malta, although cluttered up with stores and passengers, Knox had been ordered to maintain patrol for twenty-four hours off Benghazi. *Regent* arrived in her patrol position at 0800 one morning and had a thoroughly un-comfortable day with constant enemy A/S patrols and no targets. Since the submarine was ten years old and on its way to refit, and was laden with internal stores, and had about 100 tons of externally stowed petrol, he knew that even a distant depth-charge might cause a slight leak and so expose his position. In fact Knox dis-approved of his orders.

Before surfacing Knox had withdrawn some distance but enemy A/S vessels were still sweeping inshore from him. Whilst charging batteries an engine broke down, so two E.R.A.s were needed to make good repairs under the supervision of the engineer officer. The Outside E.R.A. had the middle watch on the diving panel. At 0400 the Chief Stoker arrived in the control room and said that due to engine repair work he had been told to take the morning watch on the diving panel. The Outside E.R.A. refused to turn over his duties and demanded to see the Engineer Officer to whom he stated that he would under no circumstances turn over the diving mechanism and his watch responsibilities to a man who had never served an apprenticeship and had no trade certificate. The Engineer Officer countered, 'I order you to do so. The competence of the Chief Stoker is my responsibility and he is far more experienced than you are.' The man still refused to turn over his duties, and demanded an immediate relief from his watch by a man of equivalent trade qualification 'in accordance with trades union practice'.

The captain was called from the bridge and having listened to the case gave his order for the duties to be assumed by the Chief Stoker, which was done. The Outside E.R.A. then refused to turn over his duties verbally by telling the Chief Stoker the state of the machinery, the air bottle groups available and the 'readiness to dive' and trim situation. He re-stated that he would not obey his captain's order which was not in accordance with factory floor practice.

Knox gave me his report. I took it to Admiral Ford who ordered a court martial.

Fortunately November was a fairly quiet month, only some seventy-five air raids occurred, and so the delay to *Regent* did not cause her loss; the niceties of British justice were observed without prejudice to Britain's survival.

Captain Angus Nichol of the *Penelope* was President of the Court. Lieutenant Knox, the Engineer Officer and the Chief Stoker were witnesses for the prosecution. There were no witnesses for the defence.

It fell to me to prosecute and I appointed Lieutenant J. D. Martin, the spare submarine commanding officer to be 'Prisoner's Friend' or, in civil parlance, 'Counsel for the Defence'. The Court assembled in the ancient dungeon of Fort St Angelo, which had been converted into an air raid shelter. As the case opened the sirens wailed, heralding an air raid.

Everything was as perfectly staged as for a court martial in the after cabin of HMS *Victory* at Portsmouth; the Deputy Judge Advocate to supervise procedure and all the pomp and all the fairness of a naval court martial conducted by naval officers, without learned counsel in wig lending a hand with all their judicial training.

I called my witnesses who stated what had occurred and they were not cross-examined by the Prisoner's Friend, except that Knox was called upon to give his opinion of the accused's character and competence. Knox very rightly told the Court of his earlier experience which had resulted in his recommendation for the accused to receive an award.

In summing up the case for the prosecution I said that the accused had shown himself as professionally competent and hitherto a responsible person. However, he had volunteered for naval and for submarine service in war and he therefore accepted

177

the conditions of that service. Whether he did or did not, he was subject to the Naval Discipline Act and very well knew that – he was also reminded of it by his captain at the time. To imagine that his petty pride and prejudice fostered on a factory floor should not be subordinate to service discipline and mutual safety was ridiculous. In any other Navy but ours the accused would be before the court on a capital charge, for hazarding his ship in time of war and in the presence of the enemy, but despite the enormity of his offence the prosecution would be satisfied if the accused was disrated to E.R.A.–5th class, dismissed from his ship and removed from service in submarines forthwith.

I sat down quite pleased with my eloquence and the magnanimity of my demands.

Young Lieutenant Martin stood up and said that the Court had heard what the captain of the *Regent* really thought of the accused. His name was quite possibly at that very minute being considered by the Honours and Awards Committee in the Admiralty for a decoration, on the recommendation of his captain. What the court did not know and were never likely to know was the personal relationship between the accused and the Chief Stoker. Therein lay the nub of the whole question and brought it into its true perspective – into the realm of piffling nonsense. As for the prosecution (I feared for a moment that Joe Martin was going to call me 'my learned colleague'), he would like to ask the prosecution what exactly he meant by 'in the presence of the enemy'. 'Here and now', he continued, you are all sitting down in very considerable comfort listening to an argument about nothing at all, whilst the enemy are as usual performing right above us. In the set of circumstances that we are considering half the crew of the *Regent* were asleep in their bunks and the enemy was miles away on the horizon on a dark night. So the prosecution's argument is not only unrealistic but it is prejudiced, unfair and a gross overstatement. I ask the Court to acquit the accused of this serious attack on his excellent character.'

By the time Joe had finished I felt as if I was the accused. However, Angus Nichol did not keep us waiting long and gave the Court's judgement. 'The Court considers all charges against the accused proven. The Court adjudges that the accused be reprimanded.'

Back in Lazaretto I said to the Counsel for the Defence. 'After your brutal attack on me this morning I demand a gin.' Which I got and a good laugh too.

The next day my friend Commander George Naish, the ordnance officer in the dockyard, visited me and asked if *Regent* might take his son, aged eleven, back to Britain, since the lad was losing his schooling and he added that Knox had no objection. I did not care for this proposal and said that I thought there was one chance in six of *Regent* being lost on passage. Naish said he realised that. The boy embarked.

At night, south of the island of Marettimo, *Regent* encountered a southbound supply ship and chased and sank it by gunfire. I am sure that this lad must be the youngest man to have been in action on board a submarine in the Second World War.

It was on 18 December that Malta's surface forces suffered a deadly reverse. The Commander-in-Chief, noting Force K's repeated successes, decided to double its strength and put an admiral in command, so the cruisers *Ajax* and *Neptune* with Rear-Admiral Rawlings on board arrived on 29 November, the whole force to be under the operational control of the Vice Admiral Malta. Shortly after arrival *Ajax* left Malta for Britain so *Neptune* commanded by Captain Rory O'Conor was flying the flag of Admiral Rawlings. As O'Conor was senior to Captain Agnew in *Aurora* this meant that whether the Admiral was on board or not, the flagship remained senior officer and Agnew who had just conducted three convoy sinkings in as many weeks was no longer in charge, despite his current experience. As things turned out I think this was unfortunate, however at the time it was just a routine matter that a reinforcement had changed the command structure. It was a fact that all three cruiser captains were particularly good friends and would form an understanding team.

Neptune with two destroyers went to sea on the seventeenth and met Force K escorting to Malta the fast supply ship *Breconshire*. The combined force entered harbour during the next forenoon and Admiral Rawlings arranged to play golf with his secretary at the Marsa club after lunch.

I happened to make one of my regular calls at the operations room of Naval H.Q. about 3 pm on the eighteenth. When I arrived, Admiral Ford, his Staff Officer (Operations) and Captain O'Conor had their heads down over a chart and almost immediately O'Conor said, 'Right, I'll be off,' and with his red hair, flashing blue eyes and cheerful smile he dashed from the room and down the 200 steps to his boat.

As soon as Admiral Ford had left I said to Martin Evans, the S.O.O., 'What's happening?' He explained that an important escorted Axis convoy had been located well on its way to Tripoli, which it would be approaching from the east and entering that night. The question was a matter of time. Had the ships left early enough to intercept well east of Tripoli? How far east would the force have to be to evade all mines? What a horrible low featureless unlit coast to approach at night at really high speed. The project seemed highly dangerous to me and I said to Commander Evans, 'I fear the approaches to Tripoli, since I lost *P32* to the north and *P33* to the east in early August.'

Evans reassured me that O'Conor knew that minefields existed in the port's approaches, but that nobody could say what radius from the port they might be expected. He added that this opportunity could not be ignored. All sorts of things might happen, the convoy might have its speed reduced and so fall into our hands. Only the man in command could decide how and where to intercept the enemy. All this was straightforward sense; risks had to be taken and the man on the spot made the decisions. I fully agreed, but I still felt unhappy because of the ghastly temptation for an officer full of offensive enthusiasm to cut corners in order to fall upon the convoy, and Rory O'Conor was a dashing leader.

Rory O'Conor did not cut corners; he kept about twenty miles east of Tripoli but after midnight all three ships were mined; *Neptune* being lost, and later the destroyer *Kandahar* who had gallantly gone to rescue *Neptune*'s crew. Only one man from *Neptune* survived; the crew of *Kandahar*, whose stern was blown off, were rescued from the minefield thirty hours later by the destroyer *Jaguar* with a fine display of gallantry and seamanship.

A few days later I found myself on a Board of Enquiry into the loss of *Kandahar;* the president of the enquiry was Admiral Rawlings, who said to me, 'I feel rather stunned by this whole sad business. I was returning with my secretary from golf in a horse cab and arrived on the waterfront to see my squadron leaving harbour with my flagship in the van. Within twelve hours it was almost wholly sunk or damaged. It is difficult to accept as fact.'

So ended Force K as a highly efficient fighting squadron. I

think everyone realised the dangers but decided to accept them. The prize was high; with hindsight I suggest the proper solution was to sail the squadron immediately the convoy was located, and send O'Conor and Force K their orders by cipher, rather than sending for O'Conor to H.Q. which must have lost forty minutes, which was perhaps a vital margin.

The day after this catastrophe I called in on Admiral Ford's staff at naval H.Q. Martin Evans said, 'Really frightful news has come through. Italian midget submarines have got into Alexandria harbour and put *Queen Elizabeth* and *Valiant* on the harbour bottom, but fortunately there were no casualties.'

I could not see what possible difference this could make to the war except to deprive the Commander-in-Chief and his staff of duty free liquor and cigarettes. The loss of Force K was a hard knock; the loss of two battleships seemed virtually irrelevant so far as the Mediterranean was concerned. My views were of small comfort to my good friend Commander Evans, who very naturally, like all specialist officers, held strong views about the sanctity of the battleship.

In summing up this turbulent hard-hitting three months in the Mediterranean other events need mention. In early October Admiral Horton sought to take the opportunity to visit his three submarine flotillas at Gibraltar, Malta and Alexandria and signalled the Commander-in-Chief suggesting this. Admiral Cunningham replied, 'No objection.' Under the circumstances this seemed a hard and bitter reply to an important colleague. It did not dissuade Horton at all.

I have remarked earlier that Horton was a 'lone wolf'. He belonged to the Travellers Club and to no naval club. Most of his friends were civilians and golfing companions. From sub-lieutenant to captain he had served in submarines, untramelled by tradition, latterly with much distinction in war. During the peace he had proved himself just as competent in command of cruisers, or battleships, or as a Flag Officer. He never served at the Admiralty, had no friend in the 'Establishment' and sought none. Alone and on his own merit he stood with all the self-confidence necessary to refuse Admiral Backhouse's endeavour to banish him to Australia in January 1939 and to decline the high honour of command of the Home Fleet in October 1940.

These two great men, for whom I held such an equally balanced and high regard, were both born in 1883, Cunningham being some ten months the elder. Both won three D.S.O.s in the First World War. Cunningham served from 1908 to 1920 continuously in T.B.s and destroyers. Horton served continuously from 1904 to 1920 in submarines. Both had a high professional regard for the other but were not friends, nor had they real friends in common.

It seemed to me that these two 'fighting' admirals, so well balanced in physical and mental powers, had two different ways of translating their skill, experience and forceful qualities into leadership and action. Cunningham by humane discipline, vigilance and an appeal to tradition. Horton by humane discipline, a most unusual knowledge of material and, on the spiritual side, vision. This made for a nicely balanced expert performance by both officers.

Amongst Horton's closest friends for some thirty years was G. Ward Price, who was a war correspondent of renown since the First Balkan War and finally became Director of Associated Newspapers. Horton was therefore well aware of the power of the Press and had an advocate in court to advise if necessary.

Horton had had in the First World War the very odd experience of receiving from the Czar of Russia the Order of St Anne (with swords and diamonds) and the Order of St George, together with the Chevalier of the Legion of Honour from the president of France, before he received from his own country his first D.S.O. on 15 April 1916. As the expectancy of life in submarines was short, he was determined that officers and men of the submarines should receive their fair share of publicity and so far as possible should receive their hard-earned decorations in their lifetime.

Cunningham had good reason to dislike publicity, which seemed at times to hand valuable information to the enemy, particularly about convoys, and had been unwilling to respond to Admiralty requests. He was also a believer in the traditional phrase 'the Silent Service'. He was however appreciative and even enthusiastic about his submarines' successes.

So it was that Admiral Horton visited us for two days in late October and I had all submarines both of the 10th flotilla, and those on passage, at Lazaretto to meet him. Horton read a message from the Prime Minister to our assembled company which was a great encouragement and added his own remarks. He had long talks with many C.O.s and inquired into our anxieties and admired our excavations, now more than half completed. He gave orders to eliminate gyro failures in torpedoes, which caused circling and endangered our submarines, and finally he told me that more publicity for our submarines was both deserved and necessary and the immediate award of decorations was important to morale, then he flew away to Alexandria.

Within six weeks of this visit from Admiral Horton, Wanklyn had been awarded the Victoria Cross, and Commander Anthony Kimmins had been to Lazaretto and out on a short war patrol with Wanklyn, and his B.B.C. broadcasts followed.

During the summer months social and business life had become so normal that petty bickers, as in peacetime, brought grist to the attorney's mill. So it was that a Maltese solicitor wrote me letters with increasing frequency asking me to produce in Malta a certain Leading Stoker Capes who was then serving in a submarine at Alexandria. Capes, it was alleged, had before the outbreak of war driven a hired car which had been in collision with a *karozzin* (horse cab) belonging to the solicitor's client and wrecked it. Both sides denied liability. Would I please produce Capes so that a settlement might be reached? I said I would if submarine movements allowed this and I wrote to Captain Raw suggesting Capes work his passage in a submarine store trip and I would return him by submarine when the case was over.

Capes arrived in September, with heavy black beard and a rather self-righteous attitude of complete innocence, which for all I know may have been fully justified. After a month no settlement had occurred so I warned both parties that Capes would return to Alexandria in late November in the submarine *Perseus*, (Lieutenant Commander Nicolay) and this occurred.

On passage east *Perseus* was ordered to establish patrol west of Greece and on the night of 6–7 December was patrolling north of Zante. At about 2300 she struck a mine, which hit forward, broke her back and she sank at a steep angle but settled on the bottom on an even keel at 170 feet.

Capes was in the after compartment and with the aid of a water-tight torch shut the door isolating the compartment and found five other stokers were with him but in a dying condition. By the time he had unclipped the D.S.E.A. hatch only one other man was living. Capes opened the hatch, after flooding the compartment and equalizing the internal pressure with the outside sea pressure, and made a perfect slow ascent using D.S.E.A. equipment passing a moored mine fifteen feet from the surface. He then swam ten miles north to Cephalonia. After much wandering Capes was rescued in June 1943 by an organised caique expedition.

This escape is not only remarkable but mysterious. The war orders were that all escape and other hatches, except the conning-tower hatch, were not only to be clipped internally but also secured by a steel bar externally to prevent a hatch jumping its clips due to depth-charging; so it must be presumed that Capes was able to escape due to the negligence of ship's officers not ensuring that the external steel strongback was in place on leaving dockyard refit.

In 1952 I visited Malta and met in the dockyard, still serving in submarines, Stoker Petty Officer Capes. I shook him by the hand and inquired whether the case of the car *versus* cab collision had been settled in his favour. With a wan smile he whispered, 'Oh, not yet, sir, but I'm hopeful of the outcome.'

On 21 December the enemy's air raids were stepped up just enough to bring a Christmas Greeting for an unhappy New Year. I reflected with satisfaction that we had 120 fat porkers hanging in the government freezer. I had been repaid my £300, and the pigs were now under the enthusiastic management of the sailors' canteen committee. Our Maltese working party had hewn such fine caverns in the rock that if our Lazaretto quarters were destroyed we could still carry on from our cave dwellings.

On Christmas Eve Boris asked me to dine with the officers and ship's company of *Sokol*, who had prepared a porker into a great number of Polish dishes. I went with Commander W. G. A. Robson who had just lost his *Kandahar* in the Tripoli minefield. We had a wonderful evening. A piano was in the large Sliema dining-room and after the feast the big bearded figure of the coxswain, Chief Petty Officer Domisch, moved to the piano, whilst the ship's company sitting round the table sang carols and national songs in splendid unison.

At six o'clock on New Year's Eve the Governor, Sir William Dobbie, addressed the island over the telephone hook-up. It was a speech I shall always remember because in it he said, 'The Japanese attacked Pearl Harbour just over three weeks ago and so have thrown us into active alliance with the most powerful nation in the world. The Japanese are an obstinate and stupid people who are at this time endeavouring to land on the eastern shores of Malaya, into the mangrove swamps, the paddy fields and impenetrable jungle of that peninsula. We may have suffered the sad loss of two fine ships, the *Prince of Wales* and *Repulse*, in the first days of this Japanese offensive, but, my dear people, let me assure you that the Japanese attack will fail, and I say this with confidence since I was the officer responsible for installing the gun defences of Singapore.'

With this morale booster we moved confidently into the new year.

15

DESPITE their naval successes in the last few months of 1941 the Axis powers still had to consolidate the position. Hitler had ordered the return of *Fliegerkorps II* from the Russian front and their first task was to bomb Malta. As soon as they arrived at their bases in Sicily the air attacks started, with their quickly mounting scale. The number of civilian deaths tells the story: in the last ten days of December 1941 there were more than fifty deaths; in January 1942, eighty people died, while in February there were some 200 deaths from nearly 1,000 tons of bombs dropped on the island. March and April were, however, the real months of horror. In March 1942 over 2,000 tons of bombs were dropped on Malta while in April over 6,700 tons of bombs rained down on the inhabitants – a 'Coventry' size raid every day for over a month.

The people of Malta endured during this bombing, and for most of the rest of the year, a state of semi-starvation – often receiving below 1,000 calories daily or less than one-third of the normal ration, without any firm prospect of likely improvement. Three hundred thousand men, women and children were always hungry. Their towns and ancient buildings were seriously wrecked, their businesses ruined, their whole future suspect and insecure and their native country wide open to invasion. Yet never for a moment did they flinch, although the more intelligent may have been doubtful of the outcome. It was the discipline of the people in these circumstances that remains to me the miracle of Malta.

It is against the background of this continual assault that this and the following chapters should be read.

Admiral Horton had told me during his visit that he would try to limit the period of service of submarines based at Malta to one year so that their companies could have a target date to be relieved of the strain and tension of this service. While this was his aim events, and availability of new construction, alone could guarantee the fulfilment. To this purpose *P31* (Lieutenant J. B. Kershaw) had joined in October and *P35* (Lieutenant H. L. Maydon), *P36* (Lieutenant H. N. Edmonds), *P38* (Lieutenant R. J. Hemingway), *P39* (Lieutenant N. Marriott), and *Una* (Lieutenant D. S. R. Martin) had joined in January, while *Utmost* and *Unique* left about this time to refit in Britain.

When living under conditions of great and prolonged strain the finest tonic to the community is success. In fact it is possible for the success to be so great that calamities which might seem near lethal to further business appear as petty inconveniences. Our fleet had just lost its three battleships, which was a severe blow to its pride, if not to its influence. On 14 December *Urge*, on patrol south of Messina, had obtained one torpedo hit on the Italian battleship *Vittorio Veneto* which put her out of action for two months. This was a slight but happy riposte.

On 5 January *Unique*, on patrol in the centre of the Gulf of Taranto, in the late afternoon found herself ahead of a naval force of one battleship, one cruiser and five destroyers escorted by two flying boats. This is the precise position which any submarine officer must pray for and which less than one in one thousand sorties were likely to experience. This is the great occasion where the chances are fifty to one in the submarine's favour, provided the C.O. uses as little speed as possible and as little periscope as possible, and very little of either are necessary. He must then dismiss the escorting destroyers from his mind, and concentrate his attack upon the battleship, knowing that if his attack is a real success his escape is also virtually assured since the destroyers will be occupied life saving.

This did not occur. *Unique* went deep and opened the range from the battleship's line of advance and when he estimated the escorts were passed, took a second look to find that the battleship had zigzagged away, which was to be expected. His opportunity was passed, and a forlorn shot after a fast moving enemy failed as it deserved to do.

On 19 January we lost our grand champion and administrator, Admiral Sir Wilbraham Ford, to whom we in the 10th Flotilla owed much in both support and in the way he allowed us to run our affairs our own way. For five years he had been Admiral Malta and his confidence and foresight had largely made Malta's resistance possible. It was not only the Navy but Malta and all the three armed services who were sad to see him leave at this critical hour.

On 12 January, just after arrival and on patrol south-east of Messina, *Unbeaten* made a brilliant attack on a U-boat in heavy weather. I received this signal from Woodward, '0810 Sighted Westbound U-boat and fired salvo three minutes later. Have one survivor on board who speaks German and had breakfasted off tomatoes.' I replied, 'Well done. Remain on patrol.'

As things turned out this was a mistake on my part. The young German sailor who had been pulled half concious from the rough sea, vomiting, soon recovered. He found he was no longer the bridge lookout of *U374* returning from patrol to Messina, but was the centre of pity and concern in *Unbeaten*, being offered cigarettes of Virginia tobacco and generally made a fuss of by the crew. For a week he was messman in the C.P.O.'s mess where he settled down to his new duties. He spoke no English, was intelligent, and needed little encouragement to assume the privileged role of submarine mascot.

On arrival he was brought before me, and Woodward explained that he had written on paper his name and official number and that he came from Breslau and would say no more. Nobody had any idea what the number of his U-boat was and although this question could easily be explained with paper and pencil he had refused to give it.

Using an interpreter I explained that temporarily he would be put in a cell, which might appear to be a sentence of solitary confinement but we had nowhere else to put him. As he would be brought to the rock shelter for every air raid he would spend several hours a day in public company, and I sent him off to his cell.

I gave orders that he was not to be allowed to see or know that *Sokol*'s crew were in the base and I asked the R.A.F. to let me know some hours in advance when they could transfer him to Cairo. Before being transferred there was just one fact I wished to know – what was the maximum depth to which his U-boat could dive. That was the million dollar question, since although we had been at war for twenty-seven months it was still only possible to set depth-charges to 500 feet maximum depth, which seemed one good reason why the Battle of the Atlantic was then slowly moving from bad to worse.

188

I arranged to interview him two days later with the aid of an interpreter from the Army, with Tanner and Tomkinson to listen in and make suggestions, which could be openly done since he had no word of English. I explained that we should all appear to be solely interested in wishing to know the number of his U-boat but were willing to let him talk openly about any subject. Since his treatment in *Unbeaten* had given him supreme self-confidence I had no intention of changing the tune, all I wanted was to get him talking, so I intended to allow him to sit down opposite me.

The interview started and the young German, with smiling confidence and obvious enjoyment, explained he would never tell us the number of his U-boat. However, he was willing to tell us how very adequate the rations were for his family in Breslau, how dangerous life evidently was in Malta and how poor the food, and he could see that Germany was winning on all fronts. This was just the attitude I wished to encourage but it was altogether too much for Tomkinson. As the interpreter told us the prisoner's opinions on the shortcomings of life in Malta, Tommo said to me, 'If you will excuse me, sir, I can't stick this. This self-satisfied German puppy should be standing to attention between two sentries with fixed bayonets and not sitting opposite us laughing and criticising us. That little twirp is one of seventy million reasons why I am not with my wife and daughter and I can't stick this sort of insult.'

'O.K. Tommo, you're excused', and he left.

Tanner and I showed interest in conditions in the Reich, the excellent harvests, the lack of British bombing, the good leave arrangements and rest camps for U-boat crews, the certainty of Hitler's victory. I said that while that might be so, the fact remained that Britain was still fully active, in fact he had just been blown off his conning-tower, and I added, 'You were very nearly caught coming through the Strait of Gibraltar. That,' I lied, 'will soon be impassable to all U-boats when our new methods are introduced.'

'You had no defences a few weeks ago,' said the confident young prisoner. 'All my captain said was, "Slow both. 260 metres," and the current brought us through.'

After a few irrelevant questions I closed the interview. I felt reasonably sure he had told the truth when off guard. So 850 feet was a possible diving depth. Rather more than double ours.

Having got that I arranged for the prisoner to be sent to the civil jail where there was proper accommodation outside the target area, but I first asked Boris if there was any chance of getting the U-boat's number through a Polish stoolpigeon being in the cell. Boris replied, 'My coxswain C.P.O. Domisch lives near the German border not far from Breslau and speaks German perfectly, we will send him to prison.'

So Domisch, in overalls, posing as a German bomber crew prisoner and with orders not to speak until he was spoken to, lay on one bunk in a double cell and the prisoner from Breslau joined him. No word passed for over an hour, but when conversation did begin Domisch was immediately denounced as a Polish stoolpigeon and returned to Lazaretto rather offended.

This young prisoner arrived at Cairo some two weeks later and I received a reprimand from Major Quill, Royal Marines, in charge of prisoner intelligence, who complained that the man had been ruined by us and was completely security conscious. It took the experts six months to discover that his U-boat was U-374. I apologised but had reported what I thought important; the diving depth of 850 feet.

This was not, I think, believed. In any event deep pistols for depth-charges did not become available until 1943. Three and a half years late and very nearly too late.

In January *Una* joined the flotilla, commanded by D. S. R. Martin whom I knew and regarded as a sound chap. He had patrolled off Tunisia on passage out but had seen nothing, so I sailed him in February to patrol the southern approaches to the Gulf of Taranto and in his sailing orders was clearly stated, 'The Italian tanker *Lucania* (8,100 tons) sails from Taranto 11 February on passage to the Atlantic. She will not be zigzagging, will not be escorted and will be marked on both sides amidships with the Italian flag. *Lucania* has been promised safe passage by the British Government and is not to be molested.'

The reason for this was that diplomatic arrangements had been made through intermediaries for *Vulcania* (24,000 tons) to go via Gibraltar and the Cape to Mombasa to embark Italian non-combatants and families from an internment camp for repatriation, with the proviso that Italy supplied *Vulcania*'s fuel, so *Lucania* sailed with this object.

On the evening of 12 February I received a signal from the Admiralty ordering me to report immediately whether *Lucania* had been attacked. I repeated this to *Una* who confirmed that he had sunk an escorted tanker that morning, so I recalled *Una* immediately, and sent *Tempest*, who was on her first Mediterranean patrol, to take her place.

On entering harbour *Una* signalled that the first lieutenant was in command, the captain being sick with a high temperature. I went on board and interviewed Martin in his bunk. There was no doubt whatever that he had sunk *Lucania* without a shadow of excuse. I was told that the tanker could not have been *Lucania* because she was escorted by an aircraft and that the Italian flags were too small to identify on the ship's side. In fact the aircraft was on anti-submarine patrol and the flag markings can never have been seen, since the torpedoes were fired on a thirty degree track long before the size and colour of the flag could have been checked.

The truth was that the captain was running a high temperature and I suppose was willing to believe anything he wished to believe. I felt that I had been deliberately insulted and disobeyed; also the constant bombing was not helping my temper. I asked the R.A.F. for an urgent passage to the U.K. and got one, sending Martin home to explain to the Admiralty why he had sunk the *Lucania* and if necessary to be arraigned before the Foreign Secretary, for I was informed that Anthony Eden felt even more strongly about it than I did.

Having relieved Martin of his command and sent him packing I put Lieutenant C. P. Norman in *Una* which he commanded with distinction.

I was not told the outcome of Martin's interviews in Britain except that he was appointed to *Tuna* and sank *U644* in April 1943, earning the D.S.O. So all ended happily for him, but there was a sad riposte for us at Malta. The Italian Navy very naturally took immediate steps to seek out and destroy this marauder and on 13 February sent the torpedo boat *Circe* to search the area. *Circe*, newly fitted with asdic and trained in its use, located *Tempest* (Lieutenant-Commander Cavaye) on her first Mediterranean patrol, and sank her. *Circe*, with this success to her credit and with live practice and experience so recent, followed up ten days later by locating and sinking *P38* (Lieutenant R. J. Hemingway) when this submarine was attacking a convoy approaching Tripoli on 23 February.

Of course I did not know until the war was over how or why I lost these two submarines, but it was indeed swift retribution for an irresponsible act.

During my two year appointment at Malta under siege the behaviour of the men in my command was a reward second only to the success of our operations. There may have been occasional petty offences brought before commanding officers or the executive officer of the base but I only became involved on less than ten occasions, some of which are sufficiently odd to merit comment.

I have related the court martial on the E.R.A. of *Regent*, which took up the time of about twenty people, mostly busy officers at a very busy time, and the very fair judgement given. After that, when the air attack developed and with a new V.A. Malta, I was in no mood to refer personal peccadilloes to an admiral who could but order a court martial. I decided to disregard the law and take the consequences.

It is a poor commentary on the estate of Holy Matrimony that with the discomforts of the Malta blitz anybody should prefer to remain in Malta to reunion with his wife and family in England after three years of separation. One of the torpedo preparation party, a capable able seaman leading torpedoman, was such a person. His unorthodox behaviour led to me unorthodox reaction and to an unusual reprimand from V.A. Malta, which received no support from Admiral Cunningham. I will refer to the offender as Able Seaman Q.

In December 1941 I got a signal from the Commodore Devonport Barracks, 'Able Seaman Q is overdue for relief, home leave and requalifying course. As there is a shortage of L.T.O.s request you take first opportunity of passage to U.K.'

This suited well and it was arranged for him to take passage in *Utmost* sailing for home about New Year's day. When *Utmost* was due to sail, Q could not be found either in the base or his shore haunts and the submarine went without him. He appeared at work in the torpedo depot next morning and, when brought before Marsham, said he had no excuse except that he was very happy in his present job. Defaulters and punishments were an infliction on everyone under these siege conditions and Marsham concocted a suitable punishment to meet the crime, 'Forty-eight hours cells, deferred.'

Unique was due to sail on 27 January, so on 25 January Q was apprehended, with my full approval, and locked up in the cooler with his kit bag and hammock in the next cell, all ready to step on board *Unique* two days later. This of course entailed the employment of three sentries in watches night and day and the supervision of a Petty Officer every time there was an air raid warning, so as to accompany the prisoner to the rock shelter. This was immediately before the demolition of the base.

When *Unique* was due to sail Q was taken down to the submarine an hour before departure and put on board. The submarine's sentry was on the gangway and the crew were taking down and stowing their bags and hammocks. It was understandable that the ship's company should congregate on the Lazaretto messdeck just before sailing, to bid farewell to their friends and receive letters and parcels for delivery to wives and sweethearts in the U.K., and thus it was that Q found himself alone on board.

Going into the wardroom he found the pistol rack unlocked and found six rounds of pistol 0.45 ammunition. He loaded the revolver, went into the control room, and fired six rounds at random into the pressure hull ply lining, but not into any vital piece of machinery. So Q was brought out of the submarine and again placed in cells. This hullaballoo occurred just below the wardroom verandah.

Every machine and instrument had to be tested, *Unique*'s sailing delayed and her initial dive undertaken with particular caution. So *Unique* went on her way and we were left with Q and no prospect of getting rid of him until *Clyde* arrived on a store trip some ten days later.

I had more important matters to deal with than Q's eccentricities but he was now a major nuisance and, over a drink at the bar that evening, I said to our ancient mariner, Lieutenant-Commander 'Pop' Giddings, who had served twenty years on the lower deck, 'This man "Q" has now become a public menace, what the hell's biting him?'

'Ah, sir, that's women all over. They play hell with a man's emotions.'

'Oh thanks. I thought perhaps he was mental.'

'Oh Lord, no! It's his girl down in St Julians who's got something others haven't.'

'Thanks, Pop.'

It was clear that if I reported this to Admiral Leatham, who had now taken over from Admiral Ford, he must order a court martial, and I was determined that the Commodore R.N.B. Devonport should have this chore.

Clyde, under the command of Lieutenant R. S. Brookes, arrived and unloaded and was due to sail for Devonport a few days before the fateful Friday when mines gutted the messdecks. I ordered her to Marsamxett harbour and when Brookes reported I told him the story and that I wished to see him and his coxswain and chief stoker at 1100. *Clyde* was sailing at sunset.

When they arrived, Q was brought before me at the defaulters' table between two sentries. This was the first time I had seen him as a prisoner, although I knew him well enough as a hard-working member of the torpedo party. Brookes and his two Chief Petty Officers stood on my right. I handed Brookes his sailing orders and then said, 'Regarding the prisoner, these are his papers and these are the circumstances of his close arrest. You are to take him to Devonport and deliver him to the Commodore R.N. Barracks for court martial for sabotaging one of H.M. submarines in time of war. He is to be under close arrest until you are one mile from Malta, then he is to be under open arrest because you have no accommodation for prisoners on board. You are to tell your ship's company of the charges against him. If he gives you any cause whatever for anxiety over his conduct and intentions, you are to surface and place him on the forecasing. You, Lieutenant Brookes, are then to shoot him, dive and continue your passage. The reason why I order you to shoot him before diving is to ensure that nobody can possibly save him. Do you understand my orders completely?'

'Yes, sir.'

'Do you understand my reasons, coxswain?'

'Yes I do, sir.'

'Do you understand my reasons, chief stoker?'

'Yes I do, sir.'

'All right, take the prisoner to H.M.S. *Clyde*.'

The next day, when *Clyde* was well on her way, I sent a copy of my sailing orders for *Clyde* and my specific orders regarding

Able Seaman Q to Vice Admiral Malta with a copy to Captain *S1* as usual.

I received next day for my information a copy of this letter:

> *To* C. in C. Mediterranean   *From* V.A. Malta.
>
> I have informed Captain *S10* that his order to the Commanding Officer of HMS *Clyde* that under certain circumstances Able Seaman Q is to be shot is too rigid and most injudicious.
>
> Ralph Leatham
Vice Admiral

I knew that Admiral Cunningham would read this before *Clyde* was half-way to Gibraltar but he made no signal or comment, so my order to Lieutenant Brookes remained in force until Q was handed over for court martial three weeks later.

Some two years later, when I was Commodore Western Approaches, Commander Layard, commanding a frigate, came to see me and remarked, 'I have a leading seaman on board. I would assess him as one of my very best men, but on his service certificate is an entry that in 1942 you had given orders that while under open arrest for a month on board *Clyde* he was to be shot under certain circumstances. I have never before seen a similar entry, what on earth caused it?'

So I said, 'I suppose he is a respectable married man with a splendid young family and devoted wife.'

'Oh yes,' said Layard, 'A really steady, reliable chap.'

'I'm delighted but rather surprised,' I said.

A few weeks later, after the messdecks had been gutted and conditions were appalling, *Una* was about to sail on patrol when a considerable hullaballoo occurred near her gangway and the duty submarine officer came to my cabin and reported, 'Sir, *Una*'s gunlayer has arrived in the base fighting drunk. He's in a very truculent mood, *Una* sails in an hour and it is impossible to put him onboard. I doubt if he'll be sober in twelve hours.'

This seemed to me a very much more serious matter than the case of A.B. Q whom I had just got rid of. Q was a rating from the base torpedo party avoiding repatriation to Britain, but this gunlayer, whom I will call G, was a submarine rating about to avoid a war patrol due to drunkenness. Until then no rating had ever missed a patrol by default, and if G was allowed to do so at this moment of our trial I could see morale slipping and danger ahead. I knew that since beer was almost unobtainable the chief tipple ashore was 'red biddy', which was very raw Cypriot wine of most irregular reaction, and therefore G's condition was perhaps due to slight indiscretion rather than deliberate over-indulgence.

'Can you get his uniform off?'

'Not a hope, sir, unless he's knocked unconcious.'

'Is he in his best suit?'

'Possibly, sir, but he's smothered in dust and has been constantly falling over getting here.'

'All right, then, go with the Duty Petty Officer and tell his own messmates from *Una* to get a heaving line with a slip knot at one end, and slip it over one ankle, pull it tight and push him into the harbour. Then every time he comes up and proclaims the usual lower deck comment, pull on the line so that his head goes under. Continue to do this until something happens, or he becomes unconscious, when he is immediately to be pulled ashore and revived. Tell his messmates that I order this treatment in his own best interests. So far he is not even a defaulter.'

'Aye aye, sir.'

I went to the officers' verandah which was then still intact and watched proceedings.

My recommended treatment seemed popular. In a moment G was thrashing around in the harbour and the anticipated terms of endearment burst from his lungs but down went his head as the heaving line tightened. The struggle continued until suddenly he broke surface and was violently sick. There was a hush of anticipation and G said in a subdued tone, 'I give up.' He was helped out, carried on board *Una*, put on a bunk in dry clothes and sailed with his submarine.

In the summer of 1943 I attended an investiture at Buckingham Palace to receive the C.B.E. from the Queen. The King was visiting Malta that very day. After receiving my decoration I withdrew to a position where the proceedings could be watched and to my delight in marched Lieutenant J. D. Martin leading *Una*'s six or seven ratings who had been awarded decorations, and there was the gallant gunlayer to receive the D.S.M. 'For outstanding service during eighteen months' submarine operations from Malta.'

As I left the Palace Able Seaman G came over to me and, shaking me by the hand, said, 'Please, sir, may I introduce you to my dad?'

'Why, certainly G, and I do congratulate you – this is certainly a great day for both of us.'

I was introduced to a tall, lean, exulting Mr G senior, in dark suit and magnificent cravat with a pearl tie-pin, wearing a billy-cock hat at a jaunty angle. A costermonger I guessed.

'By jove, Mr G, you must be proud of your boy!' I exclaimed.

'Ah, God bless you, sir, I am, I am indeed.'

16

FRIDAY the thirteenth is, by repute, an inauspicious day for somebody. There was a lot of low cloud during the morning of 13 February 1942 but about noon our 'Jim Crow' boy scout sounded the klaxon and this found me near the base front gate. Obeying my own orders I ran into the nearest shelter which was off the men's messdecks.

There was a large muster of men with me, but I had an intuition that they were not all there and that some foolish ones were disobeying orders. A stick of heavy bombs fell on Pieta, demolishing the house of General Beak, V.C., who by good fortune was in his lavatory whose stalwart walls saved his life as a hit brought down his house. This was half a mile from us. A few minutes later a Stuka attack just missed us but shook the whole building, exploding in Lazaretto creek. I ran out and up the stone stairs to assess the damage and found four Engine-Room Artificers and their messman on the messdeck, dazed by shock, with windows blown in and a half-eaten meal on the table. I was naturally angry and my surprise arrival pulled them to their senses and to shelter.

It was not possible for all men to be all the time in the shelters during prolonged raids (and four or five hours was common during daylight) because some special duties had to be performed and also our W.C.s were on the waterfront thirty yards from the shelters, but having a meal was not an excuse. I passed the word that the enemy was after us and my orders issued over a year earlier were to be obeyed more precisely.

Another raid came in at 1430. It was parachute mines this time. Two hit the western end of Lazaretto where all the messdecks were and the entire roofs of two storeys, made of two-hundred-weight stone slabs, came down in one act throughout the men's quarters. Eight other mines fell on Manoel Island, three men were killed and our barracks demolished. The walls remained like empty shells, reaching thirty feet towards the sky.

This caused the ever vigilant General Beckett to place four Bofors guns manned by the Royal Malta Artillery around Lazaretto.

Raids continued, but for a while we seemed to be immune, until at 1600 on 27 February the klaxon ordered us to our burrows and shortly afterwards a cascade of heavy bombs struck the eastern end of Lazaretto, which formed the officers' quarters. At the height of these explosions the two junior Greek officers from the submarine *Glaukos* dashed into the shelter, shouting that the others were following, but they did not appear.

Three of us dashed out and past the Bofors gun, firing steadily at retreating Ju87s although their parapet was a shambles from a crater just beyond it. Just up the steps was a pile of masonry and it took three hours to recover the bodies of the Greek captain, his first lieutenant and two officers. This sad loss immobilised *Glaukos*'s refitting; it was due to the captain deciding to continue a conference in his cabin and then suddenly ordering all six officers to take shelter too late.

The stalwart discipline of the Bofors crew of the Royal Malta Artillery was admirable, and my report upon it, I was told, was recognised by suitable rewards.

About eighty yards from Lazaretto was a sub-rock heavy oil tank of about 10,000 tons capacity. It had a high gallery in front of it with a floor space of about a hundred feet by forty feet and it was twenty feet high. The floor was not level, nor very smooth, and several tons of oil and water lay in pools upon it. The officers dispossessed of their cabins moved into this stinking cavern and prayed it would not receive a direct hit. The tank itself was empty, but the stench of heavy oil pervaded everything.

Chests of drawers and a few chairs were brought down the thirty steep steps to the cavern floor and were placed on the dry spots with boards leading through the glutinous oily slush to them. So we established a changing room for submarine officers here, and also my splendid and courageous typist Miss Gomer had a desk and typewriter under one of the two lights. For two months, through air raids, she sat and typed patrol reports, and the work of my office, to the banter of submarine officers arriving at intervals with clothing and private possessions they had salvaged from their demolished cabins.

I had been lucky, since my sleeping cabin and clothes remained intact; my day cabin, which had been the office, had lost its roof. Further along the gallery Sam MacGregor was toiling for hours amidst the rubble and I enquired how he was faring. 'I'd be happy enough,' replied Sam, 'if I could only find my bagpipes.' This he eventually did.

There was no longer any question of anybody within the base sleeping elsewhere than in a deep shelter. Although crowded this could be done in long lines of two-tier bunks. For four weeks all officers and ratings messed together under the stars or the sun in relays on trestles. Fortunately it seldom rained. Our galley and hot water boiler had survived the attacks.

Our conditions at Lazaretto were probably better than those on the airfields but I suspect that since the airfields had been the centre of attack for fourteen months their well spread out amenities, such as they were, proved less vulnerable to the effect of a concentrated attack.

This demolition of Lazaretto occurred in February, before the main assault which was to be four times as heavy during April. It was early in this month that most of the submarine officers' flats in Sliema were wrecked, amongst them the *Sokol*'s top flat of a three-storey building. Boris went round to view the wreckage with his officers, and there glinting in the sun on top of ten feet of rubble was his Virtuti Militari which General Sikorski had taken from his chest.

Looking up at the shell of the building, perched on a few feet of floor that still remained like a musical box on a high shelf out of the reach of children, was the piano. Boris sent two officers to find a tall ladder which was brought to the site and Boris, with his treasured decoration once more on his breast, climbed the ladder and played the Polish Grand March.

During this bitter four months there were two attacks carried out by 10th Flotilla submarines which showed a particularly high degree of skill. During the first days of January *Upholder* (M. D. Wanklyn) was off Palermo. He attacked and missed two ships on 2 January and two days later attacked the steamer *Sirio* (5,000 tons) scoring one hit, but the steamer did not sink. This attack was an unnerving experience since, out of three torpedoes fired, one torpedo ran hot in the tube and a second circled and exploded on the bottom near *Upholder*. Wanklyn then had one torpedo left and having stirred things up locally moved eastwards to a new area intending to inspect the northern approaches to Messina.

At 0530 on 5 January the night was fair and moonlit. Wanklyn had an emergency call to the bridge and on his arrival a shell fell some way short of *Upholder*. The officer of the watch stated this was the third that had come from the darkness under the cliffs. Wanklyn turned towards the gunflash, a U-boat emerged from the shadow steering for *Upholder* and Wanklyn dived as a shell passed overhead. As he dived he felt certain that the enemy seeing him disappear would turn either to port or starboard on the surface and that he would not continue towards him or dive. The direction from which fire was opened showed that she had come from Messina and was doubtless going west to Palermo, so having decided all this Wanklyn swung *Upholder* on to an estimated firing course while diving.

On his first look through the periscope he saw a large submarine swinging broadside on and heading west, range about three-quarters of a mile; guessing the deflection angle by eye he fired his solitary torpedo and hit the *Saint Bon* amidships. He surfaced, picked up three survivors and returned to Malta.

The second attack I particularly commend was by *P31* (J. B. Kershaw) on 5 March. I had had intelligence hints that it seemed probable a single ship of particular importance and heavily escorted would pass west of Lampedusa bound for Tripoli. Near midday Kershaw sighted this convoy in conditions of flat glassy calm and maximum visibility. He noted the numerous surface escorts and air patrol overhead. He also remembered that *Tempest* and *P38* had both been sunk in the previous three weeks, pointing to efficient Italian A/S methods.

Watching the approach from great range he noted that his solitary target was steering a straight course, which allowed him to place himself accurately at ideal range, go to eighty feet and fire by asdic without showing his periscope throughout. Kershaw did this to perfection, sinking the important supply ship *Marin Sanudo*, of 5,080 tons. *P31* was heavily counterattacked despite this, but the enemy merely plastered the whole area and never gained contact.

The tough time we had experienced since Christmas was only a prelude to the late March and April attack.

As a partial counter, during the past year the R.A.F.'s aerodrome complex had been hugely expanded. Air Vice Marshal Lloyd pays tribute to the Army's work in his book *Briefed to Attack* where he says that 1,500 of the Inniskilling Fusiliers and the Manchester Regiment were pen-building and crater-filling in January to March, and this increased to 3,000 in April, while these large numbers were substantially reinforced by civilian labour. There was no earthmoving machinery and shovel and wheelbarrow were used on this front line by men on half rations.

In full cooperation with the A.O.C. Malta Major General Beckett, commanding A.A. defence, had a concentration of Bofors flak in the Ta Qali–Luqa–Hal Far aerodrome complex. I was told that an important but insuperable difficulty was caused by the spent splinters from Bofor's flak falling on to the wing fabric of dispersed aircraft. There was no material in the island to use as a light covering to pens to prevent this, and what amounted at first to superficial damage became cumulative and fatal.

The last aircraft reinforcement Malta had received was forty in mid-November 1941. Now to our surprise on 7 March fifteen Spitfires arrived with a few Beaufighters and Blenheims. So at this moment of great trial the A.O.C. was at long last presented with Spitfires and with those light spares which could be ferried in by air. With them came, automatically, the very grave problems of a change of aircraft. Nine more arrived on 21 March and a further seven on 29 March. This appears a substantial reinforcement, thirty-one Spitfires in three weeks, but they were normally fighting at odds of between five and ten to one, and when exhausted of petrol and ammunition would be chased to their landing by an Me109.

It was a nightmare life for brave men, and guts alone cannot counteract numbers and sheer brute force. It was a case of too little and too late. On 1 March there were twenty-one Hurricanes serviceable, although this number fell to as low as six on busy days, and on the last day of March only nine Spitfires and five Hurricanes remained serviceable (despite seven Spitfires arriving four days earlier). This was inevitable when fighting daily the 400 fighters available to Kesselring.

As one of the very few officers who served in Malta through both the blitzes of early 1941 and early 1942 I naturally hold strong opinions on the conduct of the air defence of the island and the tardy supply of fighters to the Mediterranean theatre as a whole during 1941 and 1942. The problem dates from the beginning of the assault on Malta but I do not propose to deal with the period before mid-1941.

When Air Vice Marshal H. P. Lloyd took over command of the R.A.F. in Malta, relieving Air Vice Marshal Maynard, he was selected, briefed and flown to Malta within a period of six days. Lloyd was an experienced bomber officer and his briefing by the Chief of Air Staff was to 'attack': to attack and sink enemy shipping as first priority; to bomb points of embarkation and discharge; and generally to carry the battle to the enemy. Air Vice Marshal Lloyd kept loyally to his brief with bulldog determination.

We submariners asked our R.A.F. friends then and at intervals, 'How soon will Spitfires be here?' The invariable reply was, 'As soon as air filters are available, any time now.' This bluffed us. It was clear the enemy could re-impose the blitz at will.

Imagining as we all did that the air defence of Malta and re-establishment of surface forces was first priority, we viewed with sympathy the perilous insecurity of the R.A.F., while their prowess won our admiration. Lloyd carried out his orders with a grand display of guts and force of character. He arrived from Britain at the moment the Luftwaffe attack was petering out. It is just possible that he agreed with his brief.

There had been another change in command at the same time, which was to affect us. Lord Tedder in *With Prejudice* describes how the A.O.C. in C. Middle East, Air Marshal Sir Arthur Longmore, had often represented the lack of aircraft, in signals home, and how Tedder had warned him that the Air Staff were becoming irritated by such realistic signals. On 3 May after sending just such a signal, Longmore was recalled to London and Tedder was appointed in his stead. Longmore had started his career as a naval officer and so held an informed and sympathetic attitude to the needs of the fleet in air matters, so the Navy lost a friend. Tedder probably did all he could. Only he could judge what and how much he could ask for without sudden recall and possibly to follow Longmore into limbo. He was sandwiched between fighting a war without weapons and being sacked if he asked for them too strongly.

Tedder, throughout 1941 and 1942 supported the aerial offensive from Malta without the insurance of adequate fighter protection. Did he believe in this? Or was he tactfully supporting the Air Staff policy?

But perhaps the Air Staff had not dictated this policy. Presumably the Cabinet and the Chiefs of Staff Committee, under the powerful influence of Winston Churchill had approved it, and this is substantiated by the quite remarkable exchange of signals between Admiral Cunningham on 16 March 1941 asking for help and the annoyed refusal of Admiral Pound, the First Sea Lord, who stated, 'I trust you will disabuse Longmore that the reinforcement of Malta with Hurricanes will become a routine affair, which I suspect he hopes for. Although glad to use carriers as air transports in grave emergency, I feel this is wrong when it can be avoided by looking ahead sufficiently.'

The trite answer to my assertion that the wrong policy was employed is to state that it was the only one possible. To disprove this consider the following facts: the Battle of Britain was won by a small margin by about fifty fighter squadrons, and the Spitfire was proved in action superior to the Hurricane; fourteen months later at the end of 1941 there were about 150 squadrons of fighters in Britain. On 19 April 1941 Lord Beaverbrook wrote to Sir Charles Wilson (later Lord Moran) who had begged him to reconsider his resignation from Minister in Charge of Aircraft Production, 'As for my special responsibility, there are more aircraft than the Air Ministry can use.'

If it is argued that Spitfires could not be operated from Malta for reasons of logistics (lack of spares, machine tools, jigs, etc.), it should be noted that there were already six different types of aircraft operating from Malta at this time – Wellingtons, Blenheims, Hurricanes, Swordfish, Beaufighters and Marylands. It is reasonable to suppose that Spitfires could have operated then, as they were to do one year later under worse circumstances. Shortage of petrol can be discounted. If Spitfires in adequate numbers had replaced Hurricanes and Wellingtons there would have been enough.

The acid question is, would it have paid a dividend in enemy discomfiture if the R.A.F.'s first priority had been to give Malta adequate fighter protection? I contend that this could have been done more easily than the policy actually undertaken, and that its result would have altered the whole face of the campaign since it would have stopped the war in North Africa. The only argument against such a course is that if Britain had achieved this, it would have left no front on which our armies were engaged against the Axis. Our threat to the Axis coastline between the North Cape and Salonika would have caused Hitler acute anxiety.

It is not my intention to surmise the course of events if the North African campaign had been won by Britain before Japan's entry into the war. It is evident that while it would have caused Hitler great anxiety it would have saved him immense losses in material and manpower which might or might not have been used with terrible effect against Russia. But it is my intention to point out that if the British Government had decided to use its air power and sea power in their proper roles, instead of becoming hypnotised by the former, the campaign must have ended before December 1941.

I have been greatly assisted in assessing debatable questions by the Historical Branch (Navy) of the Ministry of Defence and on this question of policy regarding the defence of Malta I have received this brief,

There is no simple answer to the shortage of Spitfires in Malta in 1941–42. Certainly delays in their tropicalisation was one of the factors, though by no means the most important. It was a period when there were delays of all kinds in the three Services due to shortages. There was a marked lack of air filters in the Middle East.

The need for tropicalisation of aircraft for Malta, where they operated from all-weather airfields for the most part, was not as important as for the Middle East, where sand was the bugbear, but the Malta fighters came from the Middle East reserves and in point of fact the first Spitfires destined for the Middle East were retained for the defence of Malta.

There was also an over-insurance in the United Kingdom against enemy air attack, while the threat of invasion still lasted, and, even sporadic attacks by enemy 'hit and run' aircraft caused considerable disruption in industry. In retrospect this might seem to have been a short-sighted policy, but priority had still to be given to the protection of the centre of government and, in particular, of production. The ordeals of the Battle of Britain and the bombing of London and other cities were still fresh in people's minds.

Perhaps the most intractable problem for the air reinforcement of Malta was one of geography. With Malta under siege and the Cyrenaican hump occupied by the enemy the campaign in the Middle East had become largely a struggle for air bases; reinforcement of Malta by short-range aircraft was only practicable by the use of the time-consuming Takoradi route or the use of aircraft-carriers in a major naval operation. These reinforcement aircraft when deck-borne suffered from corrosion and the additional hazards from intensive enemy air attack when they landed. Also there were severe limitations on the use of petrol.

I am grateful for this but it does not alter my opinion.

My criticism would be unfounded if there were no Spitfires available in Britain to send to Malta, but the official figure of fighters available in Britain in December 1941 was nearly 2,000.

This should be compared with the situation in 1940. On 9 July 1940 there were fifty fighter squadrons and in late September 1940 there were fifty-eight. This does not mean that Fighter Command was stronger at the end of the battle than at the beginning since 450 personnel including many of the most experienced pilots had been killed and a further number had been wounded. No precise figures for the number of fighters available on these two dates appear to be known, but it can be said that, discounting the few squadrons of Blenheims and Defiants, the numbers of Spitfires and Hurricanes available on both dates would be between 600 and 800.

From these facts it is clear that up to 200 Spitfires could have been spared for Malta in July 1941 and still have left about double the fighters in the U.K. that were available to Dowding for winning the Battle of Britain.

Since the government decided to tell the R.A.F. to do what the Navy was built for and concurrently to neglect what its Fighter Arm was built for, it is worth studying the result during the sixteen months between Germany's invasion of Russia (which precluded simultaneous attack on Britain) and the victory at Alamein, that is, between 22 June 1941 and 7 November 1942.

There were six convoy operations to Malta which succeeded in landing about 231,000 tons of supplies of every kind. There was the ruse to run two merchant ships through Vichy French waters which failed. There were also four successful visits by the 2,600 ton minelayer *Welshman*, one by her sister ship *Manxman*, and about thirty by store-carrying submarines. These combined efforts added a further 6,000 tons to the total.

The large fast merchantmen employed were the Western Allies' most valuable type of cargo carrier. Statistics of the six convoys show:

	Merchant Ships	Battleships	Aircraft Carriers	Cruisers	Destroyers
Involved	50	8	8	32	118
Interned	2				
Damaged	7	1	1	7	8
Sunk	20		1	2	7

If there had been Navy and Air based on Malta and in charge of the situation, convoys must have been larger, with additional tankers, but undoubtedly casualties would have been a fraction of those suffered. Concurrently the R.A.F. would have had that opportunity which was sought to force the enemy air to come and fight over a small defined area. It was just about the only situation in this world wide war where the protagonists of 'wing' and 'balbo' fighter tactics could have exploited their theories.

17

AFTER the attack of 6 March on our base, when *P36* and *P39* were both seriously damaged and my command ship, the fuel lighter HMS *Talbot* sunk, as soon as I had established that the damaged submarines were in Sam MacGregor's capable hands and that Marsham and Pop Giddings were getting assistance for our cut water main and electricity supply and telephone, I set out across the harbour to report our situation to Admiral Leatham.

I needed exercise to clear my head of diesel fumes which we had been inhaling from our oil-soaked base, so instead of the short cut up the ditch and through the R.A.F. offices I landed at Ferry Steps and climbed the stone stairs to Palace Square and scrambled over the occasional debris in Strada Reale towards the demolished Opera House and then down steps to Naval H.Q.

As I passed the lace shop of Carmella Cassar, noticing with joy that it was intact, Carmella came to her doorway and said, 'Please, captain, come in for a minute. I have something to ask you.' I entered and she led me to her back room where a velvet cloth covered something on the table. Carmella continued, 'These, captain, are of no further use to me, as was once the case to their previous owners, will you buy them from me?' Lifting the cloth I saw two priceless Fabergé jewel cases both of solid gold, both about $1\frac{1}{2}$ inches deep. The smaller was about 4 inches by 3 inches internal measurement in deep prussian blue external enamel and a motif of red roses on the blue background. The larger stood on four claw legs and was about $5\frac{1}{2}$ inches by 4 inches internal measurement. The colour of the enamel I cannot recall with certainty but I think it was the same deep blue, for my attention was drawn to the splendid spray of diamonds on the lid's centre in a 'Prince of Wales' feather motif, with the diamonds at the ends of three 'feathers' about the size of the cross-section of a standard lead pencil, the clasp was also heavily jewelled.

'Where on earth did you get these, Carmella?' I exclaimed.

'A member of the Russian royal family's staff sold them to me when HMS *Marlborough* called here in April 1919. They needed sterling currency then and that is what I need now, captain.'

'Well, how much are you asking for them?'

'Just the same as I gave for them, £300.'

As I sat and gazed in amazement a feeling of revulsion set in. Here was I with two damaged submarines at the base and no amenities for the flotilla, bargaining for loot from the Russian revolution.

I replied, 'Thank you, Carmella, I will let you know very shortly, but at the moment we are in a bit of a pickle over at Lazaretto and I must report to V.A. Malta at once.'

These two caskets were, I am told, worth between £5,000 and £25,000 at the time and now are beyond estimate. They were the jewel cases of the Dowager Empress.

I forgot about them for a week, and then thought I should not let such a chance pass by, so I went to Carmella again and said, 'I will give you £300 for those caskets.'

'I'm sorry, captain, but I sold them that evening.'

This I have never regretted, for I feel sure I would have taken them with me when I left Malta, and as I spent 4½ hours in the sea north of Tobruk on that occasion, these priceless works of art would have ended at the bottom, possibly with me still clutching them. The situation was unsuited to antique dealing, or to money grubbing.

It was during March that a heavy bomb hit the quadrangle at Lazaretto devoted to farm pursuits and the sailors' pets. At that time it was tenanted by a sow and her litter, a large number of rabbits in hutches, the property of individuals, and one irascible turkey cock whose bad temper was attributable to sympathetic sailors who would soak dried peas in their tot of rum and then feed them to him.

I made a signal to a submarine returning from patrol to remain at sea a further two days since a direct hit on the farm compound had killed stock which must be cleared up.

The C.-in-C. signalled, 'Report farm casualties,' and I replied, 'One sow and litter, about 100 rabbits and one turkey. Casualties from shock are mincing down satisfactorily.'

That was virtually the end of farm and pet keeping, largely

because walks to gather rabbit food were no longer a sane re-creation.

It will be seen that the situation recorded in my official report (in Appendix 3) became really serious in March after Lazaretto was largely demolished and the heat was turned on to the submarines either in port, in the dockyard or on the harbour bottom. It was now that I thanked God for my gallant commandos, who, organised into working parties, worked through the nights in the dockyard changing battery cells with cracked containers. A difficult, slow, precision job with each two-volt cell weighing three hundredweight, and with sulphuric acid slopping from the cracked cells while air raids were in progress overhead.

The dockyard workmen did not work when a raid was on, nor can men work day and night on the starvation ration of 1,000 calories a day or less. How glad I was at this time that all those porkers were available to our flotilla and base staff to keep us fully energetic.

Had it not been for the military working parties of my commandos any submarine that got into dockyard hands would never have got out again; as it was we kept up the circulation of submarines going on patrol, which averaged about four always at sea and a similar number hidden on the harbour bottom to be repaired at night unless damage prevented their diving. A nice rest on patrol was indeed popular, while the submarines' successes steadily took their toll.

The heavy attacks during March led to damage to *Upright* on 2 March and to *P36* and *P39* on 5 March, as well as the sinking of HMS *Talbot*. Meanwhile *Urge* was undergoing refit from 26 February on.

The serious events of 5 March had made me order all submarines to be dived in harbour during daylight hours and, as a consequence *P35* was seriously damaged on 8 March. We had suddenly started losing submarines to the dangers of repair on the surface at the rate of one every two days, and I only had ten submarines.

On 9 March I summoned a staff conference with all C.O.s attending. *P31* (Kershaw) and *Una* (Pat Norman) were on patrol, and so was *Sokol* but the First Lieutenant, George Kowziolkowski, was in command in order to give Boris a rest, so I sent a message to Commander Boris Karnicki asking him to be with us.

Those attending were Tanner and MacGregor and the following C.O.s: Lieutenant P. R. Harrison (*P34*), Lieutenant S. L. Maydon *P35*), Lieutenant H. N. Edmonds (*P36*), Lieutenant N. Marriot (*P39*), Lt.-Cdr. M. D. Wanklyn (*Upholder*), Lt.-Cdr. E. P. Tomkinson (*Urge*), Lt.-Cdr. E. A. Woodward (*Unbeaten*), and Commander Boris Karnicki (*Sokol*).

Certain things were common knowledge to all of us when we assembled at this meeting and I knew no more than anyone else. Above all was the encroachment of the Luftwaffe over Lazaretto and Marsamxett harbour. Due to shortage of A.A. ammunition an order had had to be given that only bombers could be engaged by our A.A. defences. As early as December submarines entering harbour had been machine-gunned by fighters and Pat Norman (in command) had been shot in the neck when off Fort St Elmo.

Now in March the Me 109s patrolled Marsamxett harbour at 200 feet and I had watched these fighter pilots give a leisurely wave of the hand as they passed Lazaretto. I remember in particular a young submarine officer running into our shelter as a bombing raid was approaching and commenting, 'The Luftwaffe are down to their pansies now. A fighter pilot just waved to me and the bastard had painted finger nails!' If he had had painted finger nails such a detail might well be discernible. We had the impression that the enemy was crowding in for the kill.

It was in this situation that I addressed the meeting. I said that I needed to know my C.O.'s candid opinion on one matter. How could we most effectively fight back? It was clear that we must not lose more submarines and in my opinion this meant keeping our submarines at sea. I was sure that all would agree that to leave Malta was unthinkable, it would be a direct blow to civilian morale. If we could keep five submarines at sea we would be doing as well as we ever had. To achieve this it seemed to me that there was only one way. The submarine on return from patrol must enter harbour after sunset. The old crew would then refuel and embark torpedoes. A new crew, made up from submarines sunk or under repair and spare crew, should then embark and take over during the middle watch, so as to sail and clear the harbour before dawn. In fact we must do what British submarines had never done before, use two complete crews for each submarine.

This, I continued, seemed our best course in this tough situation; we should remember, however, that just a year earlier things were bad, but by May the Luftwaffe had left Sicily for other duties, so it seemed possible that since Spitfires were now actually operating from Malta our future should be assured if we could adapt ourselves to these temporary inconveniences. It seemed probable that the enemy would leave us shortly to campaign elsewhere. I asked for their frank opinions.

Wanklyn said, 'I would be quite happy to do that, provided I always return to *Upholder* on alternate patrols and we don't get shuffled round the whole Flotilla.' I confirmed that he would only operate *Upholder*.

Boris Karnicki said, 'Speaking for the Poles, we would wish to be in on this and I assure you that we will play our full part.' This was a remarkably handsome offer which I greatly appreciated, but I heard later that his superiors in London considered that he had exceeded his powers of decision. They were not in a position to know or to judge our desperate needs. Other C.O.s agreed without enthusiasm that there seemed no other choice, except Tomkinson who remained silent.

MacGregor spoke of the advance report on defects he would require by radio the night before arrival to ensure a timely turn round. It seemed that my proposal was accepted and I concluded that Tanner and I would work out a roster and we dispersed.

Half an hour later there was a knock at my door and the tall figure of Tomkinson entered. He was overcome with emotion and could hardly speak. 'Sir, I must tell you that *Urge* is mine and I cannot agree to your proposal. Of course you are right, we cannot leave Malta at this juncture, nor can I hand over my submarine to another C.O. and another crew. This is something quite different from the spare C.O. taking an occasional patrol to rest the C.O. This means that *Urge* is handled and looked after by a completely new crew, that my work and my training of her ship's company will count for naught on alternate patrols. Why? Just because some enemy airmen are piddling around overhead? My *Urge* is one hundred per cent efficient and my duty is to command her and to beat this devilish outfit. Sir, I cannot leave my ship in a crisis, that is the last thing I can do, and if you insist that this scheme is essential I must – yes, I *must* – resign my command!' He broke down and wept.

I was deeply shaken. 'But Tommo, if that is the way you feel then that is how things must be. I was only flying a kite, and I thought you were all in agreement. Why didn't you say this at the meeting?'

'I could not trust myself not to make a fool of myself, nor can I go against your judgement in this matter. It was only when the meeting was over that I came to the definite conclusion that I cannot follow you in this, and because I know I can't and I hate to be disloyal I have no way out. Please let the rest of the flotilla carry out your scheme but leave me in my own ship, I beg you. I can stand continuous patrol with confidence and come in to refuel and embark torpedoes as necessary.'

'I assure you,' I replied, 'that nobody but you and your ship's company shall take *Urge* to sea. As regards the others I shall see how things go.'

It was now clear to me that the views expressed by Bickford to the then First Lord, Churchill, in December 1939 were indeed idle chatter (as Admiral Horton told me later in the war). The fact was that my C.O.s, whose opinions I respected and whose loyalty was always certain, accepted my proposal only as a 'last ditch' decision, while one officer, whose whole character was powerful yet utterly loyal, refused, and broke down in telling me so. I sat and thought for a while, chewing over and appreciating Tommo's remark, 'Just because some enemy airmen are piddling round overhead.' It seemed to me that although they had already knocked down our Lazaretto roofs, converting us to troglodytes, and damaged three submarines, perhaps Tomkinson was right; perhaps I was exaggerating future difficulties due to recent misfortunes. At the moment I must send the maximum number of submarines to sea which was far safer than in harbour, and not resort to double crews in any submarine until I was forced to do so, which was not yet.

Admiral Cunningham's original directive to me was very clear. 'Do what you think, Simpson, and if I do not agree with you I will very soon let you know.' He had kept to his word precisely and the decision was up to me.

In the next few days I sailed every operational submarine and was richly rewarded, but before continuing my narrative I wish to conclude my observations on the very important matter of the British sailor's personal pride in his command and in his ship's company, which is absorbed by the whole team and so creates an unbeatable spirit which only dies with the ship or in this case with the submarine. A concrete example of the overriding power of spiritual values over material considerations.

While preparing this book I wrote to Admiral Sir Charles Little to inquire his opinion and whether to his knowledge exchange crews had ever been resorted to in his experience. I received this reply from Admiral Little, who joined submarines in 1902.

My dear Simpson,

I agree with all you say about splitting crews but it will interest you that on the very first submarine manoeuvres in 1904, the five Hollands and *A1*, defending Spithead against the Home Fleet, lasted for a week and we did split our crews, but had one half the proper crew in each lot. I had Holland No. 4 then and Tubby Keyes (Sir Roger's brother) was my opposite number with my sub. We worked alternate days.

Although *A1* was lost with all hands the Admiralty decided the submarine had some military value and continued to develop them.

In my letter to Admiral Little I had also asked him why Admiral Horton had told me of difficulties during the First World War through Winston Churchill seeking opinions direct from junior officers. He replied, 'Winston always had that habit of trying to check the opinions of senior officers by engaging their juniors. In the first war when he was so much younger than the admirals this was particularly difficult.'

This is an interesting comment which made me realise that when Churchill was appointed First Lord of the Admiralty in 1911 he was (with all his talent and military experience) at least twenty years younger than the naval members of the Board of Admiralty, the Commanders-in-Chief of our Fleets, our Home Ports and our foreign stations. In fact, they were all old enough to be his father. His inclination to doubt their wisdom is surely as old as human nature.

Following the conference on 9 March I sent every seaworthy submarine, four in all, to sea in the next few days, and since I was informed by Admiral Leatham that a convoy operation from Alexandria might be attempted at very short notice, I sailed them all northwards to patrol focal areas so as to be available at short notice to form patrol lines to intercept units of the Italian fleet if there was a southerly move against the Malta convoy. This had a most fortunate result.

On 14 March, at about noon off the east Calabrian coast, *P34* had closed the shore in an abortive attempt to intercept an escorted ship. Taking a brief final look at his target against a background of the land Lieutenant Harrison was amazed to see a large Italian U-boat surface and stop directly ahead of him. He crept within close range and put two torpedoes into the U-boat *Millo;* then he surfaced to pick up survivors. He recovered four officers and ten ratings but was so close to the shore that a machine gun opened fire on him and he withdrew, sailing direct for Malta to land prisoners.

Harrison said to me on arrival, 'I asked an officer, "Why on earth did you surface and stop in broad daylight?" The reply was, "The captain wanted to smoke." ' This surely deserves to be a famous epitaph for a submarine captain.

P34, having embarked torpedoes, returned to patrol. *Unbeaten*, following her northward, encountered the escorted transport *Pisani* and hit her with one torpedo but she did not sink. The next day Woodward sighted the Italian U-boat *Guglielmotti* making surface passage and promptly sank her. There were no survivors.

Upholder and *P36* followed on 14 March and, since no date for the Malta-bound convoy operation had been fixed, I told Wanklyn to mark time by keeping an eye on Brindisi, but warned him to keep clear of probable minefields. *P36* was to go direct to a central position in the Gulf of Taranto so as to be there in any sudden emergency.

On 18 March, off Brindisi, Wanklyn sighted a U-boat returning to port down the swept channel. He at once closed the enemy, passing straight through the protecting minefields, and sank the U-boat *Tricheco* within a mile of Brindisi breakwater. He then withdrew southwards and that night sank one trawler and damaged a second, with his twelve-pounder gun, in the Otranto area.

So it was that these four submarines on passage to their cover positions sank three U-boats in four days, and caused other havoc. This was a quick reply to our troubles in harbour and emphasised the importance of their vigilant efficiency.

Urge had been undergoing annual refit from the end of February and Tomkinson had been most anxious to get her to sea.

On 23 March *Urge* and *P31* (Kershaw) both sailed for the Tyr-rhenian sea. *P31* was to establish patrol off Elba and advertise his presence in an endeavour to draw A/S forces north from our usual hunting grounds. I felt that Tomkinson had been under great strain in shooting down my policy for survival, and that a bit of jollity and an Army companion would do him good, so Captain Wilson, Royal Artillery, and his commando partner a marine corporal, with the tools of trade (canoe, explosives, etc.) sailed in *Urge*, which was to operate between Naples and Messina and do very much as he pleased for the confusion of the king's enemies.

He had a highly successful patrol. Finding no targets off Naples he moved south to the Gulf of Policastro and on the night of 29–30 March blew up an electric train, which was seen to roll down the embankment. Immediately the demolition party had re-embarked a ship was sighted to seaward and Tomkinson decided on surface gun action, however after scoring three hits the target replied with effective gunfire, and *Urge* was repulsed. Course was continued southwards towards Messina and at 0900 on 1 April the Italian cruiser *Banda Nere* was sighted northbound at 21 knots, escorted by two destroyers on her way to Spezia to dock.

The cruiser was promptly sunk and no counterattack was made since both destroyers were occupied rescuing survivors. *Urge* had no torpedoes left so quit the scene, arriving at Malta on 6 April. She remained in port for only two or three days before leaving our 'bedlam' for the life Tomkinson preferred – in his beloved *Urge* with the company he had trained to such efficiency and to the command he would under no circumstances, through enemy duress, reliquish. He had fully justified his point of view.

So at sea the flotilla's operations reached their peak of success against naval targets at this time of crisis.

P31, off Elba, attacked a small convoy and although nothing was sunk the ships turned about and retired, so our presence in the northern waters had been advertised.

Our fortunes at Lazaretto, in Marsamxett harbour and in the Dockyard must now be followed from mid-March onwards. On 17 March *Sokol* returned from patrol having sighted no targets in fourteen days off the east Tunisian coast and her captain, Com-mander Karnicki, rejoined his ship. The next morning while manoeuvring to come alongside the base for rapid overhaul bombers attacked her and a near miss shattered many cells in her battery, which put her out of action and made a period in the dockyard imperative.

The gallant fight put up by *Sokol* during the next thirty days of hiding by day and repairs by night is detailed in Appendix 4. She finally sailed from Malta before dawn on 17 April with four patches on her pressure hull and over 200 holes through the casing, both battery sections exuding a small amount of chlorine gas, and only one propeller functioning.

I had acquired a small motorcycle now that boats and cabs no longer existed and I drove slowly through the night for the nine miles from Lazaretto to Dockyard Creek to bid farewell to my gallant Poles. It was a good starlight night and there were remarkably few bomb craters or obstructions on the road. One jetty light came on opposite *Sokol*'s conning-tower and Boris came down and bade me farewell.

'You must let me know, Boris, when you are west of Sardinia then I shall be able to stop worrying about you, but make your signal short.' He had just got back on his bridge when I added, with all the naïve optimism which invariably controlled my thoughts and actions, 'I shall be seeing you soon, Boris, but if I should miss you in England what will be your address in Poland?'

'My address in Poland?' said Boris in his deep voice and with obvious surprise. 'Ah, now let me think.' His officers and crew, who were about to cast off the wires, were all listening intently, as Boris pronounced. 'Captain! When you come to Poland after this war just ask for the office of the Commisar for the Socialisation of Women and walk right in.'

There was subdued laughter fore and aft and a good laugh from me. It was the first time that I had had an inkling that *Sokol*'s company were in their hearts fighting solely for a cause rather than for their country.

Sokol slid forward from the wharf into the night. Two days later while doing the long haul at 100 feet through the Sicilian Channel minefield, with the crew coughing from chlorine, she took a dangerous angle bow down and seemed to fall bodily to 300 feet – she had run into a sea-bed fresh water spring. It was a close call in its unexpectedness. Six days after leaving Malta I got a signal '*Sokol* to *S10*. Proceeding.' It was all I wanted to know.

On 20 March a convoy left Alexandria for Malta. It comprised four ships, *Breconshire*, *Clan Campbell*, *Pampas*, and *Talabot*, while the naval force to fight it through under the command of Admiral Vian comprised four light cruisers and eleven destroyers, and also detailed for smoke laying were the old cruiser *Carlisle* and the *Avon Vale*.

This convoy operation, which led to the 'Second Battle of Sirte', is fully described in the official history and was a brilliant success against great odds, culminating in *Pampas* and *Talabot* arriving intact in Grand Harbour, *Clan Campbell* being sunk and *Breconshire* damaged, but anchored, in Marsaxlok bay on the south east of the island.

As soon as I was informed that the convoy was sailing I disposed my four submarines (sent for this purpose a week earlier): *Upholder* to support *P36* in the Gulf of Taranto and *P37* and *Unbeaten* to the southern approaches to Messina.

Shortly after midnight 21–22 March, on a black night with low cloud, the Italian striking force passed within asdic listening range but out of sight of *P36*. Lieutenant Edmonds listened and made his estimate and at 0400 made an enemy report of probably one battleship, six cruisers and a destroyer flotilla. There were in fact one battleship and four destroyers, while three cruisers and three destroyers passed undetected close in shore from Messina to the north of *Unbeaten*.

After the battle the Italian force was heard by *Upholder* at 1720/23 as they were returning to Taranto in rough weather and rain squalls. Wanklyn closed at full speed and sixteen minutes later he could identify the upper works and funnels of a battleship. He fired a full salvo at 4,000 yards, but this failed due to an enemy alteration of course at the same time. The Italian cruiser force returning to Messina passed up the Sicilian coast inside the patrol position of *P34*, a disappointing result, but as already stated one of these cruisers was sunk by *Urge* on 1 April.

The Italian force having returned to harbour the four submarines were recalled, arriving at Malta on 27 March except for *P36* who arrived two days later.

It will be noted that three days after Kesselring had arranged to mount his blitz which nothing was to survive on his Fuehrer's orders, half of a vital convoy arrived unscathed in Grand Harbour, due to the brilliant conduct of the escorting forces, the low cloud that favoured us and the extreme efforts of the fighter cover on the last day during the approach to harbour. It can well be imagined that the huge air resources of the Axis in Sicily were thrown in to redress this defeat, but still, with weather favouring defence and the tenacity of the R.A.F. fighters, these two invaluable ships remained intact for two more whole days – but what is even more important for three whole nights which were virtually air raid free. Very little cargo was unloaded.

From Lazaretto nothing could be seen of what was occurring in Grand Harbour, and it must have been on 26 March that I was visiting naval H.Q. and met Air Vice Marshal Lloyd on my way. His tenacious but normally cheerful face brooded thunder. 'It's a disgrace, a most damnable affair! Three whole days and nights of inaction and now they're both hit and on fire! Its disgraceful,' and passed on.

The A.O.C.'s rage was surely fully justified. The extraordinary effort and skill required to get the ships to port, the blessing of continuing cloudy weather after arrival and the tense minute by minute defence by his fighters against fearful odds, and now our salvation a bonfire. In his book *Briefed to Attack* Sir Hugh Lloyd has given a vivid description of this whole episode, and he quotes the total cargo discharged as 807 tons, about half of which a volunteer R.A.F. party seeking out Spitfire spares had landed and carried to safety. In the official naval history Roskill quotes 'only about a fifth of the 26,000 tons loaded for Malta was safely landed.' I think this very big discrepancy between 807 tons and 5,200 tons is due to Lloyd's figure referring to cargo discharged before the two ships were sunk and Roskill's figure including all the cargo salvaged from the burned-out ships in shallow water. Salvage went on for some months and I understand a considerable quantity of tinned foods was usable, nevertheless it is difficult to believe that anywhere near one-fifth of the convoy's cargo came ashore since nothing came from *Clan Campbell* and *Breconshire*.

There was a desperate shortage of cranes and lighters, and I do not think there was one operational tug, although there were several power boats. I gained the impression at first hand that there was a stunned tiredness due to the weight of the daylight attack and also that the stevedore labour was half starved. Under these conditions the well-known and popular personality with the Maltese workers and the dynamic leadership of Admiral Ford was sadly missing.

It was unfortunate, but presumably there were very good reasons for the general post in the top naval appointments in the Mediterranean at the very moment of Malta's crisis. This is what happened.

On 19 January Admiral Ford, who had been for five years the powerful and trusted personality around which Malta's naval improvisation and defence had been formed, was relieved despite his offer to stay on. Admiral Leatham took his place as problems rose to a crescendo. Leatham was experienced, able and imperturbable, but new to a job that was a nightmare. He was not known by the rank and file. He was more an intellectual and administrator than the 6 foot 2 inch commanding extrovert that Admiral Ford had been. Almost immediately Leatham took over Sir William Dobbie's health broke down. In fact, on arrival in Britain, Dobbie at once entered hospital for a major abdominal operation. Leatham was automatically Dobbie's successor pending another appointment from the British Government and during March and April his duties were divided between 'Understudying the Governor' and 'Vice Admiral Malta'.

On 1 April Admiral Cunningham left Alexandria and Vice Admiral Pridham-Wippell took over, as acting C.-in-C. Mediterranean until relieved by Admiral Sir Henry Harwood on 21 May. On 7 May Lord Gort arrived in Malta and Sir William Dobbie, a shadow of his former self, left the island the next day.

To what extent the failure to unload *Pampas* and *Talabot* between 23 and 26 March was due to the Navy I do not know. I do know that a state of affairs already chaotic was not simplified for Admiral Leatham at this time.

18

On 1 April *Urge* sank the cruiser *Bande Nere* at 0930 north of Messina and retribution followed in five hours. Between 1430 and 1500 an intense air attack on submarines developed. *P36*, alongside Lazaretto, was sunk by a direct hit and was held to the pillars of Lazaretto until the berthing wires snapped. *Unbeaten*, lying on the bottom of Lazaretto creek, had her torpedo tubes distorted and so was rendered operationally useless but still seaworthy. *Pandora*, unloading torpedoes at Hamilton Wharf in the dockyard, was cut in two and sank with the loss of twenty-six lives. The first lieutenant and engineer officer from the destroyer *Lance* in a nearby dock dashed to her rescue and were mown down as the first lieutenant lost a hand and the engineer lieutenant a leg in their brave endeavours. In an hour I had lost three submarines.

On 4 April the Greek submarine *Glaukos*, which had been refitting for three months and was ready to sail, but with her officers killed in Lazaretto, was also sunk. *Pandora* and *Glaukos* were not of the 10th Flotilla, and our strength was now six operational submarines and also *Sokol* and *Unbeaten* beyond repair. My hope was that these two could be sailed for Britain. This was finally achieved.

Somehow the dockyard had got *P35* repaired although her forward compartment had been flooded throughout. The efforts of Mr Joblin, the constructor officer were beyond all praise, while he had the daunting task of endeavouring to repair the destroyers *Lance* and *Havock*, and the light cruiser *Penelope* in addition to our problems.

I could only form my own opinion of the future and keep it to myself. It seemed that invasion was imminent and the presence of submarines the only slight insurance against seaborne transports. To quit Malta was more than ever unthinkable.

At this moment, unknown to me, the acting C.-in-C. at Alexandria was being asked by the Admiralty to give his views on sending the 1st Flotilla from Alexandria to Colombo to strenghten the situation against the Japanese fleet in those waters and to move the 10th Flotilla to Alexandria. Admiral Pridham-Wippell was strongly against this, pointing out that the U class submarines were too slow to be of service except from Malta. This was indeed true.

At Alexandria Captain Ruck Keene had taken over the submarine command and it was decided that he should fly to Malta at the first opportunity to see me. Admiral Leatham, (V.A. Malta) quietly imperturbable, assured me he would back any decision I might be forced to make but hoped I would find that the flotilla could stay, for he could only rely on submarines if seaborne invasion started. (It is now known that this was intended for mid-May.) Admiral Leatham however warned me that German E-boats had arrived in force at Licata on the south coast of Sicily and were laying mines at night both in the approaches to the Grand Harbour and to the south of the island and could be picked up on radar but the mining positions could not be fixed. This was most serious news. I asked whether radar-fitted Beaufighters could shoot them up but was told that this was impossible with the extreme efforts to maintain even a few day fighters.

This was the position on 5 April and I then realised that only a decisive reinforcement of Spitfires sufficient to gain control of the air and change the picture could justify our remaining. It was the unknown extent and position of mining which was the decisive blow; we had more or less learned to live with the Luftwaffe by mid-April.

Upholder was ready for sea and Wanklyn asked to return to the Adriatic, his experience off Brindisi having whetted his appetite. As I considered his sinking of the U-boat entering Brindisi had been highly dangerous I sent him in the opposite direction to land two Arab agents in the Gulf of Sousse and to rendezvous with the *Unbeaten* on 10 April off Lampedusa, to transfer his commando canoeists for passage to Britain. This was done. *Upholder*'s rendezvous with *Unbeaten* on the night of the 10–11 April was the last that was heard of the gallant *Upholder*, Lieutenant-Commander Wanklyn, V.C., D.S.O. and two bars, and his brave company.

Unbeaten, with her twisted torpedo tubes, and her gallant band under the stalwart command of Woodward, got back to Britain. *P31*, *P35*, *Una* and *Urge* all carried out short patrols in the area between Cape Bon and Lampedusa during April so that they had the 'sanctuary' of patrol conditions rather than the harbour blitz. They were not in considered offensive positions, but were within forty-eight hours recall if the need arose. Nevertheless *P35* torpedoed one ship and sank another, while *Una* also sank a southbound 5,000 ton ship.

P34 was being overhauled at night and spending daylight on the bottom in seventy feet of water between the torpedo baffles, which were near the entrance to Marsamxett Harbour.

I cannot pass on from this first half of April without referring to the supreme efforts and appalling experience of the five surface ships in dockyard hands. I visited *Sokol* every few days when she was unable to dive and hidden beneath camouflage nets. On 5 April this brought me to the dockyard and I met Lieutenant Robin Watkins (whose father had saved my career after attacking *Hood* in 1935). He had been in command of *Havock* at Matapan, then through the Crete operations and his ship had limped into Malta damaged in the last convoy operation. Despite his smart appearance and usual confident smile I could see he was strained to the limit. 'How are you, Robin, and will you be getting away?' I inquired.

'Yes, tomorrow I hope if our luck holds.' It did, and in the middle of the night of the 6–7 April *Havock* ran aground south of Cape Bon, his company and passengers becoming Vichy prisoners. I know nothing of the circumstances but can well imagine that all were at a pitch of fatigue where navigating a ship at thirty knots in order to be clear of air attack by dawn was beyond their endurance and judgement.

The cruiser *Penelope* undocked on 8 April, a bomb falling in the centre of the dock just afterwards. That evening Captain Angus Nichol, although wounded, took her to sea and at full speed to safety, arriving Gibraltar on 10 April. Her ordeal for the past fortnight while she had been the centre of air attack can only be vaguely imagined unless actually experienced.

The destroyers *Lance* and *Kingston* were both heavily hit in dry dock and destroyed with many casualties; the captain of *Kingston* was among those killed. The destroyer *Gallant*, completing a long refit from war damage, was seaborne at a wharf where she was holed and subsequently beached, never to float again. The agony of our wounded surface forces was over; the cruiser alone survived.

During this first half of April, when the fury was turned on the harbour area, bombing became general over the whole district from Vittoriosa north-west to St Julian's bay, where Surgeon Captain Cheeseman was killed with his wife when their house collapsed upon them only fifty yards from Greta and Gravy Tench's home. Three 'rest flats' for submarine officers were flattened and we felt that casualties would be certain amongst the sailors' flats. Somehow Hubert Marsham contrived transport for operational crews to the seaside rest camp at Ghain Tuffiela on the far side of the island, while their submarines were tended, submerged by day and refitting by night, by submariners whose submarines were sunk.

The marine pensioner in charge, delighted to be in commission again, hoisted the White Ensign on the flagpole. The wide-ranging enemy fighters spotted it, and that day wrecked the whole camp with cannon fire. The sailors were mostly bathing, there were no casualties and by the evening the men were back to the sanctuary of the Lazaretto shelters.

On 17 April I was told that forty-eight Spitfires were expected in the next two or three days. What, I wondered, was the magic number of Spitfires needed to win a substantial victory over the island; to be followed by the advantages of defence aided by radar over offence from airfields sixty to ninety miles distant, so that the R.A.F. could regain balance and acquire reinforcement. What was the critical number? Was it forty-eight? That seemed slender indeed. Perhaps this number was seventy or even a hundred, but soon we would know. Once the R.A.F. got a short respite and reorganised after devastation I was sure A.O.C. would mop up the E-boats with night fighters in quick time. It was the E-boats and minelaying which were lethal to submarine operations. I knew our fighter pilots were proven to be superior by a remarkable margin of skill, while the Spitfire was feared by the Luftwaffe. Would forty-eight do the trick? I wondered with hope as I called in at the office of the Group Captain Air Staff.

I greeted my friend and airman collaborator in operations, we were both of the same rank. He confirmed that forty-eight Spitfires were due on the 19th or 20th, so I inquired, 'Will that number turn the tide? It is splendid news, but can forty-eight Spitfires fight a decisive battle?'

He replied, 'I doubt it. We shall, of course, only be using twelve at a time!'

'What,' I exclaimed, 'when you have at last a consignment of forty-eight you are going to have them shot down in penny numbers?'

'You don't understand the problems of servicing on arrival, refuelling, ammunitioning, plus the long passage just flown, plus briefing and all these problems. To imagine we can have more than twelve airborne at a time is just wishful thinking. I'm sorry to disappoint you but it just isn't a practical operation.'

I dared not make a further remark, I went straight to Admiral Leatham and said, 'This decision spells doom, sir. If that is all they can do, what are these Spitfires being ferried here for? Not for the relief of Malta, that is obvious. It means my flotilla must withdraw before we are utterly mined in or all sunk. Please sir, will you go and persuade A.O.C. to organise things so that all forty-eight can go up and fight?'

Admiral Leatham replied very quietly, 'No, I can't, Shrimp. It would be wrong for me to go to A.O.C. and interfere with his arrangements, also it would be useless. It would endanger future cooperation, I fear. I agree that what you say should be done if it can be done, but I must not interfere and I'm sure you understand why. I have no objection to you pressing your point of view as strongly as you like, but not to A.O.C. personally, he's got enough worries and I am sure would do this if his staff put it forward as practicable and the right course.'

I went immediately to Air Commodore Bowen-Buscarlett, the senior air staff officer, and put forward my contention most earnestly. He replied, 'That's easily said but is operationally impossible. It simply cannot be done.' He paused and added, 'I am not at all sure that it is the right thing to do either, to risk everything in one fling.'

The rest of our conversation was fatuous, but since I remember it perfectly I will add it.

'Sir, if you were to go out into the street and ask the first ten children you met over the age of eight whether it would be best to send up forty-eight Spitfires initially or to send up twelve and hold thirty-six in reserve I will wager £5 that they would all say forty-eight.'

225

'Yes, possibly, but then children are not always right,' he said thoughtfully and not unkindly. With this crushing rejoinder I retired.

Now all was clear in my mind; as soon as I learned the Spitfires were destroyed the 10th Submarine Flotilla would leave for Alexandria but not until then. On 19 April I was told the Spitfires would come in next day.

I think it was sometime in the afternoon that, without the slightest warning, I suddenly saw the stalwart figure of my old friend Captain Philip Ruck Keene walking towards me at Lazaretto. He had, I think, flown in during the previous night and been to see V.A. Malta. We settled down to a talk and he asked me what my intentions were, in view of the situation. He brought no directive from C.-in-C. Mediterranean nor any comment from V.A. Malta, but he said, 'Max Horton told me to tell you that he realises the difficulties of your decision at this moment, but I was to tell you that since your losses on 1 April he feels it is time you pulled out because he cannot possibly replace such losses, particularly in trained officers, and he told me this before the loss of *Upholder*.'

'The decision,' I replied, 'has already been made. The Spitfires arrive tomorrow and will be elimated, chiefly on the ground, then I shall leave with a clear conscience.'

An air raid developed and all officers assembled in our dormitory tunnel with a rock blast screen in front of it. We sat in a long line facing the two-tier bunks and I chatted with Ruck Keene. Two 1,000 kilo bombs fell directly overhead, smothering us with rock dust and Sam MacGregor said, 'That's the Herrenvolk, but my bagpipes are down here.'

When the all clear went, Ruck Keene bade me farewell and assured me of a warm welcome at Alexandria. Just how he came and went or travelled back to Alexandria I am not sure. His visit was typical and helpful. I had had a common sense message from Admiral Horton which supported my reluctant decision.

Next day, 20 April, the Spitfires arrived, Kesselring reacted with all his might, the Ack Ack put up a terrific barrage, and the defence was inadequate. Some Spitfires were lost in the air but more were lost in their pens by flak damage. At dawn on 21 April there were twenty-seven operational and by that evening seventeen. On 30 April there were seven.

On the morning of 23 April I knew that U.S.S. *Wasp*'s effort on our behalf had been wiped out. I went to V.A. Malta and said that if I stayed longer we would lose all and gain nothing. He immediately agreed and told me to go ahead and he would inform the C.-in-C.

Departure under these circumstances took time. *P34* had been kept in harbour for refit alongside Lazaretto at night and at dawn each day she was moved to deep water near the harbour entrance and just inside the torpedo baffle. This consisted of mooring buoys joined by a 4½ inch steel wire supporting an old torpedo net.

Lieutenant Harrison and half his crew had taken over in preparation for sailing for Alexandria and dived his submarine beside the baffle at first light. German reconnaissance photographs showed nothing floating in either harbour and Lazaretto a shell, so on 24 April the Stukas dived on Marsamxett harbour and bombed it back and forth several times. On their last sortie, at about 5 pm, a 1,000 kilo bomb fell immediately to seaward of the baffle, displacing it. We immediately started calling *P34* on our submerged oscillator installed at Lazaretto. No oil appeared on the surface so we hoped she was still in one piece; after twenty minutes *P34* replied.

When darkness came *P34* signalled that he was stuck at 15 feet, so I pulled over with Sam MacGregor in a dinghy with a hacksaw and found the 4½ inch wire tight as a violin string across the conning-tower. Sam cut through it until it snapped with a report like a pistol shot and *P34* jumped to the surface. The bomb apparently exploded before hitting the bottom and material damage was negligible, but the crew were badly shaken.

Although bombing continued no further mishaps occurred.

The flotilla left Malta over the fortnight from 26 April:

P31 on the 26th;
Urge on the 27th;
P34 on the 29th;
Una on 4 May;
P35 on 10 May.

Mr Richard Casey (now Lord Casey) was flying to Cairo to take over the duties of High Commissioner Middle East and he kindly gave a lift to MacGregor and myself in a Lockheed Hudson that seemed chiefly full of mailbags; we got to Heliopolis at

0900/4 May and so to *S1* aboard HMS *Medway* in Alexandria harbour.

Hubert Marsham remained behind in command at Malta.

From the outbreak of war with Italy no press reporter had been allowed in Malta, but in February 1942 a freelance journalist then attached to the *News of the World* had thumbed a lift from Alexandria in a Beaufighter. He came to me in some distress in mid-April, saying that A.O.C. would not give him a passage back, that so far he had been prevented from sending a dispatch and that he was stuck on the island; we befriended him and Tomkinson agreed to take him to Alexandria.

As the days passed on board *Medway* the 10th flotilla slowly assembled. All except *Urge*, and so it gradually became a certainty that she was lost, most probably due to an E-boat mine a few miles from Malta. Lieutenant-Commander E. P. Tomkinson, D.S.O. and two bars and his brave company had survived their close friends in *Upholder* by only two weeks.

The four survivors of our small flotilla felt the loss acutely; it was natural that we all felt that if such olympian exponents of skill and judgement fall, then the odds against survival were slender. Worse news was to follow. *Porpoise* (Lieutenant Commander Bennington) brought in stores from Alexandria on 29 April and returned successfully, but *Olympus* arrived on 5 May from Gibraltar and left on 8 May with many survivors from *Pandora* and *P36* on board, making a total complement of eleven officers and eighty-seven ratings (six officers and thirty ratings as passengers) for return to Gibraltar. At dawn on 9 May military shore posts east of Valetta saw naked men struggling ashore. Twelve had swum six miles from *Olympus*, which had been mined, but not immediately sunk, shortly before midnight. These were the only survivors. In three weeks about half my fine command had been killed.

As I reflected bitterly over the losses and wondered how I might have avoided them I noted that none of these (*Upholder*, *Urge* and *Olympus*) had been sunk by the Luftwaffe. Nevertheless the lethal antennae mines laid in lines parallel with the shore a few miles off Grand Harbour could never have been laid by E-boats if radar-fitted aircraft could have operated by night, which during Kesselring's assault was impossible.

19

Our return to Malta no longer depended only upon gaining decisive and lasting air superiority. That would be stage one to be followed by the arrival of modern electronic minesweepers. Malta was our home and place of duty, we followed the island's fight from day to day.

I will quote from two sources to show how the R.A.F. regained air superiority and never again lost it. My source is the book by the man best qualified to know, the A.O.C., Air Vice Marshal Lloyd. His eye-witness account gives an accurate picture of events. (I have slightly abridged the account, but without altering the meaning or the impact.)

The setting of this narrative is that on the night of 8–9 May the USS *Wasp* with forty-eight Spitfires on board and HMS *Eagle* with seventeen were steaming east under heavy escort to launch their aircraft for Malta from a position south-west of Sardinia. Concurrently HMS *Welshman*, a 2,600 ton, 40 knot minelayer with Spitfire spares and smoke-making canisters on board, accompanied them, ready to break away under disguise with an extra funnel and other petty deceptions. She was to move into the Tyrrhenian sea to the eastward at leisurely speed, then to Malta at full speed during the night. Skill and good fortune favoured her.

Sir Hugh Lloyd's narrative states,

The night was quiet with not a single intruder; yet the sky was clear. There was no reinforcement traffic; only a Lodestar from the Middle East carrying our vital spares.

Soon after ten o'clock, Squadron Leader Grant called me from Pantellaria. 'Hold on for a few moments longer,' he said. At 10.30 he dived down over Ta Qali with sixteen of the sixty Spitfires which had been flown from two aircraft-carriers. Gracie had returned two days before and in six minutes he was sitting in the cockpit of a newly arrived Spitfire ready for combat. A few Spitfires were ready in *four minutes and the worst in seven minutes*. At 11.14 there was another alert and we all thought 'This is it.' The Germans were bound to know the time of the arrival of the Spitfires from their radar location and radio and Kesselring was certain to try to catch them on the ground before they could be re-fuelled and made ready for combat. The Spitfires roared off the runways – thirty-one of them – as about half of the sixty had yet to land. Soon the encircling patrol of Axis fighters came into view and one of our new pilots, on arriving over the Grand Harbour tried to do some formation flying with what he thought were those of his kind, but he woke up when a big piece had been blown out of his fuselage.

I did not like the look of the raid, as there was a far bigger time interval between the arrival of the formations of Spitfires than we had anticipated. Twenty-eight were still flying around the aerodromes or approaching the island when the A.A. bursts pointed out another forty German fighters at 12,000 feet and many of the Spitfires stood in grave risk of being bombed as they landed. However, twelve Ju88s seemed to come out of a hole in the clear blue sky at 17,000 feet, to drip down by easy stages of 2,000 or 3,000 feet at a time; and behind them, but much higher, were five Italian Cants in perfect formation, with forty or fifty fighters and possibly others too high to be seen. No one knew which aerodrome was to be the target until the last dive. I thought it would be Luqa, but, at the last moment, as it were, they all turned and went down to Hal Far. Huge clouds of dust and smoke began to rise which was to hang in the air for hours and, until it was blown out to sea in a fairly compact cloud mass, would restrict visibility. Two civilians and three soldiers had been killed and six soldiers and three civilians had been wounded and Hal Far was unserviceable for a few hours. We scanned the sky for more Ju88s and 87s but none came. It was an anti-climax.

The next alert was not until 1.30 and by that time we were in a strong position and improving on it with every hour. Another alert came at 2.40 and, since it was another fighter circus of twenty 109s to circle the Island, we decided to stay on the ground; we did not wish to become involved in a chase of the 109s and be caught re-fuelling. At 3.44 another gang of thirty fighters came into view and as the plan was to kill the bigger game – the bombers – there was nothing to do but wait in the dispersals.

The Axis flew about in our air until 1640 when there were signs, at last, of the bombers assembling over Sicily and the Spitfires were off – fifty-eight of them. Forty 109s appeared at 8,000 feet and higher in the sky, later on I counted fifteen Ju87s, ten Ju88s and five Cants. Although Luqa was normally a hot favourite, all of the bombs fell on Ta Qali, which made it necessary to switch the aircraft based there to Luqa and Hal Far. Two soldiers had been killed on the aerodrome, and in the fighting we had lost one pilot killed and two Spitfires damaged against an enemy loss of four destroyed (including three of the Cants) nine probably destroyed and seven damaged.

I do not suppose that anyone would have laid any odds against a strong attack at dusk. It seemed inevitable. As it did not come we were disappointed. The night which followed was not particularly noisy either – only sixteen intruders, of which a Beaufighter shot down one and the A.A. another.

The following day, 10 May, the *Welshman* was due in the Grand Harbour at 6 am. Her precious cargo of stores included such items as powdered milk, canned meat, dehydrated food-stuffs, ammunition, spares for the Spitfires, etc. *Welshman* arrived dead on time.

The day began with an alert at 5.40 for forty-five fighters and although we refused to have anything to do with them I thought they were subdued. They kept their height; well away from the island, and they did not even attempt a dive at the Safi strip. At 8.20 thirty-two more fighters came over and again we refused to be drawn. But at 10 o'clock there were signs of the bombers over Sicily, and soon fifty-two fighters circled the island, followed by the Ju88s and 87s and as they dived down on the *Welshman* I counted the close escort; there were sixty-two of them at least. Other alerts later in the day were for more fighters. At 18.10 however, the Spitfires were off again to meet the next bomber raid, which was also aimed at the *Welshman*; but not one bomb fell near her and having unloaded her freight she left that night.

The 10th May had been a great day and despite having been

on duty all day at the dispersal points (and they were due there again long before dawn the following morning) officers and men waited around for the final score. It was not unlike waiting to hear the result of a Grand National. The final score was twenty-three destroyed, seventeen probably destroyed and twenty-four damaged for the loss of one pilot missing and one Spitfire. All this counted for nothing however, when compared with the evening's news from Rome radio, which said that thirty-seven Axis aircraft had failed to return from the day's operations over Malta. The announcer then went on to say that a powerful naval force had been attacked in the Grand Harbour and that forty-seven Spitfires had been destroyed, but he omitted any mention of damage to the naval force; indeed, except for the *Welshman*, it did not exist. And just in case his listeners had wondered why the island still existed after the previous months of bombast the announcer explained that Malta was built of solid rock and could take a lot of punishment.

My four surviving submarines, *P31*, *P34*, *P35* and *Una* were enjoying a well-earned rest. The 1st Flotilla were covering the Aegean and west to Benghazi. *Torbay* arrived in mid-May with about twenty soldiers evacuated from a bay in south Crete. The fleshpots of Egypt were welcome and routine seemed uncannily peaceful.

I went to Cairo at the end of May to stay with a cousin, a doctor who had practised in Egypt since 1908 and had a large house in Heliopolis, where I found a younger cousin, a captain in a Highland regiment, quartered; he was apparently on the staff. He told me one evening (I imagine it was 26 May) that Rommel was on the move again. I browsed around in the splendid library carpeted with Persian rugs, the doctor's lifetime collection from purchase and grateful patients, ate delicious meals served by his devoted and numerous Egyptian servants and drank gin slings in his shaded garden. I might have been in Beverley Hills or Darjeeling, except I think it was quieter and the service better.

About three days later a New Zealand sergeant, a friend of the doctor's, arrived and brought with him a travel-worn corporal and asked if they could have a bath. They were invited to stay as long as they liked, so I learned a lot about trout fishing in New

Zealand from the sergeant, who was on staff duty in Cairo, and far more about front line conditions from the corporal, whose story went something like this.

'We were in laager in the Knightsbridge area having breakfast at about 7 am and due to break laager at 8 o'clock. Suddenly we saw a dust storm to the south-west which looked unusual and before you could say knife they were on us and round us. We were all "in the bag", General Messervy and all, but after a short time the Panzers had to engage our forces coming from the north and we got "out of the bag", the general included. My tank was shot to pieces so I took a ride on the back of one still working and we went like hell to the east for a bit and contacted another armoured unit, so I left the tank and hitched a ride in an east-bound lorry, but we ran into a formation of Panzers again, and my transport convoy were all "in the bag" again. It was just getting dark and most of us got away, but not the transport which had been shot up, and a bunch of us met another eastbound convoy and hitched a ride. Thank gawd, we didn't get "put in the bag" again and as I had no tank I came right through. The doctor's bath here is bloody marvellous!'

After a couple of nights in bed and days in the bath he left us to find his unit. It was the only time I heard a first-hand account of desert warfare. The position 'in' or 'out' of the bag was continuously referred to. He seemed to have acted resourcefully after losing his tank. I returned to HMS *Medway*.

About 5 June the Chief of Staff to the C.-in-C., Rear-Admiral Edelsten, sent for Ruck Keene and me and said, 'A convoy for Malta, code name "Vigorous" is being planned to sail about the 12th to arrive simultaneously with a convoy "Harpoon" from Gibraltar. It seems certain that the Italian battlefleet from Taranto will endeavour to intercept our convoy and I have been wondering to what extent your submarines can help. I have thought that a continuous line of both flotillas spread east and west and moving at four knots westward on the critical day might form an effective mobile minefield through which the Italian fleet would have to pass to get at the convoy to the south of it. Do you chaps think this a practicable use for your submarines?'

We both thought it a very good idea and it was decided that my four U class, which only had a surface speed of 10 knots, should be to the westward whilst *S1*'s T class would prolong the line to the east so that they could regain ground at night, at about 15 knots, if cover was required towards Alexandria. The submarines were to be disposed at five mile intervals. The submarine line was to be about forty miles north of the convoy route. The submarines were sailed accordingly and were all in position at dusk on 14 June.

At 0400, 15 June, Ruck Keene and I arrived at the combined operations room in the H.Q. of No. 201 Naval Cooperation Group, where we found Admiral Harwood (C.-in-C.) and Rear-Admiral Edelsten (C.O.S.). Air Marshal Tedder (C.-in-C. Air) arrived a few minutes later in order to (in Roskill's words) 'conduct the intricate movements in intimate collaboration'. I suppose this was the idea but hardly in accord with fact.

The fact was that there can have been no man more critically preoccupied than Air Marshal Tedder at dawn on that June morning except General Auchinleck. His forward airfields were over-run, the army was in disorderly retreat on the Egyptian border and he was due for a conference with the Army Commander as soon as he could get away from the orderly, prosaic battle laid on by the sailors. He nodded good morning with a cheerful smile, lit up a sulphurous pipe and began to patrol a beat backwards and forwards on one side of the room, which he kept up for the next two hours. I was the junior boy present so was doing the plotting. I am virtually certain that Tedder never came near the chart nor looked at it. Why should he? His strikes from Egypt and Malta were laid on since the previous day; he was really there out of politeness.

Continuing this story of 'intimate collaboration', neither Ruck Keene nor I had been told that any air strike had been laid on. Nor was the subject mentioned by Harwood or Edelsten, who were soon to bring me the first enemy report from a Maryland reconnaissance. There were I think three enemy reports brought in during those two hours and they proved remarkably accurate. Each signal was brought by a messenger to Harwood who, having read it, would intercept Tedder at the end of his beat, show it to him, then give it to me for plotting, and we four sailors would remark on it.

Throughout these two hours there was of course no other signal. I plotted the convoy's 8 knot advance some forty miles to the south of the submarines' line and progressed the submerged submarines at four knots to the west as they spread their cover in the direction of Malta. We knew that Vian and his cruisers were somewhere near the convoy and for him to break radio silence would have been not only unnecessary but folly.

By 0615 I was feeling definitely excited and said to Edelsten, 'If those air reports are really accurate, sir, they are going between *P34* and *P35* and we should have news any moment now.' C.O.S. nodded agreement and Ruck Keene hoped they would pass through his flotilla. At this moment a messenger came in with an air report which read, 'Air strike successful enemy in confusion several hits on battleships and cruisers.'

A broad smile came over Tedder's face, and rightly so. He knocked out his pipe and said to Harwood, 'Well, I'll be off' and left the room.

I was speechless with rage. 'Robbed,' I thought, 'Simply robbed at the last minute! Why the hell can't the R.A.F. co-ordinate their strike to be after our attack and south of our line?' It was a bitter disappointment.

Of course my attitude was not only unreasonable, it was ridiculous. The air needed to get in their attack at the earliest possible moment, when the enemy fleet was as far north of the convoy as possible and when advantage could be taken of the half-light conditions of dawn for the torpedo bombers silhouetting the enemy ships against the eastern light and getting the maximum protection from the western gloaming, and this they had done to perfection. The latitude in which the air strike occurred, if properly timed, depended upon the latitude of the southbound enemy fleet at first light. In this instance it happened to be between one and two miles north of the submarine line.

This was my first and last experience of a battle from a combined ops room and its intimate collaboration. I gained the feeling that both admirals would have been as surprised as the air marshal if the submarines had really achieved anything. What subsequently occurred is fully described by Roskill.

The heavy cruiser *Trento* was stopped and *P35* later sank her.

On arrival of *P35* at Alexandria some four days later Lieutenant Maydon told me with deep disappointment that, as he raised his periscope to fire his salvo, the enemy, surrounded by bomb splashes, turned stern on to him, and his opportunity was gone.

Recently he sent me the following extracts from his navigator's notebook with entries made as they occurred.

05–24 Position by stars 36° 02′ N, 19° 07′ E.
05–29 Dived course 300°
05–40 Loud H.E. bearing 320° [This means that loud propeller noises were to be heard to the N.W.]
05–45 Sighted two large vessels bearing 310°
05–50 Altered course to 270° [west]. Full speed submerged.
06–02 Enemy identified as two battleships and two cruisers in line ahead escorted by two cruisers and eight destroyers. Course 175° speed 26 knots (220 revs.)

[At this juncture whilst he was making his final adjustments to the attack there are no entries].

06–11 Bombing started. Range 5,100 bearing 305° enemy turning away.

Commander Maydon's commentary to me by recent letter is

I remember hoping against hope in the early stages of the action that the enemy would not come within range until there was sufficient light to see him clearly through the periscope. As it was, *P35*'s aborted attack was in visibility only just permitting reasonably accurate periscope observation.

It was a very hard stroke of fate.

If you plot the situation on squared paper, for which there is all the necessary data, it will be seen that at 06–11 when Maydon put up his periscope to fire, his sights would have been on. He would have fired a salvo of four 21 inch torpedoes, range 4,000 yards, speed of torpedo 42 knots. Running time 2 minutes 33 seconds. If Maydon's estimates were precise he would have got two hits. If they were about ten per cent in error he should have got three hits, because it was our practice to fire a salvo covering one and a quarter lengths of the target at ranges over 1,000 yards, a slight error being usual.

I have given details of this incident for two reasons. I think Roskill's official history underestimates the potential of the air-cum-submarine defence which failed narrowly (3 minutes) due to coincidence. It nearly proved very effective.

Secondly, whilst admitting that my annoyance in the combined ops room was due to my narrow-minded failure to appreciate the whole picture, I think that Air Chief Marshal Lord Tedder's comments in his book *With Prejudice* need correction. His opinions here expressed might be taken seriously. He states:

I thought no doubt not only that air action had been handicapped by complete lack of information from our own ships, but that Harwood himself had been gravely handicapped and blindfolded.

Tedder knew that radio silence by the cruisers and convoy was mandatory.

One of our submarines observed numbers of hits on the battleship *Littorio* while one *Trento* class cruiser was set on fire by bombs and another sunk by a torpedo. Naval observers in the Liberators saw a cruiser and destroyer hit by torpedoes.

He states that he wrote in his official report:

Suggest that the main lesson from this strike is that given the right aircraft with the right bombs we can restore the situation in the Mediterranean, deny the sea to enemy capital ships and so free our own sea communications, and at the same time deal piece meal with his own supply ships.

This book was published in 1966, just ten years after he knew officially that the result of this strike was one cruiser stopped and *Littorio* hit once, causing superficial damage. That Lord Tedder should have formed these opinions in 1942 is remarkable. That he should have published them in 1966 is incomprehensible.

Admiral Vian, with the 'Vigorous' convoy, had to turn back. After heavy losses to the convoy and its escorting force two ships from the 'Harpoon' convoy, with 15,000 tons of cargo, were fought through to Malta, postponing the date of certain starvation by some two months.

So out of seventeen ships in the two convoys just two had arrived, but during the battle for 'Harpoon' in the Sicilian straits a most important thing was occurring. Commander Jerome was leading four small, inconspicuous modern minesweepers around Cape Bon and they got to Malta without interference. This factor ensured the 10th Submarine Flotilla's return if our air supremacy held.

On 27 June Ruck Keene said to me at breakfast, 'All your flotilla are in port so please look after mine for a couple of days – I am off to Cairo and here's my telephone number.' He caught the morning train. That afternoon a Squadron Leader called to see me and said, 'I am from central intelligence and I call to ask whether you can help in a vitally important matter. We have reason to suppose that a fast tanker with a cargo of cased petrol is due to arrive at Tobruk at noon tomorrow, 28th, or it might be later, but I am confident that its arrival is noon one day very soon. Since the R.A.F. is concentrating on the non-stop bombing of Axis communications between that port and Matruh can you take over this target?'

'Yes, I can. I will recall *Thrasher* from north of Benghazi and put him north of Tobruk, he will be there by dawn tomorrow.'

I told *Thrasher* (Hugh Mackenzie) to move to ten miles north of Tobruk to await a fast southbound tanker, that his quarry was very important and he should expect it at noon on 28, 29 or 30 June.

I thought no more about it for other affairs intervened. An officer called from C.-in-C. to say that Alexandria was to be evacuated, *Queen Elizabeth* and two fleet repair ships were sailing at dusk the following evening for the Suez Canal and Admiral Vian's cruisers and the *Medway* and submarines were to leave port for Haifa at dusk on 29 June. I recalled Ruck Keene and got busy organising our move. The next evening, about two hours after the battleship, two repair ships and six destroyers had left, Axis aircraft came over and dropped mines in the swept channel which could not again be swept effectively.

So that both flotilla captains would not be in the same ship I took passage with Captain ('D') Micklethwaite in *Sikh*. The cruisers crept out, followed by *Medway* and destroyers and the Greek submarine depot ship, all ships making about six knots on the eastern side of the channel. As *Sikh* sailed northwards an Egyptian tug came chugging down mid-channel belching smoke and looking busy and, when abreast *Sikh*'s bridge, was blown to pieces so close that all of us on the bridge were soaked by sea water and one of *Sikh*'s boilers was put out of action. At 0920 next morning *U372* torpedoed *Medway* and she sank in twenty minutes but fortunately with the loss of less than twenty from a complement of over 1,100. The destroyers entered Haifa next morning.

The loss of *Medway* at this hectic moment in Britain's fortunes in the Western Desert and Mediterranean seemed catastrophic. We had lost our finest depot ship, her full repair facilities and, worst of all, the entire outfit of ninety spare torpedoes embarked as upper deck cargo. There were 1,100 survivors to be accommodated immediately from the escorting destroyers while everybody, including the two submarine flotillas at sea, but arriving Haifa steadily, had lost all kit and possessions except the salt-soaked clothes or the submarine clothes that they stood in. Our two submarine flotillas were in danger of being immobilised.

U372 reported the sinking of a transport and the German Admiralty did not realise the importance of their success for some months.

The situation entirely suited the competent ebullience of Captain Philip Ruck Keene. On being pulled out of the sea by a destroyer he signalled, 'Regret to report *Medway* sunk by U boat in position X. It was a beautifully executed attack,' – An opinion unlikely to raise much enthusiasm in Whitehall. On arrival in Haifa he merely asked me to look out for the submarines on patrol, and in no time at all, by means that I never discovered, we were well accommodated in this hospitable Jewish city.

A search party, presumably destroyers, were sent to search for torpedoes and recovered forty-seven floating in the vicinity of the sinking.

An officer was sent to Cairo to obtain furniture for a new shore base and to lead a convoy of trucks north with our domestic requirements.

In forty-eight hours we were all comfortably housed and victualled. A German restaurant's iced lager and Wiener-Schnitzel seemed unbelievably delicious. On 3 July Ruck Keene was away to meet General Spears and persuade General Catroux that Beirut was where his flotilla should be based. All was agreed and he was back in about six days to divert the furtniture convoy from Cairo through to Beirut. The sebsequent base at that port, previously used by French submarines, was a very great success and it opened for the use of the 1st Submarine Flotilla about 16 July.

On 5 July Admiral Leatham signalled C.-in-C. that the air

situation over Malta, and the sweeping of mines, justified the return of submarines when it suited him; that was not just yet, not until the Levant submarine base was organised.

To return to operational matters, at Haifa on 6 July *Thrasher* secured to the jetty with his 'Jolly Roger' flying. 'I got him on 29 June,' said Mackenzie. 'Well done, Rufus. I'm sure that tanker was particularly important,' I replied and thought no more about it.

I was deeply upset because on my last minute transfer to *Sikh* at Alexandria I had left, in an attaché case in *Medway*, all the original records of my Malta flotilla written up by the Commanding Officers, also the only copy of the Lazaretto magazine edited and produced monthly by Bob Tanner, being a record of unique contributions both grave and gay from men who were now mostly dead.

Settling in at Haifa wasn't all plain sailing and I had to have three boards of inquiry in five days and to apply for them personally to the formidable Sir Philip Vian. He could not have been more understanding and, when on the last occasion I reported that a young officer sitting on the sill of his hotel bedroom window had fallen out and broken his neck, he remarked 'Troubles usually come in threes, you should be clear of them now.' We gave a lunch party to him at the German restaurant and I seated him in the centre of the long table surrounded by the young submarine C.O.s so that they could meet and talk with this brilliant fighting admiral. It was a happy occasion.

Lieutenants Skelton and Pitt, two young C.O.s, suddenly arrived unannounced and explained that they came from Iskenderun (Alexandretta) where they had turned over two submarines to the Turkish navy. These had been built by Vickers Armstrong at Barrow, and Pitt and Skelton had been appointed in command with the Turkish officers and crew on board to ensure that on this occasion Britain honoured her contract and Turkey received her ships. They had of course brought them through the Mediterranean in war routine, diving during daylight hours and not relying upon the Turkish flag for safety.

This was in contrast with Britain's requisition of the battleship *Reshadieh* in August 1914. She had been paid for by Turkey from public subscription and street collection, and had been taken over by Britain and re-named *Erin*. This caused wide popular ill feeling

240

throughout the Turkish nation and assisted German diplomacy to swing Turkish public opinion to an anti-British attitude months in advance of Turkey's October alliance with Germany.

Pitt and Skelton told me that the Turkish General who was the fortress commander had inspected and accepted the submarine with pleasure and given a luncheon party in their honour. His knowledge of English was limited to the alphabet and an ability to count to seventeen; there was an atmosphere of gaiety and the General had been most obliging when responding to toasts, repeatedly demonstrating his alphabetical and numerical prowess to the joy of his numerous guests.

Skelton was later ordered home by air to a submarine command elsewhere and was in the aircraft with the great actor Leslie Howard which was shot down over Biscay on 1 June 1943, the Luftwaffe having been informed that a man resembling Churchill had embarked at Lisbon. Churchill was returning from Algiers.

Ruck Keene returned to Haifa and sent me on short leave to Beirut with orders to inspect Famagusta in Cyprus as a possible advance base for my small submarines should V.A. Malta change his opinion. I flew there in a Walrus amphibian to find the harbour and resources illusory, but for my entertainment the Resident Naval Officer introduced me to a Greek professor who showed me round historical places. After the ruined battlements we visited the cathedral where the marriage between the Black Prince and Queen Berengaria was solemnised. As we left he pointed to the massive wooden doors stating, 'On these doors, after the failure of the crusades, the skins of Greek Christians were nailed after they had been flayed alive by the Turks.' He then told me that British rule and compromise was no longer acceptable. I hope he is happier now.

I flew back to Malta with MacGregor and Tanner on the night of 21–22 July. The island seemed uncannily quiet. Lazaretto was more or less habitable, with tarpaulin roofs in places. Marsham and Pop Giddings and their merry men had been joined by an old friend, Commander Jerome, in charge of minesweepers, who had cleared the harbours and approaches, making the return of submarines possible. The recent air battle during the first week of July had been won. Starvation seemed the only spectre; an ominous and close one.

241

I am sure that history will pass judgement that the first six months of 1942 was the critical battle in the Mediterranean and that 4 July was the approximate date that Rommel faced defeat. Certainly a fierce and glorious campaign lay before the Eighth Army in the next ten months; what I feel with certainty is that Rommel's defeat by every means of land, sea and air occurred round about early July 1942. Furthermore I believe that history will pass judgement that while all forces involved fought on both sides with rare and sustained tenacity, the decision came through mistakes of high policy, and the Axis lost through making the bigger mistake.

I believe that the British government's policy to use Malta as an air strike base, rather than a secure naval offensive base from early 1941 was a gross error, only over-ridden in its stupidity by the Axis failure and procrastination in not capturing the island. By 4 July Rommel knew this, and he knew that his tactical brilliance and success had led him to disregard his sound strategic pronouncement in Berlin before his campaign in Africa started: 'Without Malta the Axis will end by losing control of North Africa.'

Everyone had had to dance to Rommel's tune until about 28 June, when Auchinleck and Tedder put the brakes on and he knew that he had failed. It is hardly surprising that as a result Rommel's health broke down – after all this extraordinary dynamic leader was mortal. If you read the long letter from Rommel's aide, Lieutenant Berndt, to Frau Rommel, dated 26 August, it is clear how ill he was. Professor Horster, Rommel's medical adviser, examined him in August and the following signal was sent signed by Horster and General Gausse: 'Field Marshal Rommel suffering from chronic stomach and intestinal catarrh, nasal diptheria and considerable circulation trouble. He is not in a fit condition to command the forthcoming offensive.' That was 'Adam Halfa'.

If a man is reduced in a week from a prospective world conqueror to a powerless individual in a desert with the remnants of a defeated army around him, and he knows he has wrongly advised his government twice in three months, and that that government is a vengeful maniac, it is only human nature to look for an excuse. It seems to me that this occurred. In fact in *The Rommel Papers* he blames the supply authorities in Rome for not appreciating 'that the African war was approaching a climax'. He then becomes very specific in certain paragraphs and states, 'The protection of our convoys at sea was the responsibility of the Italian Navy. A great part of its officers, like many other Italians, were not supporters of Mussolini and would rather have seen our defeat than our victory. Hence they sabotaged wherever they could. The correct political conclusions, however, were not drawn from this.'

These are extremely harsh words and in my experience quite untrue. The Italian Navy even went so far as to use cruisers to carry stores and petrol to the army and suffered serious loss as a result. As the war progressed their convoy escort efficiency did not decline, it improved. It improved to a frightening extent.

Interservice cooperation needs a lot of goodwill and under-standing. International interservice cooperation at a time of defeat needs the qualities of a saint to avoid criticism.

This brings me to an interesting point which came my way by a fluke. In March 1951 I was serving as Flag Officer Germany and naval adviser to the British High Commissioner. It had been decided to approach the West German Government to consider German rearmament and John Ward (now Sir John Ward, G.C.M.G.) was chairman of the committee to discuss this matter with officers selected by agreement between Bonn and the Oc-cupying Powers. General Speidel and General Heusinger were the officers leading the German team and discussion proceeded with goodwill and social contact. I did not attend any of these con-ferences.

One day Ward said to me, 'I believe you served in submarines during the war, so I am sure it will interest you to hear a remark General Heusinger made to me after our last meeting when we were discussing war experiences over coffee. He said, "There is one officer in the British forces who above all deserved the highest decoration your country could bestow upon him; that is the captain of the submarine north of Tobruk on 29 June 1942 who sank a fast tanker and stopped Rommel's advance to the Nile.'

When I started writing this book and read the very large num-ber of books bearing on the campaign I decided to investigate to what extent my friend Rufus Mackenzie, whom I had positioned north of Tobruk, had influenced history. I am deeply indebted to Sir John Ward, Admiral Ruge, the German naval historian, the Italian naval historical branch and above all to General Heu-singer, who wrote confirming his opinion.

What happened was this. With the fall of Tobruk it was essential to get the port working immediately as the chief supply route supporting Rommel's thrust. Mussolini had had a yacht built on a destroyer's hull, of 1,600 tons and capable of over 30 knots. At this time she was lying at Spezia and a port working party of four officers and 290 men were embarked. This yacht *Diana*, then known as a destroyer transport, was sailed to arrive Messina 27 June.

Naval Command Rome made a signal to Naval Command Messina at 10 am 27 June, 'Please confirm in confidence and with utmost haste, if *Diana* could possibly take on board 200 tons of cased petrol without having to disembark the personnel. Consideration should also be given to the possibility of disembarking the above-mentioned personnel.' This signal was not acted upon, all personnel remained on board and no petrol was embarked. *Diana* was sunk at 1230/29 June with the loss of 336 lives.

The New Zealand Division were in the thick of this battle. The New Zealand Quartermaster General has kindly investigated this problem most thoroughly for me and has stated that even if 200 tons of cased petrol had arrived at Tobruk on 29 June it would have made no difference to the battle, since the R.A.F.'s round-the-clock bombing of the Tobruk–Matruh supply line was by then preventing all but a trickle of support to Rommel's armour. Admiral Ruge supports this view.

The scene I think emerges clearly. Field Marshal Rommel demanding of his quartermaster. 'Where the hell's this petrol?' and the quartermaster in a fix, but who nevertheless expected 200 tons at Tobruk, exclaiming, 'The tanker's been sunk Sir!'

'That's the last straw, the bloody navy let us down again. Tell O.K.W. that!'

Since *The Rommel Papers* have long been published with his censorious comments, it seems only right on clear evidence to put the record straight on this particular incident anyway.

I hope that as an interested player in the opposing team at that time I have not trodden on anyone's corns.

20

G IVING a clear narrative of flotilla operations during the last half of 1942 has been complicated by Churchill's insistence in October and November of that year that no submarine was to sail under a mere number. Each one was to have a name. In fact if nobody else could think of names he would do it himself. His keen interest was appreciated but I do not think it was important, the U class names being uninspiring.

At the outbreak of war submarines built, and those launched, had names, e.g. *Utmost, Unique, Urge, Upholder, Una*, etc., but those ordered on the expanding war building programme were merely numbered *P31, P32*, etc.

For purposes of clarity I will continue to refer to the Malta veterans by their numbers, but their new names are given below in brackets. The reinforcements I will refer to by their new names and their numbers are given below in brackets.

The Tenth Submarine Flotilla reassembled at Malta as follows.

The veterans.

P31 (Uproar), Lieutenant J. B. Kershaw, 30 July.
P34 (Ultimatum), Lieutenant P. R. H. Harrison, 30 July.
Una, Lieutenant C. P. Norman, 2 August.
P35 (Umbra), Lieutenant S. L. C. Maydon, 15 August.

Reinforcements from Gibraltar.

Unbroken (P42), Lieutenant A. C. G. Mars, 20 July.
United (P44), Lieutenant T. E. Barlow, 21 July.
Unison (P43), Lieutenant A. C. Halliday, 2 August.

The submarine depot ship *Maidstone* (at Malta before the outbreak of war) had been stationed at Gibraltar since late March 1941. On her was based the 8th Submarine Flotilla. In 1941 and until October 1942 the flotilla's duties were mostly the final training and mechanical perfection of reinforcements for the 1st and 10th

Flotillas. Patrols off south French ports were seldom fruitful but good training.

In mid-1942 operational S class submarines began to become available for Gibraltar and by October 1942 four had arrived and the flotilla was operational under Captain G. B. H. Fawkes.

About the time of our reassembly at Malta Commander C. H. Hutchinson joined, a submarine veteran from the Norwegian campaign where he had sunk the cruiser *Karlsruhe*.

At Haifa, devoid of all encumbrances but the clothes he stood in, was Paymaster Midshipman George Hardinge who had had to swim for it from the cruiser *Naiad* and then *Medway* in quick succession; however on the assumption that the cliché 'Third time lucky' was based on experience he took passage in a submarine in order to keep my office in order.

Hubert Marsham, always on the look-out for untapped talent, and considering that Marsamxett harbour had become hazardous from sunken booms and the oil lighter, appointed our Temporary Surgeon Lieutenant (D) Gwynne, R.N.V.R., a keen yachtsman, to be official pilot for new arrivals on their first entry. Our Gibraltar reinforcements soon learned that we were not hidebound by tradition when boarded and directed alongside Lazaretto by the dentist.

When calling on Admiral Leatham and his staff who gave me a warm welcome, I learned that Air Vice Marshal Lloyd, after his tremendous burden, his great victory and his prolonged fearless personal leadership had turned over his duties to Air Vice Marshal Sir Keith Park of Battle of Britain fame. I rang his aide and was invited to call right away.

Sir Keith, a lean 6 foot 2 inches and straight as a telegraph pole, welcomed me and got down to business right away. He said, 'I want you to know, Simpson, how really important your store-carrying submarines are to me. For instance, here is the date that my petrol runs out at our average expenditure of forty-five tons a day, and the critical date isn't so far off. A windfall by submarine advances that date by forty-eight hours, which might seem trifling but it isn't. It may well prove the necessary margin to pull us through. Submarines have been the regular source of keeping the air supplied with 18 inch torpedoes; now that your flotilla is back you must freight in 21 inch torpedoes for yourself and I admit they are the more important. If we get into a critical fix over torpedo supply come and discuss it with me. May I return your call at 1100 tomorrow morning?'

I was deeply impressed by this encouraging, and practical, friendly interview, and so it continued until I left Malta.

Next morning I met the A.O.C. at our upper entrance and he explained he could stay only five minutes. So we looked down on the shell of Lazaretto and piles of rubble, and I explained that our shelters running into the rock beneath where we were standing were a lot tidier. 'What a ghastly shambles, and furthermore how unnecessary.' With this pungent comment he departed to his airfields.

Except in October 1942 when there was some heavy air fighting over and around Malta we hardly saw an enemy aircraft. The air raid warnings sounded and flights of Spitfires would leave, gaining height, but I gathered that the fighting occurred over the sea towards Sicily.

In 1968 I had lunch with Sir Keith Park in Auckland, New Zealand, and I inquired, 'Do you happen to remember what you said to me in July '42 when you visited Lazaretto?'

'Yes, certainly I do. I said, "What a ghastly shambles and how unnecessary"' he replied like a flash.

'What exactly did you mean by "how unnecessary"?'

'Well, Dowding and I won the Battle of Britain with fifty squadrons in the country. That was October 1940 and by December 1941 there were 150 squadrons looking for a job in Britain.'

'How was that, sir?'

'Ever heard of empire building?'

Sir Keith Park was born and bred a New Zealander. Their amazing fighting record in two world wars is not associated with good luck or special weapons but with determination, quick appreciation and a flair for improvisation. It is their heritage from pioneering days. They are extremely adaptable individualists who will form an unbeatable team at the shortest notice. That is why their martial qualities are so formidable. I fear that with the spread of urbanisation these qualities will mellow markedly, but so long as the land is their main source of wealth these national characteristics will predominate.

This diversion is to show why Park's remark on Malta carries particularly weight with me and happens to endorse and so reinforce my own opinion.

From late July until I left Malta six months later the dangers to the operational submarines in the central Mediterranean had entirely changed since April. Lazaretto was a secure base with poor but habitable messdecks and cabins; the plague of sandflies from the piles of rubble was a nuisance. Our underground workshop was becoming well equipped with machine tools. Electricity, water and the telephone were always available. The lethal E-boat antennae mines in Malta's approaches had all been swept.

On the other hand the efficiency of the Italian naval escort forces had steadily risen since the beginning of the year and were to continue to do so through the months ahead.

The Axis desert army's needs were as demanding as ever before, their acute difficulties were in shipping the oil fuel. Their air and surface convoy escorts were maintained at full strength to the detriment of the mobility of their battlefleet. This was the broad picture.

As before about half the strength of the Malta submarines were kept on short patrols of one to two weeks and met with steady but moderate success. I will confine my narrative to outstanding events or individual exploits of particular merit and importance. The event of this chapter was action surrounding the fighting through of convoy 'Pedestal' in mid-August 1942.

The object of Operation 'Pedestal' was to force through a convoy of fourteen merchantmen to Malta before mid-August when food would be exhausted and starvation would ensue with catastrophic suddenness and finality. With the convoy were four aircraft carriers, three to fight off enemy air attack and *Furious* to ferry in thirty-eight Spitfires. The escorting force under Admiral Syfret and cruisers under Admiral Burrough was of unprecedented strength. The convoy passed Gibraltar early on 10 August and eventually four merchant ships and one damaged tanker arrived at Malta between 13 and 15 August. I will now confine my story to events little recorded or for obvious reasons not recorded at all.

The 10th Flotilla's contribution was to be to provide one submarine to cover the northern exit to Messina (*Unbroken*), to provide one submarine to land a specially trained commando for aircraft sabotage (*Una*) and to provide three submarines to join a line south of Pantellaria to prevent enemy cruiser interference during the last stages of the run to Malta. These dispositions were part of the extensive overall plan from the Admiralty. It was in fact Malta's last chance.

'Pedestal' was of the greatest importance as can be seen from a conversation I had at this time. I walked on the evening of 10 August to visit Greta and Gravy Tench at St Julian's bay. I received the usual warm welcome and Greta, looking adorable as always, chatted with me, while Gravy, the head censor and in charge of food distribution and who was just in from his office, seemed deeply preoccupied. After a while Gravy interrupted our gossip by saying, 'Shrimp, I know you have ample problems of your own, but given the following problem, which is now on my plate, what would you do?

'The present island-wide soup kitchen arrangements are fully organised and working well. The tinned and dehydrated ingredients are issued from secure lock-up centres daily to the responsible organisers who concoct the necessary witch's brew on field kitchens and distribute it from fixed points to the towns and villages. These ingredients are ideal for control and orderly administration but the last issue – the absolutely last issue from island reserves – occurs on 15 August, in five days.

'After that we are down to the slaughter of horses and goats, which you may remember was cheerfully considered to be adequate for six months, but on his arrival Lord Gort ordered a census of these animals and it was found that the vast majority had been eaten already. The present census of animals in the island is estimated to last from five to ten days.

'Now, thinking ahead, you will see that on sixteenth a precise number of horses and goats must be requisitioned, slaughtered, skinned and boiled down into soup, a procedure entailing knives, blood, protestations and all done in public more or less, but it would have to be done, and I feel that if this was a last and final act it might well lead to riots.

'To forestall this tendency to panic it seems to me that tomorrow I might have a government broadcast made to explain that we must test alternative methods so the first schedule of horses and goats will be killed on the twelfth and thirteenth and then we will revert for a day to tinned food. In fact if I chop and change without causing panic we might last to the twenty-fifth. What would you do?'

'I would trust to the convoy, or a bit of it, getting through forty-eight hours in advance of your deadline, Gravy, because if it doesn't Malta's "had it" anyway, while if it does your splendid organisation can carry on smoothly.'

'Thanks, Shrimp, I am so glad you have said that, it reassures my opinion but it's all a close thing!'

I knew about 'Pedestal' well in advance and my flotilla's duties were clear and practicable. There was one thing about this, it was the only occasion in the war when I was told where to put my submarines, but I wish to emphasise that I wholeheartedly approved the Admiralty's broad dispositions.

Before sailing *Unbroken* on 30 July I explained, in some detail, to Lieutenant Mars, who was about to set out on his first patrol from Malta, just what he was to do. He was to go up to the Capri area and look for targets. He was not to expend more than four torpedoes in this area and must retain a full salvo for the vital phase of his patrol which was covering a Malta-bound convoy. He was to leave the Capri area at his discretion but not later than 7 August because I particularly needed concrete evidence that his new U class innovation, a 3 inch gun with accurate sights and fixed ammunition with flashless cordite, was effective. He should pick his own chosen position for this test against, I suggested, a south-bound goods train. He should then continue south and establish patrol in the north-west approaches to Messina in the vicinity of Cape Milazzo. If A/S sweeps were too hot in this area he was to retire northwards to the vicinity of Stromboli.

In accordance with my invariable practice I told *Unbroken* where to go and in which direction he should retire if circumstances demanded it. My reason for ordering retirement north towards Stromboli was to ensure that he cleared the probable area of an A/S search on the Messina–Palermo route, which I knew to be covered by probably the most experienced and competent submarine commander then afloat, Commander B. J. Bryant in *Safari*, who was stationed off Palermo.

I was very surprised when Lieutenant Mars objected that the Milazzo area was too dangerous and asked why must I send him there. I told him it was my interpretation of a broad Admiralty directive to cover the northern approaches to Messina. He left me dissatisfied. It was an unhappy interview and alien to my past experience.

Unbroken found targets off Capri, firing at two ships but missing, which was an unfortunate disappointment. Having moved south a train was demolished at 2230/8 June, one mile north of Longo-bardi, every shot finding its mark at a range of 1,000 yards and confirming the effectiveness of the 3 inch gun. Moving to his position north of Cape Milazzo he was detected by what seemed like shore-based asdic working in conjunction with A/S patrol vessels and he was uncomfortably harassed, so in accordance with my orders he withdrew to the Stromboli area which was quiet. *Unbroken* took up an excellent position 10 miles WSW of Strom-boli. At about 0800/13 June *Unbroken* fired a torpedo salvo at four escorted Italian cruisers, range 3,000 yards, and scored one hit on the 10,000 ton *Bolzano* and one on the 7,000 ton *Attendolo*. A prolonged counterattack ensued but the enemy did not gain con-tact, although over a hundred depth-charges were dropped.

I recalled *Unbroken*. It had been a splendidly successful patrol and several signals of congratulation arrived. Neither cruiser was repaired in time to take further part in the war. The incident covered several paragraphs of criticism in Ciano's diary.

I was of course very proud of *Unbroken*'s success, but I do not think that Lieutenant Mars fully appreciated my gratitude for his careful examination of the Cape Milazzo area, whose dangers were entered in Bob Tanner's flotilla information book and may well have saved a submarine on a later patrol. The proven effectiveness of the 3 inch gun was also important news.

Commando raids carried out from submarines were frequently and often successfully made in the Mediterranean, and a school for training commandos had been instituted in 1941 at Ismailia on the Suez Canal. Of my original commando under Captain Taylor, who joined Lazaretto at much the same time as I had done, only Lieutenant Schofield and seven men were prisoners. Three officers and fifty-three other ranks were still with me, and I had only carried out one raid of any size using this force. I cannot trace the date since it failed and has not been recorded, but Lieutenant Walker and about sixteen men were put ashore about three miles east of Gela on the south shore of Sicily.

My orders were that they were to go to Gela aerodrome, used by German fighters, and destroy as many on the ground as possible by using sticky bombs with time fuses. This aerodrome was about six miles inland and I impressed on Walker that there was nothing to be gained by persisting in this raid if he met opposition early on, when he had this stiff night cross-country journey in unknown terrain. In the event this party had to turn back after the whole countryside had been alerted by farm dogs and the neighbourhood was on the move looking for the cause. I had told Walker not to become involved with civilians.

So it was that our original commando from Paignton had been of invaluable assistance to us in forming emergency working parties repairing damaged submarines in dockyard, but had not recently been out raiding.

Since late 1941 it had become rather a habit for C.-in-C.'s staff at Alexandria to suggest a raid and fly in their own commandos from the Ismailia school to carry it out, and this happened several times. It was naturally resented by Taylor and his men but there was nothing we could do about it and the Ismailia commandos had the latest in equipment.

So it was that in early August I was told by C.-in-C. that commando personnel to be landed by submarine on Sicilian shores would be flown in from Egypt before dawn on 7 August. I selected *Una*, Lieutenant C. P. Norman, to carry out the operation.

Captain G. E. A. Duncan (Black Watch) with his party, Lieutenant E. Newby (Black Watch), Sergeant W. Dunbar (Argyll and Sutherland Highlanders) and three commandos arrived at Lazaretto 0300/7 August. Captain Duncan explained that all the equipment would arrive at the same time the next night in charge of Lieutenant H. A. D. Buchanan, Grenadier Guards, and two commandos, making the total force up to nine.

At next day's conference the R.A.F. representative told us that the targets should be one of the following aerodromes – Commisso, Gela or Catania, which were twelve, six and one mile from the sea respectively and so far as the air was concerned all three were packed with enemy planes and they had no preference. I said that to put the commando ashore at a precisely arranged spot on the open beach to the south of Commisso or Gela might be difficult, but had the advantage of being free from enemy naval patrols. Catania was best for an accurate landing but there were three Italian M.A.S. (motor gun-boats) at Catania harbour and four German E-boats at Augusta, so the operation and in particular the recovery would be more dangerous.

Captain Duncan said that from the commando's point of view

the distance and the farm watch-dogs made Commisso and Gela useless targets and it must be Catania, so that was decided upon. The attack to take place at 0200/12 August. *Una* to sail from Malta, after dark, 9 August.

These things decided, Captain Duncan and Lieutenant Norman, captain of *Una*, remained with me to plan details of the landing and the much more difficult recovery of the folbots. It was decided that after launching the canoes *Una* would lie on the bottom until 0300, then surface and expose a dim blue light towards the shore for five seconds every two minutes. If nobody arrived *Una* would dive and retire at 0400.

If recovery of folbots failed *Una* would approach to one mile off a prominent rock on the shore line at the south of the bay forty-six hours later and show this dim blue light at intervals for fifteen minutes, and then return to Malta.

The meeting over, Duncan remained a minute and said, 'Captain, tonight Lieutenant Buchanan arrives in charge of stores. I am afraid he may make a poor impression on you. I promise you he is an admirable lad, full of guts and initiative. I picked him for this operation. He is a young Guardsman and I have a feeling that his bearing and flippant veneer may offend you, but he's the man I need, so please be tolerant. He's about nineteen, I think.'

'Of course, Duncan. He should have a good lie in tomorrow morning. He will have been perched in a transit plane all night and be off in *Una* the following evening.' Duncan's description interested me.

I arranged for a steward to awake me in time and to be on duty in our wardroom at 0300, and have sandwiches and coffee. I sat in a chair and waited, but not for long. Soon the duty officer led in a most engaging young man. He was clean-shaven, with straight fair hair, of average height and the enthusiasm of youth in his eyes. He wore a tweed hunting jacket with corduroy slacks and brown suède shoes. In his left hand was a portable gramophone and record container, while under his right arm was a chestnut-brown dachshund with white feet.

'Lieutenant Buchanan, sir,' said the duty officer.

'Good to see you, Buchanan. I hope you've brought all the explosive stores?'

'Oh yes, sir. They're all right and unloaded and in store up top.

I say, sir, I hope you don't mind dogs in the mess but Socks is perfectly house trained.'

'Not at all, put him down for a run. Would you like some coffee and sandwiches or would you rather go straight to bed? You happen to be in the next cabin to me so I can take you right there.'

'Oh, I'd like coffee and sandwiches. What fun! I thought you were all starving here. You see, I have just had six hours solid sleep since leaving Heliopolis.'

'Good. Steward, please bring coffee and sandwiches.'

'How quiet everything is! Malta seems to be very normal. I say, sir, you have just remarked that I am in the next room to you. Do you mind jazz before breakfast? I always shave to jazz.'

'Not a bit, Buchanan, but I hope Captain Duncan will give you a good lie in. This time tomorrow you will be six hours by submarine from here so you must make up sleep now.'

'Oh, that's O.K., sir. Do you think the captain of the submarine likes jazz? I do hope so.'

'Lieutenant Norman is much younger that I am and even I like jazz before breakfast!'

'Oh, good. Sir, I am sure submarine life wouldn't suit Socks, do you think I could leave him in your care for a few days, until I am back?'

'Yes, certainly. Well, let's go to our bunks.'

What a delightful and refreshing experience I thought, here's a lad unspoiled by the ghastly realities of war, I pray to God he may survive.

At 0700/9 August I was shaving, when a jazz record started up through the wall. I knew that Desmond Buchanan, Grenadier Guards, was starting his day with customary enthusiasm.

Una arrived off Catania bay on schedule but a north-east breeze made the sea choppy and, due to damaged folbots, the commando had to be reduced from nine to six persons. They paddled west into the night with about $1\frac{1}{2}$ miles down wind to travel for the beach. *Una* dived at 2300 and surfaced at 0330, then flashed with a dim blue light directly ashore. Just before 0400 a firework display occurred east and to seaward of *Una*'s position. Automatic weapons were firing briskly only half a mile from where *Una* lay. 'Looks as if the M.A.S. from Catania have spotted something,' thought Norman, who had my strict order that the commando

254

was expendable but *Una* was not. He rightly dived and crept to seaward, reporting failure to recover the commando.

I made a signal to *S1* of the position, and he replied thoughtfully. 'Triumph was lost trying to recover landing party two days after an operation.'

I decided not to alter the agreed arrangement. *Una* closed to one mile from the prominent rock and showed a blue light, after fifteen minutes of no reply she sadly returned to Malta.

Pat Norman reported to me what had occurred and of course since he was on the sea bed during the raid he had observed nothing, he only remarked, 'I think they got there since when I surfaced the whole area was in darkness.' He continued, 'I know, sir, that wills and last letters to wives and dependants are harrowing affairs which you are rightly not troubled with. I hope very much that our friends are prisoners of war, but in this case Captain Duncan handed me letters for delivery which are all straightforward except for this which is addressed personally to me from that charming lad Lieutenant Desmond Buchanan. I am afraid it needs your attention.'

I read:

In the event of my not returning I would wish.
1 That the wardroom of HMS *Una* accept my gramophone and records, in appreciation of our happy journey.
2 I would ask Captain Simpson to send my dachshund, Socks, to the Princess Aly Khan at the Hotel Angleterre, Beirut.
3 I would be grateful if the cash in this envelope be sent to my mother, address———, Poona, India. [a sum of £42 was in the envelope].

'Yes, Pat, I'll look after two and three if I can,' I muttered. I was suddenly for the first time arrested by the grim reality of how war tore youthful gaiety to shreds, as it had broken mine in 1917.

My young sublieutenants in submarines seemed so mature and matter of fact compared with this gay lad from England and undoubtedly from privilege, but his spontaneous, youthful, good-mannered zest had been a tonic to my calculating tough outlook. So that, I thought, is what experience must kill, how very sad.

Socks took passage in the Submarine *Parthian* to Beirut and I sent a cheque to Poona.

It was nearly four years later that I met Desmond Buchanan for lunch at 'Rules' in Maiden Lane.

'Do tell me just what happened.'

'We six landed down wind and easy paddling with our supply canoes in tow. We hid our folbots in scrub above the sands and set off to attack at 0200. When we got to the edge of Catania airfield the whole area was floodlit and there stood the bombers with a German sentry armed with a tommy gun standing beside every aircraft. It was evident that six of us could do nothing in the circumstances; it seemed doubtful if we could destroy one aircraft.

'Captain Duncan said our best target was to blow up a large pylon nearby supporting the electric power leads to the aerodrome. It took all our explosive and at the last moment we were spotted and in an exchange of fire one of our party was killed. Immediately afterwards the charge went off and subsequent darkness allowed our escape and re-embarkation. We had to paddle into a choppy sea and I think we were a bit early on the rendez-vous. Spray prevented one seeing very much but we kept together until we were certain we were to seaward of *Una*. When we finally stopped and could see no signs of *Una* and it was about 0350 Captain Duncan ordered us to fire all our weapons in the air to attract attention, but nothing eventuated.

'The wind and sea increased, we three folbots kept together but at first light it was evident that they could not long be kept afloat. Furthermore I knew that Captain Duncan could not swim far, but as I could it was decided that I swim for the shore. I stripped off my clothes and that left me with a Grenadier Guard's button tied round my neck. On the swim towards Catania I saw a fishing boat and got to it and directed it to the folbots. We were taken ashore and I had the odd experience of being marched through the town of Catania with only a Grenadier's button round my neck, and I must say I hated it.

'There was, for a day or two of interrogation, a threatening attitude towards me, that I was a "franc tireur" without uniform and stateless; but I suppose Captain Duncan's evidence helped to squash that.'

We talked on about prisoner of war experiences and his escape at the time of Mussolini's temporary fall. This was an exceptional adventure, Buchanan explained, 'I was with one other P.O.W., moving south at night near a main road, and reached a village some forty miles north of the front line. We went in starving desperation to the small hotel and explained our situation. The Italian host and hostess accepted us and gave us quarters through a trap hatch into a loft below the rafters with straw mattresses to lie upon in the dark. Nobody else in the village knew of our existence. It was simple for three days, but the German line was in retreat.

'After about three days the Germans arrived and set up a Divisional Artillery H.Q. in our small hotel which they requisitioned. It was just two storeys with our loft above, its trap hatch plainly visible. The Germans were there for ten days, and every day at some moment within the twenty-four hours the rooms below us would apparently be unoccupied, and our brave Italian hosts would pass up an old-fashioned chamberpot full of delicious food and two bottles of water, concurrently removing yesterday's chamberpot full of our excrement. This lasted for ten days. Ten whole days lying above divisional H.Q. and then the British over-ran the place and we were free.'

It was of course the same Desmond Buchanan to whom I was speaking. A mature man of the world. I dared not ask what he was doing or intended to do. I felt afraid he would answer, 'Well, fortunately I have a few directorships and I am a chairman of an insurance company.' I hope it is nothing so prosaic.

The three submarines for the east west defence line south of Pantellaria joined forces with three submarines from Gibraltar; nothing came their way. The four merchantmen and the tanker *Ohio*, which got to Malta, saved the island, literally at its last gasp. A situation which most people did not know. This convoy therefore sealed the fate of the Axis armies in Africa, whose defeat at the hands of a revived and reinforced Eighth Army under the skilful direction of the Alexander–Montgomery partnership was only a matter of time.

This is not a statement based on hindsight. It was confidently felt in the 10th Submarine Flotilla that after the limited, but substantial, success of 'Pedestal' we had reached the top of the hill, were on level terms and had an exhilarating downhill run before us.

'Pedestal' cost the Merchant Navy nine fine ships. It cost the

Royal Navy one aircraft carrier and two cruisers sunk, two cruisers torpedoed and one destroyer sunk.

As is reported in Roskill's official history, published in 1956, four of the merchant ships and one destroyer were sunk by enemy aircraft, one aircraft carrier and one cruiser were sunk by enemy U-boats, which also damaged two other cruisers, and five merchant ships and another cruiser were sunk by fast torpedo-carrying, motor boats. These facts have been covered by two lines in Lord Tedder's account published in 1966, 'A convoy of fourteen ships set off in August, but only five got through. The rest were lost through enemy air action, as was the aircraft carrier *Eagle*.' Lord Tedder in full flight of his fancy continues, 'The accounts I received in September, however, were by no means reassuring. . . . Gort apparently told Park at least once a day that he did not wish to be "in the cooler". Similar talk about the "cooler" was becoming habitual amongst some of the other senior people in the Navy and Army.' These statements can only be thought of as rubbish.

About one week after the arrival of 'Pedestal' a large diesel-driven air compressor was installed just above sea level on the Valetta side of Marsamxett harbour opposite Lazaretto. There was also a labour force of about twenty men. Much noise and activity attracted my attention.

After about a week an impressive arched entrance had taken shape and was progressing into the limestone under the City. I telephoned the civil engineer in the Dockyard to enquire what all the activity was in aid of. 'We've just received approval for the submarine shelters recommended in 1934. We have been told to go right ahead with them.'

'When do you expect to finish the scheme?'

'If there is no shortage of fuel and we can get more machinery we should finish by 1946. That would be the whole scheme of five tunnels.'

I asked Admiral Leatham if he could stop the noise, and it ceased by 1 September. The scar of this folly remains as a monument to British methods of waging war.

September 1942 was a peaceful month for Malta with the Spitfires firmly in control overhead, some food in the granaries and

Jerome's minesweepers keeping channels clear. A veneer of normality crept across the island, but not to the government which knew the slenderness of our resources.

In August *P31* had sailed for Britain. *P34* was to follow this month, leaving me with only *Una* (Pat Norman) and *P35* (Maydon) from those who had experienced the 'blitz'. I wondered how good our 'Second XI' would prove as reinforcements to the flotilla steadily arrived. I need not have had a moment's doubt for they were splendid. I have recorded that *Unbroken*, *United* and *Unison* arrived at the end of July. In the next three months six more U class joined the flotilla: *Unrivalled* (P.45), (Lieutenant H. B. Turner); *Unbending* (P.37), (Lieutenant E. S. Stanley); *Utmost*, back after refit in the U.K., (Lieutenant J. W. Coombe); *Unruffled* (P.46), (Lieutenant J. S. Stevens); *Unseen* (P.51), (Lieutenant M. L. Crawford); and *P48*, (Lieutenant M. E. Faber).

On 19 September Commander Ben Bryant arrived at Lazaretto in command of *P211*, an improved S class submarine. His youthful appearance and offensive spirit seemed unchanged from Malta in 1939. When I went on board I saw a ship's crest hanging in the wardroom with *P211* at the top, then a camp-fire with cooking pot in the centre, and the motto 'On the Boil'.

'I don't get the message,' I said, so Bryant explained that perhaps it truly belonged to *P212* but as the figure was only one degree short of boiling point he had adopted it for his submarine's crest and motto. A few weeks later he was delighted when Admiralty's confirmation was signalled confirming the crest he had proposed and stating that from then on his submarine's name was HMS *Safari*.

Safari was sent on loan from the 8th Flotilla at Gibraltar. I sent her on a freelance patrol in the southern Adriatic which had been too long undisturbed. Bryant was the chief exponent in our submarines of the use of the gun. The ideal gun in a submarine is the 4 inch, which was rather big for the S, and *Safari*'s was a 3 inch gun, (the same as *Unbroken*'s). To get results and survive requires precise judgement, training and nerve, but in the central Mediterranean at this time when large targets were becoming distinctly scarce Bryant's fireworks were extremely valuable for keeping up the pressure and dissuading coastal traffic, in addition to his expertise with the torpedo.

In cold figures, from this date of arrival at Malta until he relinquished command on 14 April 1943 Commander Bryant sank twenty-nine vessels of all sorts, totalling about 40,000 tons. His offensive reached crescendo on his last patrol which moved the Commander-in-Chief, Admiral Cunningham, (not prone to exaggeration) to describe it as one 'which will rank among the classic exploits of the submarine service'.

Safari continued a further three months in the Mediterranean under command of Lieutenant R. B. Lakin who added ten more ships totalling 10,000 tons to this submarine's remarkable record.

I received broad and important orders through V.A. Malta, in anticipation of the 'Torch' North Africa landings (the arrival of the American Army and British 1st Army under General Eisenhower) and the desert offensive leading to the victory at Alamein. I was to be in command of all submarines operating between longitudes 8°E and 19°E. I would initially receive reinforcement from both east and west so that I had thirteen operational submarines which I was to dispose to prevent the Italian fleet from interfering with the 'Torch' landings. Admiral Cunningham was at Gibraltar and I was to send him my proposed dispositions.

At this moment my trusted and experienced Staff Officer Operations, Lieutenant-Commander Bob Tanner, was sent home, and he deserved a break. His routine habits, sound submarine knowledge and judgement, had been invaluable to me. He was relieved by Lieutenant-Commander W. D. King (Bill King of *Snapper* and *Trusty* fame) who needed better food than we could supply in Malta, his digestion having suffered in the Singapore campaign. I sent him to Beirut.

His relief was Lieutenant-Commander P. S. Francis, a very experienced submarine commander with a brain like a knife, but judgement less calculatingly experienced than Tanner's. On 8 February 1942, when in command of the submarine *Proteus*, based on Alexandria, he was on patrol on the surface at night south of Cephalonia, and sighted the bows of an enemy patrol craft approaching at high speed. Francis went full speed ahead on the surface and steered directly for the enemy. The resultant impact missed centreline by about two feet which resulted in *Proteus* losing her port hydroplane and the bows of the Italian torpedoboat *Sagittarius* being cut below the waterline for twenty feet. The contestants in this 'joust' returned slowly to their respective bases. Francis I found an admirable S.O.O.

I proposed to Admiral Sir A. B. Cunningham that my thirteen submarines be disposed, two close south of Messina, three loosely north of Messina avoiding Cape Milazzo, five on a patrol line WNW from Palermo and two south-east from the south of Sardinia. In my detailed dispositions I explained that the smallest submarines were inshore and the larger to seaward. My dispositions were approved without comment.

So as to be in immediate touch with V.A.M.'s cipher staff and full-scale operations room Francis and I moved to V.A.M.'s operations room and set up two camp beds under a large trestle table where we slept for the next six weeks. I visited Lazaretto daily.

The bulky, deep-blue volumes of the naval side of the operation were given to me, one copy for each submarine, and inside each was a detachable slip which read (from memory, since my copy is on the sea bed): 'You will be glad to know that submarine operations in the central Mediterannean at this decisive moment are in the competent hands and the long experience of Captain G. W. G. Simpson, Commanding the Tenth Submarine Flotilla based at Malta. This confidence I share with you.'

What a truly great man, I thought, to remember me with all his responsibilities. This is from A.B.C.

I was disturbed from purring satisfaction by my S.O.O. Francis, 'What stupid outfit wrote these orders, sir, and printed on the cover in white lettering "BIGOT" as the code name for the naval part of operation "Torch"?'

'What's the matter, Francis. It is a clear brief word for communication?'

'Well, sir, can't you see it's "To Gib" backwards, and they haven't even got there yet!'

I could see that Francis wasn't likely to miss much.

While September was quiet over Malta it also showed few sinkings at sea, due it seemed to lack of opportunity. More happened in October but I will refer only to one important convoy interception.

Unbending went out on her first patrol from Malta and I sent Lieutenant Stanley off the Tunisian coast, where I hoped he might find coastal shipping and pick his opportunity to 'get his eye in' without the ordeal of facing a heavily escorted convoy. He sank a 350-ton coaster, a schooner full of fodder, which he actually went alongside and put a match to after the crew were in a boat, and the following night a 1,900-ton coaster.

Unbroken (Lieutenant Mars) was sent to patrol off Lampedusa, and *United* to the south of the same island, whilst *Utmost* was posted south of Pantellaria. The reason for this was a conclusion from air reconnaissance of Naples and Palermo which showed shipping loading at both ports. On 17 October I told Stanley and Mars who were about to quit patrol to remain, and on 18 October I sailed *Safari* to reinforce the line to the south of *Utmost*.

The position on the night of 18–19 October was that five submarines were on an approximate line from Pantellaria to thirty miles south of Lampedusa in this order; *Utmost, Safari, Unbending, Unbroken* and *United*.

At 0100/19 October a very full enemy report was made by aircraft giving the convoy's position forty miles north of Pantellaria comprising one tanker and three merchantmen escorted by eight destroyers.

At 0840 *Utmost* attacked at long range, having been alerted by the circling flying-boats. His torpedoes missed, or possibly never reached the target, but *Utmost* surfaced at 1030 and passed an invaluable enemy report which allowed the submarines to the south to come on to the line of advance, except *Safari* who found himself out to the west.

Unbending sighted the convoy forty-five minutes later from right ahead and Stanley, in cool confidence on this his first patrol, with three chevrons already sewn on his 'Jolly Roger' waited for the convoy to zigzag, which it conveniently did, and he fired a full salvo from inside the screen range at 1,000 yards, sinking the 4,500-ton *Beppe* and a fleet destroyer of 1,900 tons on the starboard screen (the *Da Verrazano*). With splendid judgement Stanley went deep at slow speed passing directly under the convoy and escaping detection. Two more chevrons on his house flag.

Unbroken attacked at 1420, firing a salvo on a broad angle abaft the convoy's beam and outside the screen. The periscope was sighted by an aircraft which dropped a marker buoy. The result was an accurate and swift counterattack from the surface escort. No. 2 battery amidships was shattered, all 112 cells smashed and twelve broken in No. 1 battery. The hull held intact and no salt water problem caused chlorine. The convoy's progress prevented a prolonged hunt and *Unbroken* surfaced after dark and reached Malta next day, with fighter protection overhead, being unable to dive. During my experience no submarine received such a shattering attack and survived to return to port.

United, well to the south of Lampedusa, was closing the convoy on a northerly course and at 2200 sighted the flares from a successful air attack. After midnight Barlow located the tanker which aircraft had torpedoed and again torpedoed this ship, the *Petrarca* of 3,330 tons, but *Petrarca* like *Ohio* of 'Pedestal' fame, was tough and was finally towed to Tripoli.

Immediately darkness allowed *Safari*, who had been creeping southward, to surface and increase to full speed and, passing *Unbroken* limping home, he followed the course of the convoy. As a fine wing-forward deserves, his immediate action and appreciation coupled with his submarine's 14 knots speed was rewarded. He sighted a ship stopped with two escorting destroyers at 0510/20 October. He at once sank the *Titania* (5,400 tons) and retired without counterattack.

So this vital convoy, with an escort of eight destroyers, was reduced to one ship intact and a twice-torpedoed tanker. A fleet destroyer also sunk. This showed the Axis that Malta's threat was unchanged.

I felt elated over *Unbending*'s performance and wrote to Captain Fawkes at Gibraltar to tell him of the result. No submarine was sent through to Malta or Beirut until Captain S8 was satisfied that training and material was up to the standard required. I also wrote enthusiastically to Admiral Horton in my monthly letter and added in lighter vein, 'Lieutenant Stanley's solution to the problem of sinking the schooner full of horse and cattle fodder bound for Tripoli was both original and effective. The wooden vessel wasn't worth a torpedo so he surfaced and engaged with his gun at 1,000 yards. A shot overhead quickly put the crew into a sailing boat and the gunlayer was ordered to sink the target. Since no hit had been scored with the range closing to 200 yards Lieutenant Stanley ordered "cease fire" and ran alongside the craft, sending for a torpedoman with a tin of shale oil and a box of matches. It burned like a haystack. So it was that the wiles of *Vernon* outshone the thunder of Saint Barbara.' (Saint Barbara being the patron saint of gunnery.)

Sir Max replied rather testily, I thought, 'The satisfactory state of *Unbending*'s torpedo armament is noted. The deplorable inefficiency of the submarine's gunnery is a matter for concern and immediate remedy. The gunlayer should be replaced at once pending his reaching a satisfactory state of efficiency through harbour training which should now be practicable at Malta.'

What needed removal was *Unbending*'s gun, a silly 12-pounder pop-gun, with open sights, used in peacetime for firing salutes. I was reminded that Sir Max preferred perfection to a laugh, although he enjoyed a laugh where criticism was not called for.

21

So far in this narrative of life at Malta and of the submarines at sea I have confined my remarks to operational matters and the hazards of war. The reader may gain the impression that the commanding officer's concern was confined to these subjects, which was by no means the case, although by maintaining short patrols his problems were simplified. As an example of the variety of his worries I will quote from the eighteen day patrol of *Utmost* from 3 to 21 October 1942.

In my earlier review of the flotilla's part in landing agents I remarked upon the very objectionable experience met by *Utmost* in landing two agents in the Naples area who got cold feet and had to be manhandled into folbots, causing a delay and endangering the submarine, I quote from Lieutenant Coombe's patrol report on this particular occasion.

Health of crew. On this eighteen day patrol this was not good. A large number of common colds broke out in the early stages but were soon cured. Other ailments included three of fever and four of boils and one of uretheral discharge. M. and B. 693 cured the fever.

On 8 October before the special operation entailing closing an inhabited coast line *Utmost* was dived 19½ hours. Four hours were then spent on the surface with only the ships ventilation running as it was impossible to start main engines in our inshore position. This was followed by 15 hours on the bottom with all lights and machinery switched off. (The two agents had been disembarked at 0300/9.)

By noon 9 October conditions were most unpleasant, trays of lithium hydroxide were laid out with only slight improvement. By 1600 most people complained of severe headaches, pulses were high and several cases of vomiting occurred.

At 1900 *Utmost* surfaced and on coming in contact with fresh air more vomiting occurred.

Lieutenant Coombe was only recently in command and in my opinion too kind hearted and tolerant under circumstances which endangered his submarine. I pointed out to him that the last fifteen hours on the bottom was caused by wasting 3½ hours of the night persuading two Italians who had been paid and trained for six months in Egypt to be spies to carry out their contract. He should either have brought them back or thrown them overboard. Nevertheless he had his full share of worry.

In my covering letter to his patrol report I wrote: 'Lieutenant Coombe's remarks re health and long periods on the bottom with colds, boils, fever etc. are noted. These afflictions are largely coincidental. Considering the state of siege at Malta, lack of shoregoing amenities, exercise etc., the health of the flotilla remains remarkably good. I am confident we will tide over this difficult period without serious loss to health or efficiency.'

The outcome of disposition for operation 'Torch' was not spectacular but certainly satisfactory.

The Italian fleet, desperately hampered by lack of fuel and I think dissuaded to some degree by the torpedoing of *Bolzano* and *Attendolo* in an abortive attempt to influence convoy 'Pedestal', encountered political pressure to remain in port.

Saracen (Lieutenant Lumby) on the north-west extremity of the patrol line from north-west Sicily, sank the Italian submarine *Granito* on surface passage to the 'Torch' operation.

Turbulent (Commander Linton) sank the 1,554-ton German U-boat depot ship *Benghazi*, steaming to Cagliari, which had on board forty of the latest German all electric U-boat torpedoes. (A slight riposte for the loss of *Medway*).

Unruffled (Lieutenant J. S. Stevens) blew the bows off the new Italian light cruiser *Attilio Regolo* to the north-west of Trapani. She was subsequently towed stern first to Palermo. *United* (Lieutenant T. E. Barlow) closed at full submerged speed to intercept to the south only to find when his battery was low that the enemy was moving stern first to the north. From air reconnaissance reports I had a fair picture of the situation and made a signal to *Safari*. 'Damaged cruiser being towed to Palermo in position "X.Y.Z." escorted by numerous destroyers and M.A.S. putting up a smoke screen. Close and investigate.'

I made this signal to Bryant because I knew the man so well.

He would know that a damaged cruiser wasn't worth suicide tactics, but if it could be sunk he would know how.

Ben Bryant was reading prayers to his ship's company, which was his routine before the evening meal each day. Before dismissing the company he was handed my signal and read it to them, then set off on the surface. He was met by darkness and smoke and since the tow had increased speed he was badly astern of any interception, and retired.

There was no other officer at sea to whom I would have made that signal. He might succeed but he would not lose *Safari* in the attempt.

At noon on 11 November I received orders to redispose my submarines. So ended the phase when I was ordered to entrap the Italian fleet should it move to interfere in the 'Torch' landings; as will be seen we might have had greater success if this order had arrived a day later.

In preliminary days to this submarine disposition for 'Torch', Commander Linton brought *Turbulent* alongside Lazaretto. I went on board and gave him his 'Bigot' orders and discussed them with him. I knew 'Tubby' Linton well. He did the periscope course with Woods, Marsham and Slaughter in 1935 when I did my 'refresher' course. He was best described as a tough front-row rugby forward who represented the Navy at Twickenham for several years. He was also a first-class mathematician, with dour determination. We sat down in his wardroom alone and he read his orders and handed me the slip in them from the C.-in-C. saying. 'You had better keep this. A.B.C. doesn't hand out this sort of stuff often.' Then he read on.

When he had studied his position and job he said, 'Well, that's all quite clear, but tell me why do your flotilla fire three torpedoes in a salvo against a supply ship, aimed to miss just ahead and just astern and one in the centre? Bloody waste of torpedoes! Why not train them to get their calculations right and hit with two, that's enough.'

I rather resented this very pointed criticism and explained that I was sleeping in H.Q. and hoped he would use my cabin and enjoy Malta now air raid free for a couple of days rest. 'No, thanks,' replied Tubby, 'one doesn't sink any enemy shipping sitting in harbour and I sleep on board, so I'll be off tomorrow please.'

He was always a blunt man and I didn't feel offended, but I did think that he had reached that stage when he preferred the hazards of constant patrol to the fleshpots, or just the comforts of a harbour break, followed by the increasing wrench of that first day at sea. He needed rest but he didn't think so.

I never saw him again and his great record of successful service very rightly earned him a posthumous Victoria Cross after his loss in March 1943. *Turbulent* was sunk by escorts after missing the steamer *Mafalda* off Bastia, Corsica, having fired two torpedoes at her.

Once Admiral Cunningham judged the threat to the 'Torch' landings to be both improbable and unimportant he immediately switched his central Mediterranean submarines to their normal and still vital duties of preventing supplies reaching North Africa, and signalled me to redispose. In the event, had his decision been made a day later a rich reward might have resulted. This I will shortly explain.

At this time I received steady reinforcement from both east and west, and my command expanded to twenty-six submarines towards the end of November. The Commando Supremo's supply organisation in Rome reacted to the severe losses to the heavily escorted convoy on 19 October by switching the main supply route to the short run from Palermo round Cape St. Vito then direct to Cani Rocks some twelve miles from Bizerta. From Cani Rocks their supply ships could go either to the port of Tunis or Bizerta as required.

Air reconnaissance soon made this clear to us and intelligence told us that new minefields had just been laid on either side of this route from close west of Marittimo almost to Cani Rocks. This meant that, in order to attack the main flow of supplies, submarines had to enter a narrow strip of sea 100 miles long and 20 miles wide with minefields preventing retirement north-west or south-east, and operate against a fast shuttle service of fleet destroyers now carrying personnel and heavily escorted supply ships. This was a natural development but a highly dangerous one for the attacking submarines.

From the start of the 'Torch' landings, while operating submarines between 8°E and 19°E, I was responsible to Admiral Cunningham, now C.-in-C. Mediterranean for what occurred west of a line from Marittimo to Cape St Bon and to Admiral Harwood now C.-in-C. Levant for submarine operations to east of this line. This worked perfectly smoothly.

On receiving orders from Admiral Cunningham on 11 November to redispose submarines I withdrew two submarines from north of Messina and one from off Augusta and prepared to intercept shipping on the routes to North Africa. That same day three cruisers left Augusta northward and eluded *Una* by hugging the shore, a technique that by now I ought to have foreseen and anticipated. Cruiser coast crawling had been employed twice before that year. The same day the three *Littorio* class battleships left Taranto for Naples and on the afternoon of 12 November steamed north from Messina. *P35* was reconnoitring the coast close eastward of Cape Vaticana but got the enemy report in time and was well placed ahead for interception. The enemy report to *P35* gave 'Course North speed 15 knots,' which was deduced from the distance run between two aircraft reports. It happened to be about right.

Lieutenant Maydon was a cool-headed expert, with several sinkings to his credit and a year's experience on the station, he had manoeuvred into position for an ideal beam shot. He is not a person to blame anyone but himself so I never got much out of him then or now. He was firmly convinced that the battle fleet had increased to full speed and allowed 29 knots and missed the target by so much that his torpedo tracks were never seen by target or escort. My explanation is that the loud beat of these three giant ships gave an impression to the asdic operator of a double effect, and 240 revs were reported instead of 120. He was quite right to accept the evidence of the asdic count, which normally is precisely reliable, since he was in no position to use much periscope.

So passed the flotilla's fourth and last opportunity to sink a battleship and in bitter disappointment I wrote in my remarks to *P35*'s patrol report 'but on consideration these battleships have never done anyone any harm'.

Shortly after this a German U-boat captain made a comparable mistake over a 'sitting shot'. The minelaying submarine *Rorqual* (Lieutenant-Commander L. W. Napier) was south-east of Sardinia, and I needed to reinforce to the south of Naples urgently. The worst feature of these otherwise excellent submarines was the size of silhouette due to the high casing to store fifty mines. I told

Napier of the urgency, but left the rest to him. He could get to the position by dawn if he went full speed without zigzagging. It was a starlit, but moonless, night and he decided to risk it. The risk was certainly slight.

About 0200 I got a signal from him. 'Four torpedoes have just passed under me between forehatch and stern. Am proceeding.'

After the war it was found that a German U-boat on patrol heard *Rorqual* and then saw her through binoculars in the dim night glow. Seeing the long flat deck the captain passed the order to change the torpedo depth setting from 4 metres to 8 metres since the target was an aircraft carrier.

The supply position in Malta was very critical in late October and a ruse was attempted by sending two unescorted merchant ships along the North African coast within French territorial waters, but they were both intercepted and interned at Bizerta. Once more, and for the fourth time, the *Welshman* ran the gauntlet from Gibraltar with food and aviation spirit and her sister ship the 2,600-ton, 40-knot, *Manxman* arrived almost simultaneously from Alexandria which just tided over the island's crisis.

On 20 November the Eighth Army reached Benghazi and a convoy of four fully laden merchantmen arrived at Malta from Alexandria. The siege was over.

The 10th Flotilla submarines, aided by *Safari* and *Sahib*, took such toll of Axis shipping running to Tripoli that the route fell into disuse during December and every submarine played its full part.

I find I must refer once more to the ceaseless offensive kept up at this period by *Safari*. On 14 November I received an urgent call from Alexandria stating that the army, in full cry westwards towards Benghazi, might meet stiffening opposition due to petrol being unloaded at Ras Ali, an open roadstead with a jetty close to El Agheila. Could a submarine stop this activity?

Safari was the closest S class so I informed Bryant who set off on the surface at 12½ knots and got there forty hours later, not having sighted a single aircraft. He sank the *Hans Arp*, a T.L.C. depot ship of 2,600 tons, but there was no explosion such as he expected from petrol, so, looking carefully at the jetty, he saw a cluster of lighters and fired a surface running torpedo which blew up the lot in a huge petrol blaze.

Safari returned to Malta for a quick docking and left again on 16 December to the area between Lampedusa and Tripoli, where he disposed of six small vessels before the end of the month. Such was his record while 'on loan' from the 8th Flotilla.

With the twenty-six submarines now at my disposal from mid-November the Axis supplies were hit hard and often and the broad open sea between Pantellaria and Tripoli, where *Safari* operated as I have just described, gave opportinities to several other submarines which also had success and together virtually closed that supply route, but now I must turn to sterner patrol conditions where events were at first fruitless and losses grave.

I sent *Traveller* (Lieutenant-Commander D. Sinclair Ford) to the Gulf of Taranto to patrol independently in an area which provided targets of fleet or supply units southbound from the port of Taranto towards Crotone, she sailed on 28 November and was not heard of again. Since no Italian claim was made it is probable that she struck a mine. This was a sad and unexpected loss.

The area most vital was the convoy route from Palermo to Bizerta and the first submarine sent there was *Utmost*, who was to enter the swept channel at the Bizerta end and work her way northeasterly. She sailed from Malta on 17 November and on 23 reported she had expended all torpedoes and was returning to Malta. On clearing the channel off Marittimo she was located on 25 November and sunk by the destroyer *Groppo*.

Patrols had to be maintained on this busy route and I thought that only the small U class could effectively do it, so I despatched *United* (Lieutenant J. C. Roxburgh) to the Marittimo end where he encountered strong A/S forces who gained contact and hunted her relentlessly. Roxburgh was on his first patrol, aged twenty-three at the time. He evaded his pursuers and lay on the bottom and by the time he was able to surface had been down about thirty-six hours and the whole crew were in a most distressed state of nausea and vomiting. He returned to Malta without having a shot, arriving 28 December.

P48 (Lieutenant Faber) was sent to the Bizerta end to operate off Cani Rocks. She was sunk on Christmas Day in the Gulf of Tunis by the torpedo-boat *Audace*.

Unseen (Lieutenant M. L. Crawford) was sent to the Marittimo end and penetrated well into the swept channel where she was three times attacked from the air and carried out two attacks on convoys. On the last occasion her target was the key ship *Ankara* who avoided the torpedoes as she had done on previous occasions. Crawford experienced a disappointing and highly dangerous patrol.

North of Marittimo was *Ursula* (Lieutenant R. B. Lakin) who I sent to that position on 25 December. He carried out a brilliant attack on a 4,000-ton, Africa bound ship escorted by two destroyers and sank it on 28 December, so moved position to north of Cape St Vito, where he attacked a convoy of three ships escorted by four destroyers on the night of 30–31 December. A broad zigzag put him right ahead just before firing. He dived to get out of the way and had both his periscopes knocked off by collision with the leading merchantman. Not being able to navigate the minefields blind he wisely and successfully retired to Algiers.

Our predicament on this vital last supply route was a desperate business, but there could be no weakening of our endeavours whilst the German ship *Ankara*, the only vessel able to embark and discharge *Tiger* tanks for the Panzer divisions, was ferrying them to Tunisia with clockwork regularity. After several escapes from torpedoing she was known to the Axis as the 'ghost ship'.

The relief of Malta and success of our armies seemed to have increased our operational difficulties.

So ended this momentous year. Statistics showed that the 10th Submarine Flotilla's record for 1942 was,

Torpedoes fired	437
Torpedo hits	102
Percentage of hits	23.3
Number of attacks	154
Successful	71
Percentage of successful attacks	46.1

22

ON the night of 19–20 December 1941 Italian frogmen, using three small submersible vehicles, made a courageous and perfectly executed attack on Alexandria harbour sinking both *Queen Elizabeth* and *Valiant*. It was known to the Admiralty that during the inter-war period both Italy and Japan were experimenting with the human torpedo.

When I joined submarines in 1921 a tall, thick-set, fair-haired, bespectacled officer, Lieutenant-Commander Cromwell Varley, was often seen about Fort Blockhouse but he seldom entered the mess. He seemed to us new entries a sort of recluse, but in fact he was a forceful personality wholly preoccupied at that time with the invention of a pump. He wore the ribbon of the Distinguished Service Cross and it was the story of this hard-earned decoration that made him an object of our interest and admiration. On 12 July, 1916 Varley in command of *H5* was on patrol off Terschelling, just another of those interminable patrols where the hazards of mine and enemy A/S searches were accepted while no suitable target ever showed itself. On this occasion Varley decided to endure the tedium no longer and set course eastward for the Weser estuary. Surfacing that night to charge batteries he decided to examine and improve the upper gland of one periscope which had become stiff to operate. Destroyers forced him to dive in the middle of repairs and all tools and equipment were lost overboard. He continued to the east with one operational periscope and, having turned south to the Weser, encountered destroyers early on 14 July and fired torpedoes at them without result. He continued south and two hours later sighted a U-boat coming from Jade road off Wilhelmshaven which he promptly sank. He then did an extraordinary thing, he surfaced to pick up survivors, was sighted by the destroyers to seaward of him and was hunted for many hours as he lay on the bottom, but was not located although scraped by a sweep on one occasion.

On return to base the flotilla captain upbraided him for his lack of discipline but gave him the fullest support in his report to the Admiralty. His first lieutenant (Lieutenant Frank Busbridge) was immediately awarded the D.S.C. but Varley was required to wait about a year for Their Lordships to relent. He was then awarded the D.S.C., in contrast to the D.S.O., which he would have got had he not shewn such a disregard for orders. A very fair judgement no doubt, but to us youngsters Cromwell Varley was a particular hero; it seemed a fine example of the 'Nelson touch' about which we had heard so much and noted so little in concrete execution.

At this time at Fort Blockhouse the Chief of Staff to the Flag Officer Submarines was Captain Max Horton, who was a known protagonist of the midget submarine which had first been suggested by Lieutenant Godfrey Herbert as early as 1909. Varley's eyesight precluded further submarine service and he retired to develop a pump of his own invention intended for submarine use. While this failed to interest the Admiralty his pump was a commercial success. His inventive bent continued and in the early 1930s he had advanced plans for a human torpedo which were officially inspected and appraised by Lieutenant-Commander Guy Sayer of the experimental staff of the torpedo school HMS *Vernon*, who brought Varley's plans to the notice of the Admiralty. The Admiralty verdict was 'Not wanted in the Royal Navy'.

This scheme of a human torpedo (which involved a large explosive charge being propelled electrically by one or two men sitting on the machine externally) having been rejected, Varley turned his inventive mind to the problems of a midget submarine where the explosive charge was conveyed to the target by three or four men travelling internally within the vehicle. That is the broad picture of how things stood on the British side when on 20 December 1941 *Queen Elizabeth* and *Valiant* were sunk in Alexandria harbour by Italian human torpedoes.

Predictably, Churchill wondered why the British lagged behind the Italians in such an effective weapon:

Prime Minister to General Ismay for Chief of Staff's Committee, Jan. 18th 1942.

Please report what is being done to emulate the exploits of the Italians in Alexandria Harbour and similar methods of this kind.—Is there any reason why we should be incapable of the same type of scientific aggressive action that the Italians have shown? One would have thought we should have been in the lead.

Please state the exact position.

A very fair question and criticism from the Prime Minister.

The matter was referred to the Flag Officer Submarines and Admiral Horton did two things. Keeping the two schemes, the human torpedo and the midget submarine separate for development, he gave Varley a free hand and full facilities to continue with midget submarine development, appointing Commander T. I. S. Bell to assist him. From this was developed the 'X craft'. Concurrently, having got an Italian human torpedo flown back to Britain, he appointed Captain W. R. Fell assisted by Commander G. Sladen to develop a British version of the human torpedo which resulted in the 'Chariot'.

The midget submarines, 'X craft', never operated in the Mediterranean but by September 1942 Fell was able to send one chariot and crew of two to Lazaretto to test Mediterranean conditions.

The captain of this vessel assured me that he could leave Lazaretto after dark with himself and his mate, in frogmen's suits, sitting on saddles astride it and enter the Grand Harbour and knock on the bottom of a hulk inside the harbour without prior detection in sixty minutes. Admiral Leatham was willing to bet this could not be done but it was achieved with a few minutes to spare.

The Grand Harbour main boom, a huge torpedo net suspended from a steel wire supported by numerous buoys, delayed the chariot only five minutes. The crew left Lazaretto with only their heads above water and arrived at the middle of the boom. They then went to the sea-bed where the crewman dismounted. Hooking a light purchase on the net about ten feet up and the other end of the purchase to the net's ground line he then hauled it up, making a V-shaped gap. The captain went ahead through the V, the crewman remounted and on went the chariot with the crew's heads again above water to the target. This immense defensive boom proving no obstacle whatever.

The Italian attack carried out by three of this type of human torpedo got through the Alexandria defences when the boom was opened to admit our own ships. A combination of skill and luck.

During the first week of December Commander G. M. Sladen flew out to Malta and told me that five chariots were arriving in a few days, with their operational crews, on board parent submarines. Also two spare chariots with trained crews were on their way by surface ship.

Geoffrey Sladen was a submarine officer of long experience and with a distinguished war record as captain of *Trident*, operating in Arctic waters and cooperating for a while with the Soviet northern-based submarines. He had energy, experience and a wealth of calculating sense and had himself, with Captain W. R. Fell, carefully selected the crews and been with this enterprise from its early days.

Immediately after his arrival the three submarines entered Marsamxett harbour: *Thunderbolt* (ex *Thetis*) under Lieutenant-Commander C. B. Crouch (two chariots); *Trooper* Lieutenant J. S. Wraith (three chariots); *P311*, Lieutenant-Commander P. D. Cayley (two chariots). Sladen set to work with night training and daylight maintenance towards perfection.

I include these chariot events in this chapter since no operation occurred before New Year, 1943.

It was good to see John Wraith and Dick Cayley back again and Crouch was a splendid man whose leadership restored the ill-fated *Thetis*, in which ninety-nine men had lost their lives off Anglesey in June 1939, into the confident, offensive *Thunderbolt*. All three of them were to lose their lives on this Mediterranean tour of duty.

I met the effervescent rolypoly figure of Cayley on the landing steps. 'Hello, sir,' he said. 'Looks as if you've had the house breakers in! It's good to be home again.'

'It's good to see you, Dick, but tell me why are you *P311*? I thought Churchill would have named you by now.'

'I've sent in my proposal to Their Lordships but maybe the Admiralty doesn't see the point.'

'What's your suggestion?'

'Well, with a couple of clumsy burdens like that strapped on my back – pointing to the two vast, cylindrical containers 25 feet long and 5 feet in diameter, forward and abaft the conning-tower – I've naturally requested "*Two Tank Amen*", or its abbreviated form

276

Tutankahmen but I suppose it'll be a while before the penny drops.'

Dick searched in his uniform pocket and produced his mouth organ and after a few familiar bars said, 'Let us now praise famous men and our fathers who begat us. Gosh, it's good to be back, sir.'

Although this chariot venture was designed to revenge the sinking of *Queen Elizabeth* and *Valiant* a year before we had good reason to disregard the *Littorios* snug in Naples harbour, because it was generally thought that there was not enough fuel for them to operate and Sladen and I looked for cruiser and transport targets.

The code name allotted to the operation was 'Principal' and Sladen and I gave Admiral Cunningham the following broad outline.

The three chariot-carrying submarines to sail from Malta 28 and 29 December for the south Tyrrhenian Sea. We stressed that this passage across the Palermo–Tunis supply route now constantly patrolled by A/S forces and new protective minefields was particularly hazardous, compared with a month before when our ungainly parent submarines had arrived in Malta. This obstacle passed, the chariot carriers would separate and attack separately.

P311 would proceed up the east Sardinian coast to a precise position east of Isle de Maddelena, but south of known minefields, and there launch chariots X and XVIII who would move with a favourable current (we assessed from navigational information) to sink the last two Italian 8 inch cruisers at anchor in the straits of Bonifacio to the north of Gallura. This long run of thirty miles was to be undertaken at slow speed. After attaching the explosive charges to the two cruisers the chariots were to make for shore and be sunk south of Cape Testa. The crews were to trek to wooded shelter at the eastern shore of the mouth of the river Russu and a folbot from the rescuing U class submarine would recover them on the nights of 8 or 9 January.

This was a very stiff schedule yet, discounting disaster from minefields, I still believe it would have succeeded. I thought the crews of chariots X and XVIII the pick of a fine lot. It will be argued that *P311* should have been sent up Sardinia's west coast for the attack so as to shorten the chariots' long assault. This was fully considered and turned down with the full agreement of Cayley and the chariot crews, because we had more information about the eastern minefields and we expected an appreciable westerly current through the straits of Bonifacio whilst visual pilotage from east to west was comparatively simple for the chariots' crews.

Thunderbolt was to attack Cagliari, where a convoy appeared to be assembling, but since it was highly improbable that a convoy at anchor off this port on 28 December would still be there five days later *Thunderbolt* and the crews of her chariots (Numbers XV and XXII) were fully briefed to attack Palermo if the convoy sailed. Operational orders and the latest air reconnaissance photos for both target ports were on board *Thunderbolt*.

Trooper, with three chariots XIV, XIX and XIII, was to attack Palermo.

Since the three parent submarines with their clumsy tophamper were judged non-operational and very vulnerable, their duties were restricted to the passage out and back and the launching of their chariots in the right place, so it was necessary to appoint small U class submarines off each port to recover chariot crews if they were able to make the return journey. *Unbending* (Stanley) was to be off Cagliari, and *Unison* (now A. R. Daniell, who had just relieved A. C. Halliday) was to be off Palermo and after recovery she was to go west about round Sardinia and recover *P311*'s chariot crews from the mouth of the river Russu. *Unruffled*, J. S. Stevens, was also sent off Palermo for recovery.

Our proposals were approved by Admiral Cunningham without amendment.

Cayley led the cavalcade along the route through the minefield he had pioneered eighteen months before, *P311* sailing 28 December, *Thunderbolt* and *Trooper* following the next day. Shortly afterwards A.O.C.'s ever vigilant air reconnaissance warned me that there was considerable A/S activity west of Marittimo island indicating the probable passage of a convoy and later reported that the convoy from Cagliari road had sailed.

I held *Thunderbolt* and *Trooper* south of Sicily, reported the danger ahead to *P311* and told Cayley to give his position when clear to the north. At 0130/31 December *P311* signalled Position 38° 10' N. 11° 30' E so he was well to the north of the A/S sweep and *Thunderbolt* and *Trooper* were told to continue passage, both to attack Palermo, and that the A/S sweep had dispersed.

This signal from *P311* was the last ever heard of the submarine and its two chariots, now presumed to have perished through a mine in the eastern approaches to the strait of Bonifacio. So passed a gallant leader and his brave company.

Due to the delay on passage the assault on Palermo was postponed twenty-four hours and took place on the night of 2–3 January, which was dark and blustery with an off shore wind; nevertheless all five chariots got away before midnight. Details of this attack and the fortunes of survivors having been recorded in another book, I will confine myself to the operational success of the enterprise which was adjudged satisfactory, but which to me taken as a whole seemed too costly for the result.

Chariot XXII (Lieutenant R. T. G. Greenland, R.N.V.R. and leading signalman A. Ferrier from *Thunderbolt*) reached the new light cruiser at the innermost wharf of the harbour, detached their chariot bow, containing a 400 lb explosive charge, and placed it against the hull somewhat towards the stern, then placed limpet mines under three destroyers *Gregale*, *Ciclone*, and *Gamma*.

Concurrently Sub-Lieutenant R. G. Dove, R.N.V.R. and Leading seaman J. Freel placed the main charge from chariot XIV (ex *Trooper*) under the 8,500-ton transport *Viminale*. Of the three chariots that failed to penetrate the harbour the crew of one was rescued, one member of each of the other two died due to mishap (punctured rubber suit and oxygen trouble). All four chariots were abandoned and sunk outside the harbour and a total of six men taken prisoner.

The main charge under the transport *Viminale* went off about dawn, shaking Palermo from a night's rest and causing consternation. However it gave the Italian destroyers time to search for and remove the limpet mines, when at 0800 the large charge beneath the cruiser *Ulpio Traiano* went off and sank her, so the two main targets were eliminated.

Thunderbolt and *Trooper* returned to Malta and *Unison* went to recover *P311*'s chariot crews from the mouth of the Russu, but finding no one returned to Malta. *Trooper*'s chariot tanks were removed in dockyard, but *Thunderbolt* embarked the two spare chariots and awaited orders.

The Eighth Army were rapidly advancing on Tripoli, which was captured on 23 January, and Admiral Harwood (now designated C.-in-C. Levant) was responsible for the Eighth Army's sea-borne supply. Air photos showed two ships close to the harbour entrance through the breakwater apparently reserved for quick positioning and sinking across the breakwater entrance. Admiral Harwood asked whether a chariot attack could immediately be mounted to forestall this closure and so allow his supply ships to enter immediately the port was captured.

There were few suggestions I had ever liked less. The approaches to Tripoli were strewn with mines, it was approaching full moon and A/S patrols would be a certainty, but the great importance was clear to all and *Thunderbolt* sailed with orders to approach from the west where the existing convoy route appeared to be. Lieutenant-Commander Crouch came in submerged to a position 8 miles, 315° from the harbour entrance and surfaced stern-on to Tripoli on a calm cloudless night with almost full moon. The chariot container doors were then opened and the business of dressing the charioteers and launching the chariots, which would take nearly half an hour, commenced. Within a few moments an E-boat was sighted approaching from the harbour clearly visible in the moonlight, but it stopped some 3,000 yards short and remained there apparently asleep for twenty minutes while both chariots were successfully launched. *Thunderbolt* quietly submerged and crept away.

Chariots XII and XIII soon became separated and had to avoid more numerous patrols near the port. Defects developed in XII who beached herself east of the harbour and found friendly refuge in a farm until the arrival of the Eighth Army. Sub-Lieutenant H. L. H. Stevens and Chief E. R. A. S. Buxton made the harbour entrance in chariot XIII and were approaching their main target, but while only 150 yards short of her two explosions shook the chariot and the ship (*Giovanni Batista*) sank before them, having been positioned as a block ship.

Stevens at once switched to the second target (*Guilio*) and attached several limpet mines widely dispersed, then sank their chariot to seaward, and landed with great difficulty. The *Guilio* sank before being moved to close the gap and although a few other small ships might have been used as blockships, this does not appear to have been done so coastal vessels were able to enter Tripoli immediately the army arrived by scraping through a gap of about sixty feet breadth.

Admiral Harwood signalled to me, 'On her return to harbour please convey to *Thunderbolt* my high appreciation of her very hazardous undertakings. If the second part of her operation succeeded the effect on the future operations of our armies in Africa will be immense.'

A handsome and hard-earned tribute.

Stevens and Buxton were sent to Rome as prisoners of war, and after some months of separation both met in Campo 50 normally used for a two or three week interrogation of officer prisoners of war in that city. When Mussolini fell from power and chaos intervened for some hours both managed to obtain Italian uniforms from a friendly guard who also instructed them how to reach St Peter's, in the Vatican and how to behave when they got there. It appears that lengthy prayer was followed by forcible ejection and when it looked as though the Italian police might turn them over to a German patrol a British diplomat from the Vatican arrived and conducted them past the Swiss guards and into the Holy See, where they were hospitably treated until Rome fell to the Allied armies in July 1944.

If, in fact, the port of Tripoli remained open due solely to this last minute chariot operation, then undoubtedly the whole venture was worthwhile, but I am not convinced this was so. If it only resulted in the sinking of a light cruiser not yet in commission and a 8,500-ton transport, then the prolonged use of three T class submarines exclusively for chariot work and the loss of one of them, seems a disproportionate price to have paid.

It was now mid-January and the need continued to make every effort to attack the Palermo–Bizerta supply route which had cost us so dear in December. As I have explained I had grown to fear this narrow funnel of seaway, heavily mined except at its extremities and giving submarines no searoom for retirement, but the fact remained that the ghost ship *Ankara* was still ferrying Tiger tanks to the Panzer army with clockwork regularity, and since this Axis supply route could not yet be assaulted in force from the air the submarine effort had to continue.

Rorqual (Lieutenant-Commander L. W. Napier) came to Malta to load up with mines and 'have a go'.

Napier had been a midshipman in *Nelson* when I served there in 1930–1 and subsequently my efficient navigator in *P27* at Aden. He was a widely read man with a full appreciation of the humanities. He found in 1935 that he disliked the naval life in general and submarines in particular so much that he came to me asking that I should forward his resignation. Using every argument I persuaded him to accept the life in view of the country's plight, for surely he was needed in this work which he carried out so well. He was a sub-lieutenant then and perhaps my assurance of his ability and value carried weight, for he agreed to forget his personal inclination for my call to service.

I had seen Napier briefly eight weeks earlier when he came to join for the 'Torch' operation, and to lay mines off Cagliari. He had seemed gay and confident, but I had on that occasion told him to dash to Naples without zigzagging and he had watched four torpedoes pass under him that night. I wondered what he thought of my judgement now.

Having loaded mines on 15 January, he came to see me and I showed him the chart and the problem and suggested that he lay fifty mines about fifteen miles north-east of Bizerta, in sight of the Cani Rocks so as to get an accurate fix and place them with precision across the centre of the swept channel in almost daily use by Axis convoys. 'What I particularly dislike,' I added, 'is that I am asking you to do this right away at a time of full moon which means you will have great difficulty in charging your batteries without detection, but you will have to surface somewhere near enemy territory to do this.'

Napier had a good look at the chart and the enemy minefields which were supposed to be accurate and then said, 'Full moon will suit me admirably and battery charging won't worry me at all. Enemy patrols won't expect anything to come through on the surface at full moon, so I will do the whole run on the surface with accurate navigation and then dive at right angles through this south-western end of the enemy minefield and lay my mines right across the channel and surface and get out of it to the west. Actually, sir, it suits me very well, it seems to me a good idea.'

If confidence was the arbiter of fate then he was all right I thought, but I had lost *P48* just there on Christmas Day.

Rorqual sailed and apparently everything went forward on the night of 17–18 January as Napier had confidently predicted. The following afternoon an Axis convoy was approaching the southern end of their swept channel when it ran into *Rorqual*'s minefield and at 1422 *Ankara* struck a mine and sank, together with her load of

Tiger tanks. At last the ghost was laid. Nor apparently was that all, since it is stated in the official history of submarine operations that on the 31 January the corvette *Procellaria* and, on 3 February the destroyer *Saelta*, 1,200 tons, were both sunk by the same line of mines.

Rorqual finished the patrol on the north Sicilian coast and, having failed to torpedo two distant targets, a bridge was bombarded and shore batteries responded with such effect that as *Rorqual* dived the top of one periscope was shot off.

I was unable to congratulate Napier on *Rorqual*'s return to Malta in early February for I had left, but he survived the war with a distinguished record.

Despite *United*'s critical experience of being kept submerged for about thirty hours during his late December patrol I sent Lieutenant Roxburgh back to the same general area west of Marittimo on 4 January. On the afternoon of 17 January in attacking a small convoy the large destroyer *Bombardiere* was torpedoed, and sunk. This success erased *United*'s recent grim experience and the youngest commanding officer of the 10th Flotilla continued the war with a fine record of submarine successes.

This chapter closes my operational command of the 10th Submarine Flotilla, which continued its work based at Lazaretto until November 1943, when the flotilla moved to La Maddalena in the Straits of Bonifacio, previously the base of the Italian 10th Submarine Flotilla. After the Allied landings in southern France in August 1944 the base was closed down and the flotilla dispersed.

Some figures are available which show the activities of this flotilla vividly. These figures are for the small U class only and do not include the many successes of submarines of other types on loan to or working from Lazaretto base. The figures start with the first torpedo fired in January 1941 by *Unique* to the 1,289th torpedo fired by *Universal* on 8 August 1944 – the last torpedo fired.

The number of torpedoes which passed through Talbot's workshop for supply to 10th Submarine Flotilla and visiting submarines was 1790.

The number of torpedoes fired by Tenth Flotilla Submarines.

	1941	1942	1943	1944	Total
Torpedoes fired	319	437	392	141	1289
Hits	86	91	115	43	335
Probable Hits	7	11	7	5	30
Percentage of certain and probable hits	29.1	23.3	31.1	34	28.2

In considering the attacks which were successful (i.e. the target was hit by torpedo but not necessarily sunk).

	1941	1942	1943	1944	Total
Number of attacks	120	154	148	48	470
Number successful	64	71	85	31	251
Percentage successful	53.3	46.1	57.4	64.8	53.4

So the figures quoted by Commander W. E. Banks on the orders of Captain Ruck Keene in April 1939 at the combined fleet conference (22 per cent hits and 50 per cent successful attacks) were fully justified and proved a slight underestimation.

The sinkings in war vessels by Tenth Flotilla was 1 Cruiser, 3 Destroyers, 2 Torpedo-boats, 10 U-boats. Damaged, 1 Battleship and 3 Cruisers.

The tonnage of merchant shipping sunk was	648,629
damaged	400,480
Total	1,049,109

The merchant shipping available to the Axis from all sources in the Mediterranean was 3,140,000 tons (made up of Italian and German owned, foreign shipping commandeered and new ships built). Of this about 700,000 tons was effective at the time of the Italian armistice in September 1943, the remaining 2,600,000 tons having been sunk or damaged by British air, surface and submarine power.

23

CAPTAIN George Phillips, who took over from me at Harwich in mid-September 1940 flew in to Malta on 23 January 1943 and took over command of HMS *Talbot* and the 10th Submarine Flotilla. I was glad to hand over my task and I refrained from telling him how much I loathed the way in which it had developed during the past two months on the Palermo–Tunis route.

Instead of some respite afforded by the relief of Malta and the success of our armies, there was that gnawing anxiety every hour of every day and night over how my men were standing up to the strain of operating within a narrow channel with barely sea room to manoeuvre, ceaseless enemy air patrols overhead and convoys to attack which now contained invariably twice the escorts that there were targets. The loss of four submarines in five weeks and no prospect of change to this hazardous task for weeks, perhaps for months.

In retrospect it is obvious that I was getting tired, and it was time I left, but I must observe that in this command I attribute much of our success to the fact that I lived and messed amongst my officers and throughout the whole of March 1942, when the officers' quarters were demolished, I messed on the general mess-deck with the men. The fact that sea patrol was then preferable to harbour conditions made my task less harrowing. Now I felt each loss more than ever.

I was to report to C.-in-C. Levant and C.-in-C. Mediterranean on the way home and I applied for an air passage to Alexandria, but while waiting *Welshman* had again arrived and was to continue on to Alexandria. So I asked my ex-submarine friend Captain Denis Friedberger for a passage and we sailed at sunset on 31 January, due Alexandria at dawn on 2 February. Denis said, 'Here's my after cabin, Shrimp, make yourself at home. My steward will look after you. Come and have a chat on the bridge any time you like.'

We slid through calm seas, zigzagging at 26 knots. I turned in and slept like a log and in the morning met and talked with officers and passengers, amongst whom was a young American war correspondent recently from Algiers, so I learned how things were going there.

The afternoon I spent on the bridge as we cut through the water at an exhilarating speed. I went down to the captain's cabin and had tea and glanced at the bookcase, picking out Eric Linklater's *Juan in America* and started to read, but I couldn't quite concentrate. *Juan in America*, what keeps nudging my memory? Why of course its *Don Juan*. It is Byron, whose name I happily managed to leave to posterity amongst the illustrious whose carved signatures still stood on the Lazaretto's shattered shell. I returned to the captain's bookcase. There was *The Poetical Works of Lord Byron* and I eagerly took it down. Surely I thought I can find something here more worthy of Malta than his bitter theme of 1811, written probably in Lazaretto. I turned naturally to his sonnets and short poems, some of which I knew very well. Then I came to, 'Elegiac stanzas written by Lord Byron on the death of his cousin Sir Peter Barker, Bart, aged 28, commanding the naval shore party storming the American camp at Baltimore, 1812.'

> There is a tear for all that die,
> A mourner o'er the humblest grave;
> But nations swell the funeral cry,
> And Triumph weeps above the brave.
>
> For them is sorrow's purest sigh
> O'er ocean's heaving bosom sent:
> In vain their bones unburied lie,
> All earth becomes their monument!
>
> A tomb is theirs on every page
> An epitaph on every tongue:
> The present hour the future age,
> For them bewail, to them belong.
>
> A theme to crowds that knew them not,
> Lamented by admiring foes,
> Who would not share their glorious lot?
> Who would not die the death they chose?

This is what that great poet unconsciously wrote for my men who sailed from Lazaretto, I thought. This he wrote for them, just as much as for his naval cousin aged twenty-eight. I read it several times and I thought 'It's grand, but is it true?'

> The present hour the future age,
> For them bewail, to them belong,

and then

> A theme to crowds that knew them not
> Lamented by admiring foes.

Could these lines be true? Not if the mood of the nation and the state of Europe was anything like I had noted after the First World War. How would posterity and the youth of Britain remember my men who had died in such a desperate battle? Unless they were told the story they would have nothing to remember. I put Lord Byron's works back on the shelf and picked up the novel.

I had been reading a while and the sun had just set, we would be at Alexandria in fourteen hours, when I heard a slight bang somewhere astern followed by a second one somewhat louder. I knew at once what this was, magnetic torpedoes exploding in our wake. Three seconds later was a third and I stood up and, after a similar interval, there was a loud crack just astern of me which shook the deck, but was very mild really and did not even lift my feet off the deck. The ship stopped and I walked on to the quarter-deck to see the ship had been cut in half, just twelve feet astern of where I had been sitting. Our speed of 26 knots had prevented any severe shock from travelling forward.

I went up to the bridge, the ship was listing to starboard some 12 degrees, and I told the captain what had happened, since he had felt nothing and had no idea why the ship had stopped. The diesel auxiliary was started at once and, on the asdic, the U-boat could be heard steadily retiring. The engineer commander sent a messenger to report that the after engine-room bulkhead was holding and being reinforced with baulks of timber. Our predicament some fifteen miles north of Tobruk was reported and we were told that two Hunt class destroyers would reach us from Benghazi at about 0100.

Everything seemed in control and the foc's'le party prepared to be taken in tow.

At about 2030 the after bulkhead of the engine-room collapsed. *Welshman* rolled over and sank in about four minutes. The destroyers arrived on time four and a half hours later, and there were 120 out of 240 of us to pick up. So ended the gallant *Welshman* who had been vital to Malta's survival.

Following the German surrender on the Western front on 7 May 1945 Admiral Doenitz was ordered to direct all U-boats at sea to enter Loch Eribol or Loch Alsh to disarm and to disembark the majority of the crew before continuing to Stranraer on Loch Ryan for internment. The final count after some weeks was 156 U-boats. Captain B. W. Taylor, group commander in charge at Loch Eribol told me of the remarkable difference in reaction between individual U-boat commanders to this order. Some U-boats would arrive already disarmed, with even the gun dismantled and all secret electronic and radio equipment together with cipher and codes jettisoned, while others arrived ready for action and inquired, 'Has war against the Soviet Union been declared yet?' One elderly U-boat commander remarked humourously, 'I know what to do since my last U-boat command I surrendered at Harwich in 1918.'

As a token force to surrender to Western Approaches command eight U-boats were escorted with full crews from Loch Alsh to Lissahally jetty at Londonderry; one British destroyer, one Canadian and one American frigate forming the escort. They were to arrive at 1400, 14 May.

It was a foul day with cloud down to 200 feet and the arrangements for Admiral Horton and Air Vice Marshal Slatter to fly to Londonderry were cancelled. On this victorious occasion Sir Max ordered his personal pilot to fly him in his Dominie aircraft at sea level, coast crawling round Northern Ireland, and arrived just in time to meet the U-boats, and have a brief interview with their commanding officers. It was a real disappointment that his great friend and collaborator Air Vice Marshal Slatter was not there too.

The splendid example of sea and air cooperation which had developed between Coastal Command under Air Marshal Slessor and Western Approaches under Admiral Horton who had, as Slessor's representative, Sir Max's friend and collaborator Air Vice Marshal Slatter, was an example which can surely in future be followed under the new combined services structure. This emphasised the resolve and sincerity in Horton's letter of 8 October 1940 (Appendix 2) where he stated that lack of sea/air cooperation was one of the most potent reasons for his refusal to accept command of the Home Fleet (and those honours consequent upon such a command in war) but showed his conviction in its practical achievement.

In the post-war analysis it was found that of the 550 German U-boats destroyed at sea by British and Dominion armed forces, 225 had been sunk by sea power and 225 by air power; a proportion being sunk jointly. A valedictory emphasis on the importance of cooperation between these sister services.

Sir Max received world-wide acclaim for his immense contribution to victory by his war service of two years and ten months in command of submarines and two years and ten months as Commander-in-Chief Western Approaches. His contribution to Allied victory was rewarded by the highest honours from our allies. His own country stuck to the precise rules, which I think he would expect and perhaps even approve. He started the war as Vice Admiral and K.C.B. He ended it as Admiral and G.C.B. Precisely what he might have expected had there been no war at all.

History will acclaim Admiral Sir Max Horton's true fame. What mattered to him was to be right over those issues involving his life's work, the survival of Britain and his service to the Royal Navy.

The fact that Britain somehow won both wars, despite political and service policy blunders, which in the opinion of foreign observers had foredoomed our future, will always be paramount.

This is why I consider that the Royal Navy was not decadent for some forty years after Jutland, nor were her sister services. It seems to me particularly important that our youth should know this, for in the main it was youth who pulled us from the desperate mire of 1939–42 under the inspiration of Churchill's leadership and it is right that this should be stated and shown to have been so.

APPENDIX 1

Information received from Bibliothek für Zeitgeschichte, Stuttgart, 2 October, 1970

Subsequent of 1924, Korvettankapitan Bartenbach (retired) who had commanded the operations of the Flanders U-boats during the First World War was active in an advisory capacity in Finland. He induced the Finnish Government to undertake at first the construction of three 500-ton submarines, using plans prepared by the German 'undercover' engineering firm – Kantoor voor Scheepbouw (I.v.S) of The Hague. The German U-boat Construction Bureau was run by the German Korvettenkapitan Blum (retired) and the Technical Director, Dr Techel, of the Germania Dockyard. The three Finnish submarines, on which work commenced 1926–27 at the Crichton-Vulcan Yard in Turku, were named *Vetehinen*, *Vesihiisi*, and *Ikuturso*. They were commissioned in 1930–31. After these were started, another small submarine of 99 tons was built at Helsinki 1928–30, using constructional drawings prepared by the same Bureau (see above), and this boat was given the name *Saukko* in the Finnish Navy. Just like the 250-ton *Vesikko* built 1931–33, these boats were intended as prototypes for German boats. At the trials of some of these boats Oberleutnant zur See Schottky took charge of the seamanship while the entire technical side was in the hands of the Naval Staff Engineer Papenberg, and these trials were fully exploited by the German Navy for the practical training of a small number of active service naval and engineer officers.

If the student of history wishes to study in detail the German inter-war U-boat activities he should read the thesis written by Dr Allison Saville – 'The Development of the German U-boat Arm 1919–35'. Here the student will find the chief emphasis laid on the three 500-ton Finnish submarines named above, and the 250-ton *Vesikko*, all built on German design under German supervision, the *Saukko* appearing relatively unimportant.

Very great emphasis is laid on the cooperation of the 'accommodation ship' *Grille* for young officers under training. The real duty of *Grille* besides being a target ship was that she was a floating laboratory for underwater acoustic experiment.

My report of February 1935 is in no way refuted. It is only shown that I was but nibbling at the resurgence of the U-boat whose activities it partly uncovered.

APPENDIX 2

Vice Admiral (S), Northways, London NW3
10 October 1940

Dear First Lord,

I appreciate to the full the very high honour attaching to your offer of yesterday morning, but after deep thought and much heart-searching, I have come to the conclusion that I cannot accept.

The chief reasons that have led me to this decision are the conditions under which the Commander-in-Chief Home Fleet has to carry out his heavy responsibilities. I spent the first four months of the war in close contact with the Home Fleet and since then have maintained this contact.

The difficulties which C.-in-C. Home Fleet suffered when endeavouring to make contact with important enemy forces or units when the enemy were active at sea before and during the Norwegian campaign led me to form very definite conclusions. I expressed some of these views to the Prime Minister when he was First Lord and also to V.C.N.S. at various times.

In brief my views are as follows:

I think it essential that the Commander-in-Chief Home Fleet should have directly under his orders adequate air forces –

(a) For reconnaissance;
(b) For sea bombing;
(c) Fighter protection.

To carry this into effect bomber squadrons would have to be placed under C.-in-C. H.F.'s orders not only for bombing enemy forces at sea, but to supplement the inadequate reconnaissance machines which is all that the A.O.C.-in-C. Coastal Command can supply.

Shore-based fighter protection for the Fleet is also necessary and must be under the Commander-in-Chief's orders in certain areas.

These forces should work and train together and with the Fleet continuously, and the personnel should not be subjected to constant changes.

Only if the above measures are put into force do I see a chance of the Home Fleet successfully fulfilling its functions.

I also formed the opinion, and expressed it to V.C.N.S. some months ago, that the C.-in-C. Home Fleet should be shore based and that the Admirals of individual squadrons should be considerably younger. Generally the age of responsible officers at sea should be reduced.

In the lull in surface warfare at sea during the last months some of the above needs may not have been so apparent, but I am sure that they will emerge again directly the enemy resumes activities with his larger units.

Lastly, I formed the opinion that the Commander-in-Chief Home Fleet did not enjoy that degree of independent judgement and action which seemed to me to be essential to the full discharge of the responsibilities of this Command.

Feeling so strongly as I do on the above matters, and realising that there is little or no hope of the principal requisite changes being made in the near future, I could not undertake with any confidence the Commander-in-Chief Home Fleet's onerous responsibilities to the Board and to the country.

It is with real pain and regret that I feel compelled, for the reasons stated, to renounce the high honour which you have offered me.

Yours sincerely,
(Signed) Max Horton

The Rt Hon. A. V. Alexander, M.P.,
First Lord of the Admiralty.

APPENDIX 3

From: Captain S10
Date: 10 May 1942
To: Captain S1, HMS *Medway*
Subject: Review of Conditions in Malta during attack of German Air force and
          circumstances which forced decision to remove Tenth Submarine Flotilla

OPERATING the 10th Submarine Flotilla under constant air attack provided many exceptional situations and experience gained may be valuable and worth recording.

2. The G.A.F. visited Malta previously – from 8 January 1941, until 11 May 1941, commencing with three attacks during fourteen days, on *Illustrious* in the Grand Harbour, continuing with heavy dive-bomber attacks on Malta aerodromes and finishing with intensive parachute mine operations against the harbours of Malta. During this four-month visit from what one may regard as the training schools and winter quarters of the G.A.F. in Sicily, Malta had a taste of what might be expected the following winter. However, no attack was made on the submarine base and from maps taken from prisoners it was apparent that as late as April 1941 Msida Creek was marked 'U-Boathousen' though any air recce. photographs must have shown our submarines lying in Lazaretto Creek. Mines which fell on Manoel Island and in Valetta caused slight damage to the base, but submarines were in general unaffected.

3. On commencing submarine operations. and taking over command on 10 January 1941 I found rock shelters had been planned, but only just commenced. These were progressed throughout the year so that by December 1941 there were adequate shelters for the safety of personnel during the day and sleeping accommodation for 24 officers and 200 ratings, and this covered our essential requirements for personnel sleeping within the base. Officers' quarters, mess decks and a hospital were all on the first floor and, therefore, some four minutes walk from the shelters. The buildings had particularly robust walls, but roofs were vulnerable to blast and particularly dangerous if they should collapse.

4. The organisation and maintenance of submarines throughout this period when our Flotilla did not constitute an objective for the G.A.F. was as follows: The submarines lay in a crescent-shaped trot (so a stick of bombs could not fall along it), each submarine being connected by a floating gangway to the shore. When an air-raid occurred submarines would remain on the surface and shut off as for depth charging. In this manner only minor inconvenience was experienced and repair and routine work could be progressed. The most serious inconvenience suffered was by submarines in the dockyard where workmen, in obedience to their orders, left work and retired to rock shelters with every air alarm; thus it will be seen that at the moment when it was essential to accelerate work to complete a submarine and withdraw it from the target area, progress slowed up.

5. About 5 December 1941, German aircraft first appeared over Malta in numbers for their second visitation and, according to German reports, their activities started

in earnest about 19 December. A general narrative of events will now be given, dates and times are approximate though in most cases accurate.

6. The latter half of December was only remarkable for nuisance raids, but each week it was apparent that the enemy was becoming bolder and the R.A.F. were losing the initiative even over the Island. On 28 December R/T interception informed Headquarters that Me 109s had been told to attack two submarines entering the harbour. *Urge* and *Upholder* had been exercising with the trawler *Beryl; Urge* dived in time, *Upholder* was hit by five cannon and many machine gun bullets and Lt Norman, temporarily in command, received multiple wounds but managed to close his conning tower hatch and the submarine was brought safely back to harbour, sailing for patrol under command of Lt-Cdr Wanklyn two days later.

7. On the night of 1–2 January a small number of rocket bombs were tried out from a height of about 5,000 feet. Probably this was an experimental raid. It is understood that the rocket is intended to give greater accuracy and penetrating power and strike terror into the inhabitants. No bomb fell within the harbour area and it was found that the terrific noise and luminous track attracted attention and gave one immediate consolation when it was obvious that the bomb would miss one. So far as I am aware, this type of raid was not repeated.

8. On 6 January a single aircraft dropped a stick of bombs through low cloud which fell across No. 1 dock, one bomb causing twenty-six perforations in the pressure hull of *P31* which was in dock for periodical docking. There were three minor casualties and damage to the steering gear delayed the submarine operating by three weeks. *P31* sailed for patrol on 29 January.

9. On 19 January *Unbeaten* was attacked by Me109s when returning from patrol and only two miles from harbour entrance, whereupon orders were given that submarines returning from patrol were to surface one mile from St Elmo Lighthouse if the red flag was not flying from the Castille and the Commanding Officer was not to come on to the bridge until the submarine was within the breakwater. Subsequently on two occasions *Sokol* was attacked by fighters within 500 yards of the harbour entrance when going from Marsamxett harbour to Grand Harbour for battery repair and unable to dive.

10. On Friday 13 February at 1430 an attack was made on Lazaretto Base, resulting in two German mines demolishing mess decks and hospital. This attack was fortunately preceded at 1230 that day by an unsuccessful bombing of Marsamxett harbour, thus personnel were careful to take over and casualties were only three killed and five wounded. Old store houses on the ground floor were at once cleared of stores and new mess decks were satisfactorily instituted within ten days. These led direct to the rock shelters, thus increasing security of personnel.

11. On Friday 27 February, an attack with 1,000 kilo A.P. bombs resulted in the demolition of two-thirds of the officers' quarters, four officers being killed and none wounded. As a result, submarine officers were put on lodging allowance, base officers remained sleeping in rock shelters and all officers messed in the ratings' dining room on general messing, the wardroom being re-instituted in a P.W.D. store, previously full of drain pipes, by 1 April.

12. A heavy attack on 2 March resulted in battery damage to *Upright* who was about to sail for the U.K. She eventually sailed with one battery section only on 19 March. In the evening of 9 March Surgeon Captain Cheesman (S.M.O. *Talbot*) was killed ashore in his house.

13. On 5 March, several attacks on Manoel Island caused no damage to submarines or establishment, but cut all electric lights, telephones and water mains for the third time. The following day (6 March) dive-bombers approaching from the south eastward near missed *Una* and *P36* which necessitated patching *P36* in two places and changing the bi-focal periscope due to a splinter perforation. Half an

K*

hour later a second wave of bombers hit the fuelling lighter forty feet from *P39*, and the lighter caught fire and sank. The whole establishment was dowsed in shale oil. *P39* received extensive damage, 172 cell containers being cracked, warheads knocked off torpedoes, bed plates of auxiliary machinery broken and many welded brackets inside the submarine snapped. She was towed to dockyard that afternoon.

14. It may appear at this juncture that steps should have been taken to forestall this attack by diving submarines during daylight, but it is pointed out that approximately one thousand air raids had taken place during the fourteen months of operation and this was the first major success gained by the enemy against the flotilla; further, that this disorganisation to repair work and routine consequent upon diving by day seem unjustified until damage actually occurred.

15. From 6 March onwards, the following routine was brought into force. Submarines dived throughout daylight hours at deep water berths in Marsamxett harbour, except for one submarine which occupied the billet alongside *Talbot* and all repair staff concentrated on her. Submarines in the dockyard also had to remain on the surface and these vessels were evacuated of all personnel, after the watertight doors and sea connection had been shut off, except for one officer, one E.R.A. and one seaman who remained in the control room as an emergency fire party. If the submarine had no battery on board all personnel retired to rock shelter.

16. In order to give crews rest in harbour, it was apparent that submarines diving by day could only be manned by half crews and either the first lieutenant or third officer, since commanding officers were given the maximum leave and freedom from responsibility. In view of this it frequently occurred that an officer of less than one year's experience in a submarine had to take the vessel to a buoy and dive it with half a crew. I therefore ordered that these submarines should secure to their berthing buoy by the bows only to avoid wires round the propellers due to inexperience and working in the dark; since divers would not work through air raids it might be impossible to use them for some days in the case of a wire becoming foul of a propeller. This decision resulted in a serious accident.

17. On 8 March, *P35* dived at dawn secured to a buoy in seventy feet of water in the middle of Marsamxett harbour; the vessel apparently had slight headway on as she submerged and the pressure hull under the *T.O.T.* tank, which is unprotected by the keel, settled on the clump block of the buoy; this made a hole about six inches through the pressure hull, flooding the tube compartment, the watertight doors being shut immediately. The Third Officer, Lt Martin, surfaced the submarine at 0940 but without sufficient forward buoyancy; she then took an alarming angle by the bow and disappeared, a smoke candle being fired ten minutes later. Inspection by D.S.E.A. during an air raid, which fortunately proved to be only a reconnaissance, showed all hatches shut and working bridge telegraph gained a reply from below. Messages were sent to the surface through the underwater gun contained in thermometer tubes and a bottle, but owing to choppy surface these were not seen or recovered. A diving boat was being placed over the submarine at 1220 when she surfaced and was moved to shallow water. *P35* docked on 11 March and completed defects by 21 March.

18. At 1430, 18 March, *Sokol* was the submarine refitting alongside *Talbot*; a single stick of bombs near-missed her and cracked thirty-six battery containers. She was sent to the dockyard on 19 March.

19. In anticipation of heavy air attack with the arrival of the convoy on 23 March, the maximum number of submarines had dockyard defects made good before that date and on Sunday, 22 March, *Urge*, *P31* and *P35* were withdrawn to Marsamxett harbour, but *Sokol* and *P39* remained.

20. At 1800 on 26 March, *P39* was alongside Store Wharf without battery or torpedoes; *Sokol* was alongside Machinery Wharf on the opposite side of Dockyard

Creek. A bomb dropped from the direction of Grand Harbour Entrance fell precisely between these two submarines, but the trajectory carried the bomb under *P39* where it exploded and split the submarine athwartships at 53 station. *Sokol* received no further damage, since by good fortune another bomb from this stick which fell on the jetty beside her did not explode. There were no casualties in *P39*, all men being in the shelter and the vessel was towed to the Marsa and beached by the stern. Stores and a large quantity of spare gear and light machinery were removed to *Talbot*, but the submarine was subsequently repeatedly hit during April and is now sunk.

21. On 31 March, *Pandora* arrived and was directed to Shell Pier in Marsamxett harbour and discharged white oils that night, entering Grand Harbour at dawn 1 April and securing to Hamilton Wharf. I visited this submarine at 1030 and decided with the Commanding Officer that he should disembark stores and torpedoes for Malta as quickly as possible, refuel and sail at 2200 that night. At this time (1030) an air raid commenced, which persisted until 1630. In view of the urgency of *Pandora* leaving Malta with the minimum delay it seemed then justified to progress disembarkation of stores throughout air raids.

22. It seems probable that the first two hours of this alarm was largely reconnaissance of the harbour areas and that an attack specifically aimed at all visible submarines was arranged for the afternoon. Between 1430 and 1500 a heavy raid of Ju88s followed by Ju87s developed on the harbour area and resulted in the sinking of *Pandora* by two direct hits. She sank in four minutes, with the loss of two officers and twenty-three ratings. At the same time *P35* alongside *Talbot* was near-missed by a medium sized bomb which fell about three feet from the port forward end of the engine room between the submarine and Lazaretto building. The officers and two ratings on board abandoned her successfully having ascertained that the control room after bulk head was fractured, all lights extinguished and chlorine gas driving them from the compartment. A three inch wire was passed round the conning tower to hold the submarine upright and to the building, but this parted before stronger wires could be obtained and *P35* rolled over into fifty feet of water.

23. Simultaneously two or three sticks of bombs were dropped north and south across Lazaretto Creek and near-missed *Unbeaten*, who was submerged, but with the top of the conning tower just awash; the resultant damage caused some distortion to the torpedo tubes which led to *Unbeaten* being sailed to Gibraltar on 9 April.

24. At this juncture it was apparent that any submarine visible to the enemy was in great danger, though it seemed that the enemy would be fortunate if they seriously damaged or hit a submarine on the bottom in deep water. It was considered improbable that the enemy would think it worthwhile deliberately to bomb open water in the harbours, though this in fact, he did towards the end of April. In view of the fact that withdrawal from Malta virtually meant stopping offensive operations against Rommel's supply line, also since the 10th Flotilla was the only remaining means of preventing the enemy bombarding Malta by heavy surface forces, and bearing in mind the bad effect on local morale caused by our withdrawal at this juncture, it was decided to maintain the flotilla, keeping all submarines submerged by day, using the crews of *P35* and *P39* and a third crew (constituted from *Pandora*'s survivors and spare officers) who looked after the submarines during their stay in harbour, whilst operational crews were sent to rest camps. After a conference with commanding officers, I reported to Vice Admiral, Malta, and proposals were forwarded to C.-in-C. Med. This decision was not over-weighted by obstinacy, but the position at Malta seemed so serious and the maintenance of the fortress so vital that a further effort seemed imperative.

25. As stated earlier, submarine officers were sleeping ashore on lodging al-

lowance. During the first week in April the three blocks of flats used by *Unbeaten, P34, Urge, Sokol* and a few other individual officers were all demolished in Sliema by direct hits. This was a pure fluke, since out of the many hundreds of houses in this particular district less than fifty were demolished in raids during this particular week.

26. On Saturday, 4 April, the Greek submarine *Glaukos* which had been refitting since November and was within a week of sailing for Alexandria, but as yet unable to dive, was sunk at Hamilton Wharf, a direct hit from a large bomb striking the last remaining fuel lighter which was alongside her. *Sokol* which was within twenty-four hours of completion, received a further near miss, cracking about seventy containers, and from this time onwards *Sokol*, unable to dive, was hidden in various places in the harbour under camouflage while work progressed on her battery during nights when power was available on the battery crane (about one night in four). *Sokol* lived a charmed life, eventually sailing on 13 April with some 200 holes in her upper deck casing from bomb splinters. The bifocal periscope had to be changed and one perforation in the pressure hull patched. The defect to *Sokol*'s periscope was not apparent until her trial dive in Marsamxett harbour after embarkation of stores for passage to Gibraltar. This necessitated the submarine once more entering Grand Harbour after dark on 11 April on which occasion she fouled the boom in a Gregale and lost her starboard propeller. However she sailed on 13 April arriving Gibraltar on 28 April.

27. The new routine of sending submarines on patrol after four or five clear nights in harbour worked satisfactorily just so long as the operational crews were allowed to enjoy rest during their brief stay, but about 8 April the rest camps were daily machine gunned and finally bombed. It was therefore apparent that the new routine could not continue beyond two patrols with one short five-day rest. It was hoped however that the strong fighter reinforcement which was known to me to be due on 21 April might gain us local air superiority and consequent respite.

28. In early April submarines hidden at the bottom of Marsamxett harbour had occasionally been shaken by the odd bomb which fell in the Creek and was directed at Fort Manoel or *Talbot* establishment, so bottoming berths were arranged outside the harbour in 120 feet of water clear of the protective minefield. This was unsatisfactory since submarines could not be readily surfaced in event of enemy heavy ships approaching and since the island was virtually without air reconnaissance it was more than ever necessary for submarines in harbour to be at short notice. After *Sokol* had fouled the boom entering in the dark, it was decided that submarines should return to bottoming berths within the harbour.

29. The Spitfires reinforcements on 21 April made no difference, except to divert air attack for about two days to the aerodromes. On 23 April I visited V.A.M. and gave my opinion that the 10th Flotilla must now leave Malta as soon as possible since conditions had not improved, enemy minelaying was to be expected, and in particular since personnel were showing signs of fatigue due to bombing of rest camps and lack of normal recreation.

30. On 24 April, *P34* lying in deep water off the Valetta terminus of the Marsamxett ferry was near-missed by a very large bomb. The commanding officer was onboard and half crew; difficulty was experienced in surfacing at 2030; the submarine was manoeuvred astern to clear a supposed obstruction on the bows and finally got caught underneath the inner torpedo baffle. After communicating by asdic and ascertaining her position by smoke candle the submarine surfaced with the 4½-inch baffle mooring wire just abaft her conning tower and she was cut clear with a hacksaw. It appeared from the raids on this day (24 April) that the enemy was searching Marsamxett harbour since many sticks of bombs fell in the water, therefore whilst preparing to move to Alexandria and in view of waxing moon conditions

298

submarines bottomed outside the harbour once more and no further untoward incidents occurred.

31. Although the difficulties of operating the flotilla were considerable and were increased by lack of electric light, telephones and other progressive nuisances, such as the demolition of the general mess dining hall, the enemy did not have everything his own way and between 1 January and 1 May 1942, the 10th Flotilla sank one 6-inch cruiser, one German U-boat and four Italian U-boats also sinking two schooners, a salvage ship and a trawler, and blew up an Italian goods train. The total enemy supply ship tonnage sunk or damaged approximated 60,000 tons.

32. During these four months under review about 1,000 air raids occurred, about 10,000 tons of bombs were dropped on target areas of the island (Manoel Island receiving some 400 hits) and I imagine that the period of alert averaged more than twelve hours out of twenty-four. It naturally passed through my mind from time to time during these four months how much pleasanter life would be if the submarine tunnels proposed in 1934 had been available.

33. On 1 January the 10th Submarine Flotilla comprised nine operational submarines. Between this date and 1 May five submarines returned to the U.K. to refit, two were lost in harbour, two were lost on patrol due to no cause connected with the G.A.F., three received some damage which required docking and could not be taken in hand at Malta. The submarine *Pandora* of the 1st Flotilla and the Greek submarine *Glaukos* were both lost in harbour due to air attack.

34. The exemplary conduct of all and their determination to 'get on with the job' despite difficulties, loss of kit and amenities, deserves remark. The exceptional work of repair parties under the able direction of Commander (E) MacGregor was outstanding – no circumstances daunted them. The Maltese ratings and workmen showed great spirit and I never heard a complaint.

35. The flotilla is now dispersed, damaged and has suffered heavy loss, but it is notable that the essentials at Malta for operation of the flotilla remain; that is to say:

At the Base   Mess decks, repair shops, periscope shop in the open with store rooms, offices and sleeping quarters under rock. (Workshops are being put under rock).

In the dockyard   Battery Shed and electrical repair shop untouched. No. 1 dock quickly repairable and two cranes in Dockyard Creed still working.

It is hoped that the day is not far distant when the flotilla can reassemble at Malta and continue the fight.

REPLY FROM ADMIRAL (SUBMARINES), NORTHWAYS, LONDON, NW3

I have read with great interest and admiration your letter J/1005/S10 of 10 May 1942 giving an account of conditions at Malta and circumstances which forced the removal of the 10th Submarine Flotilla to Alexandria.

2. I do appreciate your forethought and the splendid work done by you all to prepare for the intense scale of air attack to which you were subjected, and I had never any doubt but that the flotilla was prepared to stick it to the bitter end and at the same time continue to render an excellent account of itself.

3. Under present conditions, however, I am sure the 10th Submarine Flotilla will prove of greater value during its enforced change of base to Alexandria than it could have done under the conditions with which it would have had to contend at Malta.

4. I hope it will not be long before the submarine base at Malta which you have all worked so hard to establish will once again welcome you back to continue the fight under less exacting conditions.

5. I am passing your letter to all flotillas so that they can read for themselves how splendidly you have all done and so that they can learn valuable lessons from your experiences.

(Sgd.) Max Horton
Admiral

APPENDIX 4

The Bombing of O.R.P. *Sokol*

The following is a description of the repeated bombing of O.R.P. *Sokol* at Malta, which forms an epic story of a wonderful effort on the part of *Sokol*'s Commanding Officer, Officers and ship's company, which succeeded aided by the essential good luck which often comes to those who fight hard enough.

17 March *Sokol* returned from Patrol.

All day the air bombardment of the Submarine Base and of warships lying in Grand Harbour was continued, by the Luftwaffe.

1600 5 heavy bombs fell close to *Sokol* about 10–30 yards away, causing damage as follows:

46 cells broken. Damage to air and water lines and to the telemotor system. All manometers and guages broken. Torpedo war-heads shifted forward about 1 inch.

18 March Unloaded torpedoes and carried out a battery test under continuous air-attack all day.

19 March

0700 During passage from Lazaretto to Grand Harbour *Sokol* was attacked by two Me109s using cannon and machine gun fire. Eight hits were registered by cannon shells causing very slight damage and no casualties.

20 March Changing the damaged cells.

Because of the heavy air attack and the considerable dockyard casualties the dockyard workers had become demoralized and refused to work during the raids. As a result of this it was impossible to proceed with the work. This situation led the Commanding Officer of *Sokol* to order his crew to continue to work during the raids.

21–2 March Work on No. 2 Battery was completed. *Sokol* left Grand Harbour after dark on the 22nd and returned to Lazaretto. Heavy raids were expected on the Grand Harbour area because a convoy was expected to arrive on the 23rd.

23 March The convoy arrived and the expected raids materialised.

24 March Heavy raids directed against Grand Harbour and the Submarine Base.

25 March Heavy raids on the Submarine Base.

26 March Waves of 70 bombers carried out severe attack on Grand Harbour. All
After- ships of the convoy were hit. SS *Talabot* was on fire and was in consider-
noon able danger of blowing up as she was loaded with ammunition, torpedoes and bombs. Work in the dockyard was at a standstill and all personnel were ordered to take shelter for 6 hours. Destroyer *Legion* received a direct hit and sank. Submarine *P39*, lying in the same creek as *Sokol* received a near miss which exploded underneath her and broke her back. Most of the attacks were made by dive-bombers. About 15 bombs fell in the creek where *Sokol* was lying. The nearest dropped on the creek about 50 yards away and failed to explode! This bomb weighed 1,000 lbs.

27 March   Three heavy raids on Grand Harbour.

28 March   Weather conditions were so unfavourable that no air attack developed all day. A considerable amount of work was done.

29 March   The air raid warning was sounded just after daylight, and the raid continued until dark. Single planes came over at frequent intervals. No work was done in the Dockyard.

30 March   All work on *Sokol* was finished and *Sokol* left dockyard creek for French creek to be degaussed.

31 March   Degaussing completed. The boat was prepared for patrol. Heavy raids developed all day.

     2000   40 bombers carried out an attack on Grand Harbour. *Sokol* the Greek Submarine *Glaukos* and HMS *Penelope* were lying in French Creek. Three 1 ton bombs fell 10 yards from *Sokol* causing damage as follows:
98 cells broken. Many plates in the cells broken. Boat was full of chlorine gas. Work was carried out all night in Gas Masks and D.S.E.A. sets. It was necessary to disconnect all the damaged cells. No power was available. No work in the dockyard, no telephones, and no possibility of getting a tug to move the boat.

1 April   *Sokol* proceeded to Dockyard to remove damaged batteries. Heavy air attacks were a feature all day. They were directed against Submarines and succeeded in sinking HM submarines *Pandora* and *P36*. Several bombs fell in the vicinity of *Sokol*. Because these raids were directed against the submarines, the crews were ordered to the shelters. The cruisers were leaving the A.A. gun crews closed up, and all unnecessary ratings were sent to a shelter.

2 April   Heavy raids all day. The dockyard was again at a complete standstill.

3 April   A conference was called by Captain (S) in the dockyard to discuss the chances of carrying out repairs under the existing circumstances. The dockyard was unwilling to work at night and during daytime they were only able to remove 10 cells daily.
It was decided that the batteries should be taken out by the crew and a band of willing volunteers from the base, and from some army camps attached. *No* dockyard volunteers were in these parties.
After the batteries had been repaired and replaced where needed, by the battery shop, they were to be loaded back again by the crew and any volunteers, of which there were always more than enough. During the day (3 April) no less than 20 double red warnings were given.
The dockyard removed 6 cells all day.

4 April   Before noon the crew had succeeded in getting 31 cells out. During the afternoon no power was available in the dockyard, and no work was possible. The Greek submarine *Glaukos* received two hits and sank.
The destroyer *Kingston* and the escort vessel *Abingdon* were also sunk by bombs.
The light cruiser *Penelope* was damaged, as were also the destroyer *Havock* and *Lance*.
Bombs fell around *Sokol* but caused no damage.
Captain (S) gave orders that Submarines were to dive by day while inside or outside the Harbour.
With no power available and heavy raids in progress all day, it was deemed advisable to remove *Sokol* from the dockyard and camouflage her alongside the hull of the *Essex* (an 11,000 ton motor ship) which was lying in Bighi Creek.
Sokol left the dockyard at night.

	Sokol was lying with her bows aground and camouflaged by nets and various devices which had been found on board *Essex*.
5 *April*	*Sokol* appeared to have been seen by the morning reconnaissance and during the afternoon bombs fell around *Essex*. Captain (S) decided on a new berth for the submarine to lie the next day.
	It was decided to take out one battery that night. *Sokol* was to proceed to the dockyard for this purpose. The remaining 66 cells in No. 1 battery were removed in 4½ hours. The crew of *P39* assisted greatly in this work.
6 *April*	*Sokol* was taken to Marsa Creek, surrounded by barges, camouflaged and lay with her stern aground.
	German reconnaissance discovered this news, however, and during the afternoon raids Marsa Creek was plastered with bombs.
	Nine of the concealing barges were sunk.
	Sokol suffered no damage.
7 *April*	Army specialists were called in to assist in the camouflage work. During the day 3 heavy raids developed, directed against Marsa Creek.
	Severe damage and destruction caused to numerous buildings around the creek.
	Twelve barges were sunk but no damage to *Sokol*.
	300 bombers took part in the raids.
8 *April*	Again heavy raids. This time there were four with about 300 planes involved.
	Nearly all the buildings around the creek were destroyed, and all the barges were sunk.
	The nearest bombs fell directly on the barges immediately alongside *Sokol* i.e. 3 to 5 yards away.
	Sokol was badly damaged, and over 400 holes were discovered in the casing and conning tower, including the small holes in the pressure hull. The pressure hull was found to be leaking in several places. Water and air pipes were badly damaged.
	The camouflage was destroyed by fire.
	Repair work was carried out to the water and air system by night and No. 1 battery tank was made ready.
Also	*Sokol* was moved alongside *Essex* again and camouflaged once more. The
9 *April*	battery was not ready, but it was decided to replace the broken cells in order that *Sokol* should be able to dive.
	The raids developed during the day.
	That night *Sokol* was transferred to the dockyard and 66 cells were loaded in No. 1 battery.
	This work was greatly assisted by the help of 5 officers and 9 sailors from the Base who volunteered this help.
10 *April*	*Sokol* was moved alongside *Essex* before daylight and again camouflaged. Heavy raids were made on Grand Harbour, and no power was available in the dockyard, and there was no chance to load the remainder of the battery that night.
11 *April*	Heavy raids all day, and still no power available.
12 *April*	It was quite obvious that the Luftwaffe now knew where *Sokol* was and directed an attack against the *Essex*.
	Many bombs fell around the ship, and the result was a hit which caused a fire (on board the *Essex*).
	After dark *Sokol* was moved to the dockyard to complete the Battery.
	No. 1 Battery was complete and connected up by daylight. *Sokol* was then dived in Bighi Bay.

13 April	*Sokol* lay all day on the bottom.
	After dark she was taken to *Lazaretto* Base to prepare for sea.
14 April	*Sokol* lay on the bottom in Mersa Mersetto harbour all day, and surfaced after dark to continue work.
15 April	Dived all day.
	After dark *Sokol* was sent to the dockyard to change a Periscope.
	The night was very dark, and a heavy sea running.
	While entering Grand Harbour *Sokol* fouled the booms, and was bumping heavily on the locks for about 2 hours. Starboard propeller was broken. Having cleared the boom, *Sokol* proceeded to embark her Periscope, and was dived in Bighi Bay by daylight.
16 April	1200 – *Sokol* surfaced, and entered the dockyard to load provisions and make ready for sea.
	No raids at all during the day.
17 April	0600 – *Sokol* sailed.

(Sgd.) Max Horton
Admiral

APPENDIX 5

Hercules—The proposed operation by Italian troops transported by the Luftwaffe.

General Kurt Student and his XIth Air Corps had been preparing the airborne landing for months. The mistakes of the operation against Crete would not be repeated. 'We knew much more about the enemy's dispositions. Excellent aerial photographs had revealed every detail of his fortifications, coastal and flak batteries, and field positions. We even knew the calibre of the coastal guns and how many degrees they could be turned inland.'

The Italian leader of the operation Marshall Count Cavallero, had at his disposal 30,000 men for the air landings alone – equivalent to the whole British garrison. Besides XIth Air Corps, they included the Italian paratroop division 'Folgore' which trained by General Ramcke, had impressed Kesselring enormously – and the Italian airborne division 'Superba'.

For the seaborne landing no fewer than six Italian divisions totalling 70,000 men were ready. 'It was an impressive force,' says Student. 'Five times as strong as we had against Crete.'

Major General Conrad, now as for Crete responsible for XI Corps' transport was again allocated ten Gruppen totalling some 500 Ju52s (capacity for short journeys thirty fully equipped soldiers). In view of the short distance separating Malta from Sicily they could be expected to make four round trips the first day. He was moreover much better supplied with gliders than for Crete: besides 300 DFS230s each carrying ten men, there were 200 new type Gotha GO242s with capacity for twenty-five men.

Some 200 glider pilots had been trained in landing with crane parachutes. Conrad writes, 'I suggested that all B2 aircraft (single engine training planes) should be assembled to tow the DFS230s. As soon as the last bomb fell the latter should make pin point landings with their "crane chutes" beside flak positions, known command posts and the mysterious caves. Immediately afterwards six transport Gruppen would drop their paratroops over their allotted targets, and the four carrying airborne troops would land them on the first airfield to be captured.'

The airborne invasion of 30,000 Italian troops was immediately to be followed by 70,000 Italian troops transported by sea.

Excerpt from *The Luftwaffe War Diaries* by Cajus Bekker, published by Macdonald & Co., 1966 (first published in German 1964).

APPENDIX 6

A Chronological Table of the principal convoys to Malta, their composition, losses and the cargoes they landed from July 1940 to December 1942.

Date	Code Name	Composition	Losses	Cargoes Landed
August 1940	Hats	4 merchantmen (close escort) 4 destroyers (distant escort) 3 battleships 1 aircraft carrier 4 cruisers 13 destroyers	1 merchantman damaged	Approx 40,000 tons
November 1940	Collar	3 merchantmen 1 battlecruiser 4 cruisers 10 destroyers 4 corvettes	nil	Approx 20,000 tons
January 1941	Excess	3 merchantmen 3 battleships 2 aircraft carriers 9 cruisers 23 destroyers	1 cruiser sunk 1 aircraft carrier severely damaged 1 cruiser damaged 1 destroyer damaged	Approx 10,000 tons
March 1941	M.C.9.	4 merchantmen 3 battleships 1 aircraft carrier 4 cruisers 13 destroyers	2 merchantmen (damaged in harbour) 1 cruiser (damaged in harbour)	Approx 45,000 tons
May 1941	Tiger	Through convoy to Greece and Egypt		Approx 30,000
July 1941	Substance	6 merchantmen 1 battleship 1 battlecruiser 1 aircraft carrier 4 cruisers 1 minelayer 17 destroyers	1 merchantman damaged 1 cruiser damaged 1 destroyer sunk 1 destroyer damaged	Approx 65,000 tons

September 1941	Halberd	9 merchantmen 3 battleships 1 aircraft carrier 5 cruisers 18 destroyers	1 merchantmen sunk 1 battleship damaged	Approx 85,000 tons
March 1942	M.G.1.	4 merchantmen 4 cruisers 16 destroyers	1 merchantman sunk 1 merchantmen beached and capsized 2 merchantmen sunk in harbour 1 destroyer sunk 2 destroyers damaged	Less than 1,000 tons
June 1942	Harpoon	6 merchantmen 1 battleship 2 aircraft carriers 4 cruisers 1 minelayer 17 destroyers 4 minesweepers	4 merchantmen sunk 1 merchantman damaged 2 cruisers damaged 1 destroyer sunk 1 destroyer damaged	Approx 25,000 tons
June 1942	Vigorous	11 merchantmen 1 special service vessel (Centurion) 8 cruisers 26 destroyers 4 corvettes 2 minesweepers 2 reserve ships 4 motor torpedo boats	2 merchantmen sunk 2 merchantmen damaged remainder of merchantmen turned back. 3 cruisers damaged 3 destroyers sunk 2 corvettes damaged 1 torpedo boat sunk	nil
August 1942	Pedestal	14 merchantmen 2 battleships 4 aircraft carriers 7 cruisers 24 destroyers 2 tugs 4 corvettes 4 minesweepers 7 motor launches	9 merchantmen sunk 3 merchantmen damaged 1 aircraft carrier sunk 1 aircraft carrier damaged 2 cruisers sunk 1 cruiser damaged 1 destroyer sunk 4 destroyers damaged	Approx 55,000 tons
November 1942	Stonehenge	4 merchantmen 5 cruisers 17 destroyers	1 cruiser damaged	Approx 35,000 tons
December 1942	Portcullis	5 merchantmen 1 cruiser 1 minelayer 14 destroyers	nil	Approx 55,000 tons
December 1942	(Quad-rangle A) („ B) („ C)	14 merchantmen light (destroyer) escort only.	nil	Approx 120,000 tons

BIBLIOGRAPHY

A DOCUMENTS

Patrol Reports of Third Submarine Flotilla 1940, Admiralty Archives.
Patrol Reports of the Tenth Submarine Flotilla 1941 and 1942, Admiralty Archives.
Fuehrer Conferences on matters dealing with the German Navy, 1939; 1940 (vols. I and II), 1941 (vols. I and II), 1942 (vols. I and II), published by Chief of Naval Intelligence, Navy Department, Washington. 1947.

B BOOKS

BARNETT, CORRELLI, *The Swordbearers*, Eyre & Spottiswoode, 1964.
BEKKER, CAJUS, *The Luftwaffe War Diaries*, MacDonald, 1967.
BRYANT, Rear-Admiral B. J., *One Man Band*, Kimber, 1958.
CAMERON, IAN, *Red Duster White Ensign*, Muller, 1959.
CHALMERS, Rear-Admiral W. S., *Max Horton and the Western Approaches*, Hodder & Stoughton, 1954.
CHURCHILL, W. S., *The Second World War*, Volumes 1, 2, 3 and 4, Cassell, 1949, 1950.
CUNNINGHAM, Admiral of the Fleet LORD, *A Sailor's Odyssey*, Hutchinson, 1951.
DEANE-DRUMMOND, ANTHONY, *Return Ticket*, Collins, 1953.
DOENITZ, Grand Admiral, *Memoirs*, Weidenfeld and Nicolson, 1959.
FELL, Captain W. R., *The Sea our Shield*, Cassell, 1966.
GERARD, FRANCIS, *Malta Magnificent*, Cassell, 1945.
HEZLET, Vice-Admiral SIR ARTHUR, *The Submarine and Sea Power*, Peter Davies, 1967.
JAMESON, Rear-Admiral SIR WILLIAM, *The Most Formidable Thing*, Rupert Hart-Davis, 1965.
KING. Commander W. S., *The Stick and the Stars*, Hutchinson, 1958.
LIDDELL-HART, SIR BASIL, *The Rommel Papers*, Collins, 1953.
LIPSCOMB, Commander F. W., *The British Submarine*, A. & C. Black, 1954.
LLOYD, Air Marshal SIR HUGH, *Briefed to Attack*, Hodder and Stoughton, 1949.
MACINTYRE, Commander Donald, *The Battle for the Mediterranean*, Batsford, 1964.
MARS, Lieutenant Commander ALISTAIR, *Unbroken*, Muller, 1953.
NICOL, JEAN, *Meet me at the Savoy*, Museum Press, 1952.
ROSKILL, Captain STEPHEN, *The War at Sea*, Vols. 1 & 2, H.M. Stationery Office, 1954.
SAVILLE, DR ALLISON W., *The Development of the German U-boat Arm* 1919–1935, 1963.
SHADWELL, Captain L. M., *Submarines*, Vols. 1 & 2. Naval Staff History of the Second World War, 1955.
TEDDER, Air Chief Marshal LORD, *With Prejudice*, Cassell, 1966.
WARREN and BENSON, *Above us the Waves*, Harrap, 1953.

INDEX

OTHER MEMOIRS FROM SEAFORTH PUBLISHING

Seaforth Publishing have re-released a number of classic
World War II naval memoirs, some of which are listed below.

THE BATTLE OF THE NARROW SEAS
**The History of Light Coastal Forces in the Channel
and North Sea 1939–1945**
Peter Scott

' A magnificent story. ... To read this book is to relive the excitement,
the determination and the optimism that were the defining features
of the young men of Coastal Forces in the Second World War.'
Antony Hichens

*246 x 189mm, 320 pages, 120 colour and b/w illustrations, hardback,
ISBN 978-1-84832-035-2, £25*

THE WHEEZERS & DODGERS
The Inside Story of Clandestine Weapon Development in World War II
Gerald Pawle

The fascinating story of the Admiralty's Department
of Miscellaneous Weapon Development, the so-called 'Wheezers and
Dodgers', and the many ingenious weapons
and devices it invented, improved or perfected,
told by one of a group of officers who were charged with
the task of winning the struggle for scientific mastery.

*198 x 129mm, 304 pages, 16 b/w photographs, paperback,
ISBN 978-1-84832-026-0, £9.99*

STAND BY FOR ACTION
The Memoirs of a Small Ship Commander in World War II
William Donald

This is the gripping record of varied and almost incessant action that must rank
among the most thrilling personal accounts of the war at sea. From Norway in
1940, to convoy duty on the East Coast, the landings at Anzio and then
Normandy, this is simply an unputdownable memoir.

*198 x 129mm, 208 pages, 10 b/w photographs, paperback,
ISBN 978-1-84832-016-1, £9.99*

These, and other naval memoirs, are available through
our website at **www.seaforthpublishing.com**
Or ring our order line: 01226 734555 or 734222